Writer's Mind

Writer's Mind
Crafting Fiction

Richard Cohen

NTC Publishing Group
a division of NTC/CONTEMPORARY PUBLISHING COMPANY
Lincolnwood, Illinois USA

About the Author

Richard Cohen grew up in the Bronx and attended the University of Michigan, where he won the Hopwood Award for short fiction. He has been an editor for a literary agency, a consultant reader for a major book club, a lecturer in fiction writing at the University of Wisconsin–Madison, and is now a full-time writer. The *New York Times Book Review* called his *Domestic Tranquility* "a beautiful first novel—built on observations so minutely and constantly intelligent that one feels as intellectually engaged by it as emotionally seized." His *Say You Want Me* was the *Los Angeles Times Book Review*'s "best unreviewed book of 1988."

Executive Editor: John Nolan
Developmental Editor: Marisa L. L 'Heureux
Cover and Interior Design: Ophelia M. Chambliss
Production Manager: Rosemary Dolinski

ISBN: 0-8442-5864-4 (softbound)
ISBN: 0-8442-5819-9 (hardbound)

Published by NTC Publishing Group,
a division of NTC/Contemporary Publishing Company,
4255 West Touhy Avenue,
Lincolnwood (Chicago), Illinois 60646-1975 U.S.A.
Manufactured in the United States of America.
Library of Congress Catalog Card Number: 94-66706

8 9 0 VP 9 8 7 6 5 4

for John and Christopher
and
for Leonard Fiddle

Contents

Preface

A writer is someone who is always learning to write. For this fragile-looking but surprisingly tenacious creature, everything that happens is a writing lesson. When the love of your life betrays you, it is a course in characterization and dialogue. Surreally adaptable, writers spend their lives camouflaged as doctors and patients, priests and parishioners, soldiers, prisoners, executives, factory workers, secretaries, and spouses.

Grief, illness, failure, and loss don't become any less painful if you're a writer—perhaps they become more painful—but they acquire an added value: they are material. After they have subsided, after you have been changed by them, you can transmute pain and bewilderment into reason and form by writing them down. From life to paper, from paper to life again, writers move crabwise toward perfection.

If you think creative writing is just a subject to get a good grade in, I congratulate you: you will end up in some safer, more practical, probably more lucrative career. A writer is someone for whom creative writing is much more than just a class.

During a long self-education, I have thought about, talked about, and analyzed the efforts of thousands of people who wanted to be writers. In five years as a reader at a literary agency, I saw every kind of bad, mediocre, and almost-good writing imaginable, and even a few fine, acceptable manuscripts. Then there was teaching, and evaluating published books for a book club. As a freelance educational writer, I've worked anonymously on books that taught the craft of writing—books that did not always say the things I would have said if I had been speaking my mind.

At times I've even glanced at creative writing manuals, in case the authors knew any secrets I had missed. There were always a few good tips in addition to the dreary formulas.

But there was always something lacking in those manuals. The writers *had* to know more than they were telling—because if what they were telling was all they knew, they wouldn't be creating anything, they would just be running in a rut. They proposed "rules" that I knew were only good suggestions. They preached, "Show, don't tell," but had little to show. By following the manuals, a student could become a technically competent, unoriginal, soulless writing entity.

Other books suffered from the opposite problem. Taking a feel-good, therapeutic tone, they gave pep talks to the amateur. Believe me, you will not become a fiction writer by doing breathing exercises and keeping a journal. You might become a fiction writer by thinking, dreaming, obsessing, practicing, studying, sweating, groaning, needing—*breathing*—fiction.

I wanted to write a book that contained more technical knowledge than the manuals and went beyond the pep talks to nurture the serious inner development of writers. To say what I knew, without keeping anything back. Not just to describe good writing but to embody it. To practice what I preached.

There are no "don'ts" in this book—no "Don't write dream scenes" or "Don't write about writers" or "Don't have more than one protagonist" or "Don't begin a sentence with *and* or *but*." A writer is someone whose first reflex, on being confronted with a taboo, is to break it.

You won't find any rigid formulas here either. I will not tell you to "write every day" or "keep a notebook" or even the most nearly universal dictum, which I personally follow, "Write what you know." (Did Poe really know all that stuff, or did he invent it so well that he created the illusion of knowledge? Writers get credit for "knowing" whatever made a good story, and so the meaning of the word gets contaminated.) I've kept notebooks at times and at other times not kept notebooks, and I never noticed any difference in the quality of my fiction. Keep a notebook for its own sake if you want to, not because you think it's a duty. For writers who have to make livings, take courses, raise families, search for mates or keep the ones they've found, do the shopping and cooking and laundry, clutch the threads of a shrinking social life, and somehow steal an hour or two a night to try to write a little fiction, keeping a daily notebook may be an excessive burden.

What you'll find here is pieces of conventional and unconventional wisdom identified and discussed for whatever they may be worth to you. The attitude is not "Do it this way." The attitude is "Other writers have done it this way. Think about it, test it if you wish, then find your own way."

I am not trying to sell you my caring. If I were, you might justly suspect that I had nothing else to sell. *You* supply the caring—your writing will be better that way. I am not here to try to persuade you that writing will make you whole and happy. There is deep pleasure in writing, but it is the pleasure of struggle more than of ease.

How Writer's Mind *Is Organized*

The organization of this book is shockingly simple. Part One, "Craft," begins with some discussion of what writing is, why we do it, what a story is. From this overview we zoom down to the fundamentals of craftsmanship: plot, characterization, description, and so on. Each chapter explores a range of approaches, philosophies, and tactics within a topic, rather than presenting a single orthodox technique. There's analysis of skills and advice on how, as a writer sitting at your desk, you can free yourself to attain them.

Part Two, "Process," intensifies the focus on work habits, analyzing aspects of creativity from thinking to revision while emphasizing that the process is fluid and not a matter of compartmentalized stages.

Part Three, "Practicalities," lowers some of the hurdles of building a writing career: getting educated, getting published, handling the frustrations.

Each chapter ends with a set of exercises under the heading "Do It." In addition, exercises are sometimes recommended within the main text, at points where they arise naturally. Many of the exercises involve writing; others emphasize seeing, talking, cooperating, daydreaming. Following the instructions to the letter is not the point. If you twist an exercise around, using it as a springboard toward a different one of your own invention, you are using it as it's intended. And all the exercises can be treated as thought exercises. This book is written under the assumption that you have independent projects of your own to write and that an hour spent describing your room, for instance, is probably an hour lost from your true work. On the other hand, if you're having trouble thinking of ideas for a story or getting a grip on a technique, just about any exercise in the book might turn into a source of inspiration.

Each chapter concludes with a feature called "Writer's Bookshelf," which provides an annotated list of works that exemplify the skills taught in the chapter.

The Spirit of Writing

Technique is what can most efficiently be taught in classrooms, but technique is not the essence of writing. Writing is a matter of the spirit. It comes from sensing what's around you, remembering what used to be, feeling your own feelings, recognizing the various selves who inhabit your brain, believing that other people have inner selves, too, and using competently the language you have used every day since toddlerhood. That's all so basic that it's hard to understand why everyone doesn't do it.

Every taught technique is a product of the past, and we're living in times when it's uncertain whether anything produced in the past is a useful guide in any field. Person A might write nothing at all for twenty years but, by seeing with writer's eyes and thinking with writer's mind, learn something which she then, spontaneously, scribbles down, and it might be more valuable than the life's work of Person B, who diligently practiced the craft every day. Lots of technique is transmitted in this book, but I hope the other thing, the essence, is transmitted, too. A plain truth is worth more than a pretty lie—though prettiness has value and is at least a way of getting people to pay attention. Writing is a character trait, and this book is a character study.

Writing it is part of my learning process. I hope reading it is part of yours.

Part One

CRAFT

Chapter 1

Why We Write

As I type this, I'm exhibiting all the symptoms. I'm fidgeting and stalling. Maybe I need more coffee. Maybe I drank too much coffee already and have to wait till I settle down. Maybe I should put in a load of laundry, or do a few arm curls, or call my travel agent, or all three at once. I've already stared out the window, reread a magazine article about the President, solved several international crises in a wide-ranging discussion between the left and right sides of my brain, and performed a droll comic improvisation: "You're late!" I scolded myself as I straggled to the computer. "Sorry, boss, the buses weren't running," I wheedled.

Anything but write. Because when I finally flip the power switch and the bell rings and the screen lights up, I will be shot out of this pleasant apartment to a lonely, nonphysical place where everything I love, hate, hope, and fear is hovering, high-stepping toward me and away, teasing me into thinking I can capture it. I will be riding a roller coaster I have designed myself, where the dips and turns are not built until the moment I reach them, and where I can't get out until I'm dead. When I board this ride every morning, my breathing changes and my temperature rises; I literally get cold feet and have to put on socks. I don't hear things that are said to me; I don't even notice the pretty lake outside my window, where a brown duck is stepping through a puddle on the red slats of the dock—unless I want to describe it.

This is exactly where I want to be. As a boy, I heard rumors of this roller coaster; I read the stories of people who had ridden it. The thought that I could someday ride it seemed such an unbelievable fantasy, I didn't dare tell anyone about it. Then, one length of track at a time, I began building it. I knew so little about building roller coasters, made so many mistakes, that the ride was full of twists and turns, high slow climbs and sickening plummets, and very exciting.

What part of the course am I going to build today?

I'll find out soon enough—that's why I'm stalling. Five more minutes before boarding: I can stroll around, make conversation, pretend I'm not serious. Examine the track; do a safety check.

What if I fall? What if I can't think of anything or if I write five pages and they're bad?

In fact, what if they're good? What if today's the day the track keeps climbing, the car exceeds escape velocity, the roller coaster reaches outer space? I've lived in the daily hope of creating a character who would ride with Huck Finn and Tom Jones, a world that would shine in the sky with *The Tale of Genji* and *Middlemarch*—and with the daily knowledge that I haven't done so. If I did it, how could I bear it?

Here's the strange part: although I'm scared and don't know what's around the next curve, I am—to let you in on a secret—utterly confident. This roller coaster was built for me, after all. While it's tearing around a bend, I might decide to try a one-finger handstand. Whether it works this time is less important than I once thought. I've fallen repeatedly, and I know what happens then: I stand up and climb back on.

WHY WRITE?

Samuel Johnson said, "No man but a blockhead ever wrote except for money"—which would be one of the most blockheaded statements of all time if he'd meant it. Writing is a foolish way to try to get rich. It's not the smartest way to try to pay the bills each month, either. There's no job security in writing, no benefits, no pension, no paid vacations. Even if you write a bestseller, there's no guarantee you'll ever repeat the accomplishment; and if your next book is a flop, how will you pay the mortgage on the fourteen-room house with swimming pool and tennis court you built when you had a bestseller?

Here's a math problem. Let's say you earn a million dollars from a bestseller. Before that, you struggled for a decade with two books that made no money at all, and afterward, you're so burned out from a year of publicity tours that it's another year before you can begin your next book, which you'll finish two years after that. How much have you earned per year? One million dollars for fourteen years' work—an annual income of $71,428. That's far from poverty, but as the pinnacle of a glamorous profession, it's not much to brag about. It's much less than what successful painters, singer-songwriters, actors, and directors make. Your doctor and lawyer probably make more, especially when you add the life insurance, pensions, and whatnot they get from their firms and HMOs. The lack of benefits makes your $70,000 more like $50,000: about what a senior schoolteacher makes.

This figure is for the top rank of the profession. Most fiction writers never approach it. Most established, published fiction writers have to earn their living some other way. And the distance between the top and the average is vast. If you get published, you can expect to make about as much as a teenager's allowance.

If you *must* write fiction for money, try writing for television or movies rather than books: as a general rule, performing arts are more lucrative than nonperforming ones. The smart thing, however, is to go to medical school or law school. That's immeasurably easier. Anyone capable of writing a publishable book is capable of getting a postgraduate degree, and the reverse is certainly not true. To become a doctor or lawyer, all you have to do is climb a well-constructed ladder, joining a long line of people who are stepping on the same evenly spaced rungs in the same order, and few of whom fall off. To become a writer, you have to build the ladder yourself, and you never know how high you'll have to make it or how far apart the rungs will be.

Well, even if you don't get rich as a writer, you can become famous anyway, and that's fun, right?

No. For one thing, very few writers are famous. Even famous writers aren't famous compared to athletes or actors. Seeking fame in the literary world is like seeking gold in a copper mine. Would you recognize Alice Walker if you saw her in an airport? I wouldn't. For another thing, fame may not be the best influence on one's art. It's a rare writer whose genius doesn't shrivel at the touch of fame. Writers who become very successful usually become too easily satisfied with their work—and so do their editors and critics. They ease back, cast off the heavy burden of self-criticism, and, because they're confident the work will be published, they lose the incentive to spend a few more months on one or two more drafts, trimming extra words, trashing unnecessary scenes, goading themselves to their peak. This is one reason why many writers never match their first book. Another reason is that the kind of life that surrounds a famous writer—interviews, public readings, lectures, fan mail—is not interesting to write about and distracts the writer from what is. We all thirst for praise, but the minute easy praise arrives, in the form perhaps of adoring students and friends' blurbs, you will be tempted to coast. You have no incentive to surpass yourself. Important writing always comes from surpassing yourself. It comes from feeling that you're gambling your whole life in what you write. If you have a foundation grant and tenure, then persuading yourself that your next book is a matter of life or death becomes, in itself, a major fictional effort.

"I don't care about money, fame, or tenure, I want to express myself." Well, yes. Me, too. Everyone has something to express. But if everyone in America wrote two-hundred pages expressing all the pain and joy and grievances in their lives, the result would be 250 million poorly crafted books. And how much good would all that self-expression do the self-expressers anyway, after the first warm glow of having gotten something down on paper? Let's say you write a story about how your parents watched television every evening instead of helping you with your homework. You give your parents fictitious names and exaggerate their flaws. Then you begin to believe what you've written. In real life, you begin to react to your parents not as themselves but as your fictional characters. You interpret your parents' inner lives, as if you were an omniscient narrator, and when they dispute your interpretations, you interpret that instead of believing them. You have messed up your relationship with your parents by making them the creations of your own mind instead of giving them the dignity of their independent existence. If you don't believe this can happen, ask a few famous novelists how they're getting along with the parents, spouses, and other assorted relatives and friends they turned into characters.

There is self-expression at the bottom of every work of art, but in most well-made works of art it's distilled and transformed into something that shouldn't be confused with its model. If you want to vent your feelings and get to the bottom of your personal problems, talk to a counselor or write in a diary. That's a lot easier than writing fiction and can improve your life more. Conversely, if you start out with discontent about your parents and, years later, finally turn it into a good story or novel, the end product will probably bear so little relation to the initial stimulus that it won't affect your relations with your parents.

The reason we write is that we want to make something. Writing fiction is not a matter of explaining life or describing, recording, or analyzing life; it's a matter of creating life. And the life we want to create is beautiful. A fine work of fiction is a beautiful thing that we give to this world: a house in which we find shelter from the ugliness and suffering outside. Our readers can live in it, too. To be honest, this may not be as heroic an endeavor as saving the drowning or feeding the hungry, but it's definitely on the plus side of the scale.

This is too noble-sounding. One of the functions of good fiction is to expose false claims. What if stories do not really do the world any good except to provide idle moments of entertainment? What if the masterpieces of humanitarianism do the world some token good, but the other 99.9 percent of fiction is just chewing up trees—the literary equivalent of facial tissue?

The answer is, we have to write anyway. For one thing, you can never tell in advance what kind of story your story is going to be. It might be trash, or it might change someone's life. It might even be both. Pulp science fiction, which a lot of people consider trash, has opened a lot of other people's minds, including mine.

There's a deeper reason, still, why we have to keep writing. Writing is our cry, our call. It's how we announce ourselves to the world. This is different from therapeutic self-expression; it has little to do with revealing our private grievances or analyzing our pasts. If there's therapy here, it arises from the fact that having a call—any call at all—changes you, strengthens you.

When we write, we do what birds do when they sing. "This is me, here I am. I'm hurt; or I'm happy." A bird can say that in a few notes, the same few in the same order for each member of a species. A human being is more complex and needs many words and *must* change their order each time, because that is the sign of being human.

Not self-expression but self-creation: writers are people who become themselves by writing. (In this sense, writers resemble fictional characters, who become themselves by being written.) The other motives vary from person to person and place to place. This motive is the unvarying, necessary one. Change cultures, change eras, and it still holds true. We are here, and we have to sing about it. There are infinite ways of combining words; what counts is being able to combine them *somehow,* anew. Our writing is separate from ourselves and does not reliably explain anything about our lives, yet our writing *is* ourselves, more truly than the selves that go to the bank and have lunch with friends and play golf on the weekend. It is our calling and our call.

So it should be easy, but because it's not, people write books to share what they know about it.

Do It

1. Think about why you write or want to write. Refine your thought until you can state the reasons in a paragraph. Compose the paragraph in your head; you may or may not actually write it on paper.

2. Daydream about becoming a writer. What do you see? Where and when does it take place? What have you become, physically, emotionally, socially? Who else is present? What events are happening? Concentrate on the fantasy until the details are clear. Then write a description of it. Don't show it to anyone. Keep it and refer to it now and then, noticing how your fantasies evolve over time.

3. In a writers' group or class, let everyone take a slip of paper and write a sentence beginning with the phrase, "I want to be a writer because. . . ." All the slips of paper should be folded and placed anonymously in a hat or other container. The hat is passed around; each member in turn pulls a slip of paper from the hat and reads it. You may or may not wish to discuss the statements after you read them. Members are welcome to contribute as many statements as they wish, using a separate slip of paper for each.

Writer's Bookshelf

The Writing Life by Annie Dillard (1989)

explores the spiritual and emotional sources of the writing impulse in Dillard's incandescent prose. Dillard goes halogen in her 1987 memoir, An American Childhood, about growing up affluent in a bygone Pittsburgh.

The Courage to Create by Rollo May (1975)

is a short, inspirational, serious work by a leading existential psychologist who teaches us that any kind of creation, in art or life, requires the courage to overcome anxiety.

Ake: The Years of Childhood by Wole Soyinka (1981)

beautifully describes the coming to life of an artistic consciousness during a Nigerian boyhood of the colonial period.

Self-Consciousness: Memoirs by John Updike (1989)

shows the same developmental process at work in the white, middle-class Shillington, Pennsylvania, of the 1930s and 1940s.

One Writer's Beginnings by Eudora Welty (1984)
> *has become a much-loved book among writing students. Its title could apply to every book on this list: Welty's version is rendered concisely, gracefully, and inspiringly.*

"A Sketch of the Past" in *Moments of Being* by Virginia Woolf (2nd edition, 1985)
> *candidly discusses the psychological function of art as a way of processing childhood experiences.*

The Prelude by William Wordsworth (1850)
> *is a book-length poem that painstakingly examines every twist and turn in the growth of one supremely creative mind.*

Chapter 2

What Is a Story?

A story is the narrative of a sequence of significant events that happen to someone we care about.

There are five necessary elements in that definition:

- We care about the character.
- Something happens to him or her.
- The thing that happens is significant: it makes a difference in the character's life.
- The thing that happens is not single event but a sequence.
- The sequence is narrated: it is recreated by a writer.

THE STORY IS IN THE TELLING

The events themselves are not the story. The story is in the telling. The writer is the story.

The character can be anyone, as long as we care about him or her. The action can be any event, as long as it makes a difference in the character's life or the reader's. It can be large or small in its physical effects. It can be the destruction of the universe or a child popping a balloon—or both, if one is a metaphor for the other. It can be a sequence of thoughts in a character's mind, if we care enough about the character.

It has to make "a difference that makes a difference," as the biologist Gregory Bateson said. If a character chooses to wear a brown suit rather than a gray one Tuesday morning, that, by definition, is a difference, but it doesn't cause other things in the character's life to change. However, the clever author can make that difference make a difference by showing how the choice of a brown suit altered the character's boss's impression of the character, thus leading to a prestigious assignment that eventually makes the character president of the company, and so forth. (The classic stories on the rampaging effects of seemingly trivial choices are Isaac Asimov's "Spell My Name with an S" and Ray Bradbury's "A Sound of Thunder.")

Sequence is crucial. An isolated incident is not a story, though it may be an interesting anecdote, a story molecule. It becomes a story when cause and effect link it to other events, all of which are connected to each other in a way that seems meaningful to an observer. A story is a web of mirrors, with each event not only tied to the others, but reflecting them from different angles.

Sequence involves time. The passage of time is an element of all stories: "This happened, then this happened, then this happened." When a story consists of a single scene in a single setting, it invariably implies past and future developments. However, while a sequence of events can be charted as a line, a finished story exists as a synchronic shape in the reader's mind. The reader time-travels by flipping pages, seeing patterns the characters can't see.

Writing allows you to control time. You can stretch a split-second to ten pages or compress a lifetime into the same amount. As a writer working on a story or a reader lingering over it, you can bring back the same moment again and again, slowing it down, examining it from different directions, studying it, rearranging it. Maybe that's why stories were invented in the first place. You killed a lion and were excited, but the next day you weren't killing a lion anymore, so you told about it, and that was like killing the lion all over again. Or your father killed a lion, but he died a year later, so you told about him killing the lion, and that was like bringing your father back to life.

If we weren't upset about the way time passes, and afraid of what happens at the end, we wouldn't need to tell stories. We are afraid that life is meaningless and formless, so we have invented a machine that helps us see life's meaning and form, just as a microscope helps us see what our unaided eyes can't. Or perhaps the machine *manufactures* meaning and form. Narrative is the machine. Perhaps the machine wasn't necessary— perhaps we could have discovered life's meaning and form without it. Or perhaps the machine doesn't work as advertised—perhaps life still lacks form and meaning no matter how fervently we tell stories; perhaps the meaning we create in stories is not the true meaning; perhaps some of our stories even block our view of the true meaning. All we know for sure is that we own the machine and it's fun to use.

We use it all the time. I think narrative is a major mode of human thought whose structure is programmed into the brain, just as the structure of dreams and the structure of logic seem to be programmed. Narrative is a compromise between daytime logic and nighttime dream; it is the mode of thought specific to daydreaming. (If you want to think of a good story, lie in bed and look at the ceiling.) There's a good deal of flexibility in its structure, and, being human, we have the capacity to reprogram it within limits: we can tell antistories, stories about stories, stories within stories, and stories whose shape is partly a product of where and when we are living. Individuals can bend the structure in different ways, just as individuals have different styles of dreaming. I might dream of oceans and mountains, in color with a soundtrack; you might dream of lost friends in black and white with dialogue; but both styles are recognizable as human dreams. All stories, underneath individual and historical differences, have a recognizable common ground, as variegated and as definite as the human mind.

Storytelling is pretending, and pretending is planning. It is analog thought, in contrast to the digital thought of computers; not limited to working out algorithms, it creates scenes and people from whole cloth; to call it a logical process would be to demean it. A computer can simulate, but a person can envision. People pretended they could fly, and after thousands of years, they became able to do so. People now pretend that they will colonize other planets, that they will travel faster than light, that they will have minds made of circuitry, that they will live for centuries—and as a result of all this pretending, someday they will. Storytelling is a mechanism of human evolution. Nor is it purely verbal: it uses words to translate imagination.

So our first definition—"a story is the narrative of a sequence of significant events that happen to someone we care about"—was too restrictive. In the broad sense, a story can be any set of ideas that gives form and meaning to experience. Every culture tells a story to the individuals born into it. Whether you are a member of American culture, Ibo culture, Moroccan culture, or Chinese culture, your surroundings are telling you, "This is the way people ought to live; these are the proper values and customs." And that is a story, because no matter what values and customs you treasure, there are thousands of cultures, as human as yours, that treasure other ones.

Cultural stories are what we tell ourselves to convince ourselves we're important and immortal. The meaning of all the stories is the same: "Human beings are not just ignorant organisms who are born, mate, reproduce, and die. We are here for a reason, and we can glimpse what it is. And we will live forever." The stories tell us that working, striving, building will get us somewhere. The history of civilization is a story; the Big Bang theory is a story; New York City is a story. All have been created by human beings telling themselves, "Keep going! Don't quit! You are building something that will last!" All of them, when they lose their power of conviction, will be superseded by something else created for the same purpose. In the absence of stories, would human beings have created culture at all?

So here's another definition: *A story is what we tell ourselves and temporarily believe.*

THE STORY IS IN THE WRITING

But what we're concerned with here is the narrower definition of story, the kind you write on paper, using characters you have invented.

Our initial five-part definition is wide enough to cover myths and folktales, which are retold and recreated endlessly by the minds of many authors; plays and movies, where a different director or performers can turn the same events into a different work; Poe's horror tales and Hawthorne's allegories and Jean Rhys' sketches of Caribbean life; Faulkner's and Woolf's stream-of-consciousness novels and Laurence Sterne's six-hundred pages about how Tristram Shandy got born. It covers the *Odyssey* and it covers *Ulysses.* It covers contemporary stories in which privileged people sit around making witty observations and feeling vague anxiety about feeling vague anxiety, and it covers contemporary stories in which a series of numbered paragraphs wanly parody self-parody.

It doesn't cover stories in which nothing happens and the people it doesn't happen to are of no consequence. It doesn't cover the student story I once read in which a family took a cab, talked to the cabbie, and parted from one another at an airport, and in which at no time could the reader tell who those people were, why they were doing what they were doing, or how they felt about it. It doesn't cover the student story I once wrote about a woman who took up vegetarianism—but what happened after she did, what effect eating a vegetarian diet had on anything else in her life, I was never able to figure out.

If your plan is, "A man falls asleep and has lots of jumbled dreams," that's not a story. If your plan is, "A Dublin innkeeper, sleeping next to his wife and in the same house as his two sons, dreams the entire mythic history of the human race, in circular form, in a newly invented language full of multiple meanings," that's a story. It's *Finnegans Wake,* by James Joyce. Specificity, form, and the presence of motivated human beings (no matter how augmented by Joyce's language) make it a story.

Our definition is a measuring device for answering the question, "Is my story really a story?" *Finnegans Wake* is the farthest notch on the yardstick, until someone someday stretches the yardstick farther.

It's frequently claimed that a good story has a beginning, a middle, and an ending. Yes, very true—in such a broad sense as to be meaningless. Everything has a beginning, a middle, and an ending. A can of shaving cream has a beginning, a middle, and an ending. A football season has a beginning, a middle, and an ending. But that tells us nothing about what the course of the season will be like, or who will win any given game, or how to play football. Nor is there any invariable point at which we can say, "The beginning of the season is now over; we're in the middle." And if there was such a point, what would that teach us? The difference between the beginning, the middle, and the ending is a difference that makes no difference. In many good stories, the boundaries between phases are much less distinct than in many football seasons—or in many lives. It would certainly be easy to find adequate stories that adhere to the three-step program, but it would be equally easy to look at any wonderful story by Raymond Carver, Ann Beattie, Anton Chekhov, or Donald Barthelme and find that it is all beginning, all middle, all ending—or all three at once. Yet it is common practice to have creative writing students practice writing beginnings and endings of stories, as if those were identifiable skills.

Writing a series of story beginnings can be a useful way to get your imagination started and to brainstorm ideas. It's especially valuable if you invent several different *ways* of beginning a story rather than several examples of a single pattern. However, if you approach the exercise with a vision of an acceptable, "correct" way to begin a story and try to make your beginnings match it, you are reinforcing yourself for formulaic writing.

The minute you think there's a correct way to do it, you're doing it wrong. The way to begin a story is whatever way you dream up that makes it most interesting, most beautiful—not "Begin your story with a catchy sentence and quickly introduce the main character in conflict with a foil character, with an outside force, or with him/herself."

It's also said that in a good story, every event should seem necessary. I don't think it's necessary to say "necessary." Neither *Finnegans Wake* nor the potholes in New York City were necessary; we can imagine the world without them. "Necessary" implies that only one sequence and one outcome are possible. It's more fun to believe that at every point in space and time, an infinite number of branching outcomes are possible, only one of which comes to pass.

Your job as a writer is to decide which possibility comes true. Maybe the hero will push the button that saves the world; maybe he won't; maybe he won't, but the world will be saved anyway because the heroine, unbeknownst to him, lifted the key from the sleeping guard's pocket and disarmed the detonator.

Instead of "necessary," we should say "fitting." A good story leaves us with the feeling, "Yeah, that fits." The ending fits the character, and every step on the way fits every step before and after it, and the whole story fits what we feel and know, or didn't know until we read it, about life.

The trick is to make the reader feel, "Yeah, that fits," without also feeling, "I knew that was going to happen all along."

THE STORY IS IN MAKING A DIFFERENCE

Surprise is an element of all art. I'm not talking about gimmicky twist endings; I'm talking about the surprise of encountering something that changes us. The point is not just to sew some events together and wrap them in a pretty package. The gift must make a difference to the person who receives it. A story casts light on a part of life that was dark. A story might change the way people write stories. At the very least, a good story acquaints us with people or places we didn't know before and are glad to learn about. If it doesn't do anything new at all, it's not a story, it's an exercise.

The phrase "a difference that makes a difference" is Bateson's definition of information. The information a story conveys is not rigid and direct, but elastic and allusive. It's not, "The river is three miles northwest of here." It's about what rivers mean. The information in a story is so rich and complex that the only way to convey it is in a form that mimics life. This kind of information increases each time it's read.

What puts the information into the story? The writer's mind. (Some would say "the writer's consciousness" or "the writer's voice"—I prefer the term *mind*. It's not necessarily conscious, and it's more than just a voice.) There is no such thing as a pure event; there is no such thing as an invisible author. We never achieve objectivity, though we can adopt objectivity as a stance. Even if the event actually happened in real life, the writer selects and shapes its parts, its pace, its feel, its flavor, to make it dramatic for people it didn't happen to. In real life, a tree can fall in a forest when there's no one to see and hear it, but in fiction, no tree can fall unless there's an author to describe it and a reader to learn of it.

Do It

1. Improvise a story aloud with a group. Begin by having one member of the group say a sentence beginning, "Once there was. . . ." Each member of the group in turn adds one sentence to the story. If you wish, tape-record your story as you improvise or have someone write down a transcript.

2. Lie down—in bed, on a couch, a floor, or any other comfortable place—for fifteen minutes, then get up and write down all the fantasies that passed through your mind during that time. Look over your list and choose the one fantasy that seems to show the most story potential. Think about how you could add to, subtract from, and otherwise reshape the fantasy into a written work of fiction.

3. Randomly choose three stories by three different authors from three different backgrounds. After reading them, make a list of everything you think the stories have in common.

4. With a group of friends or classmates, invent a fictional culture. Give it a name and decide on its customs. Then make up some of the culture's myths. Possible myths: "How the World Began," "The First Human Beings," "Why There Is Death," "The Greatest Hero of the Culture," and "How the World Will End." To get ideas about your culture, discuss the following questions: What kind of climate and geography do the people live in? How do they get their food and earn their livings? What customs do they follow concerning love, marriage, and family arrangements? What are their beliefs about God or gods, the afterlife, good and evil? What kind of government, if any, do they have?

Writer's Bookshelf

The Arabian Nights (various editions)

shows what a storyteller can do under deadline pressure. Shaharazad had to invent a new tale for her husband, Sultan Shahriar, every night or have her head chopped off. She succeeded, for a thousand and one nights, and not only did she and the sultan live happily ever after, but the world gained a definitive collection of fairy tales.

The Woman Who Talked to Herself by A. L. Barker (1989)

is a novel about a storyteller who interweaves in seemingly (but, of course, not really) unrelated fashion many of the stories she tells. This excellent British author is almost unknown in the United States.

The Marriage of Cadmus and Harmony by Roberto Calasso (translated by Tim Parks, 1993)

is an erudite, contemporary attempt to match Ovid's feat of telling the classical myths as a single narrative.

Italian Folktales by Italo Calvino (translated by George Martin, 1980),

an authoritative collection by a master of fiction, is so content-rich that it's inevitably somewhat repetitious. It belongs to the indispensable Pantheon Fairy Tale and Folklore Library, which also includes African Folktales, Afro-American Folktales, American Indian Myths and Legends, Arab Folktales, The Complete Grimm's Fairy Tales, Irish Folktales, The Norse Myths, Russian Fairy Tales, Yiddish Folktales, *a collection of eighty tales by Hans Christian Andersen, and more.*

Seven Gothic Tales (1934) and *Winter's Tales* (1942) by Isak Dinesen

are unsurpassed in modern fiction for sheer narrative magic; the nature of storytelling is a recurring theme of these ornate, elegantly written stories. "The Young Man with the Carnation" is comically provocative on the hazards and rewards of the literary calling.

Metamorphoses by Ovid (translated by Rolfe Humphries, 1955)

presents the Greek and Roman myths, from the creation of the world to the deification of Augustus Caesar, as a single narrative unified by the theme of change. It has been the standard source on classical mythology for almost two-thousand years and is a great read.

Chapter 3

What to Write About

In two words: Anything. But. . . .

The question of subject matter is a touchy one.

In theory, literature can be written about any aspect of human experience, but for practical purposes, it had better be dramatic and fresh if you want to become known to the public. It is okay not to become known to the public, but the assumption of this book is that you want to be. A subject that has never been treated in the same way before, and with which readers can identify, is a reachable goal to aim for. There are few if any truly original subjects for fiction, and part of the fun of reading is comparing how different writers deal with similar subjects.

It's important to stay on the right side of the line of originality. It's okay if the reader thinks, "This story reminds me of an Elizabeth Bowen story, except that this one is about Bosnia rather than World War II Britain and is from the male angle instead of the female and [here's the important part] says something different about the effects of war on civilians." It's okay if the reader thinks, "This writer seems influenced by Elizabeth Bowen." It's not okay if the reader thinks, "This is just an update of an old Elizabeth Bowen story" or "This is derivative of, imitative of, Elizabeth Bowen." You must achieve transformation, not imitation.

New wrappings for old subjects are temporarily viewed as original. Where writers two-hundred years ago could write love stories in the form of letters, they can now write love stories in the form of E-mail messages. The inside has not changed, but the exterior has been repainted. In a few years, writing a love story in the form of E-mail messages will seem passé.

THE BIG SUBJECTS

Regardless of packaging and trends, the essential subject matter of fiction is the passage of human life through stages. We grow, we struggle, we change, and we wonder. We mate, we work, we form groups, we age, we die. To put it more specifically, the big, eternal subjects are the following:

- birth and childhood
- the passage from childhood to adulthood
- love and its loss
- marriage and the lack of it
- family life and its conflicts
- work
- war
- crime
- illness and accident
- the gain or loss of money
- adventure; physical risk
- death

Regardless of the subject, the vast majority of fiction deals with pain, suffering, trouble—to use a great Yiddish word, *tsuris.* Fiction is a magic device for turning pain into joy. The magic works by renaming and framing the pain. This pain isn't happening to us, fiction says; it's happening to those people over there—those fictional characters, who, although they strangely resemble us, have different names and descriptions and live in different houses. And it all happens in this confined area—this story, these pages. We don't have to worry about it escaping and spilling into our lives. The frame makes happy endings possible, as they wouldn't be if we had to think about what would happen after the ending. Life is difficult, fiction says, but the difficulty is limited and can be solved—solved imperfectly, if it's realistic modern fiction; solved perfectly, if it's folklore or romance.

This doesn't mean that fiction can never be about happiness. It's certainly *easier* to write about evil and strife than about goodness and contentment. Nevertheless, there have been beautiful stories about the idyll of first love, the unselfish rapture of parenthood, the bliss of being part of nature, the possibility of redemption from death. I wouldn't advise anyone to try it unless (1) they have seen goodness and contentment up close, and (2) they write so beautifully that they can make stillness exciting. Contentment doesn't make us want to go anywhere; it makes us want to stay where we are. That's why it's so hard to write about, for fiction is a motor vehicle and its engine is change. The tired old word *conflict*—opposition between a character and inner or outer forces—is important because it provides the motive for change, whether the change is from sorrow to joy, or vice versa.

Fiction is about all of life, every human experience and emotion without exception; it's "the one bright book of life," in D. H. Lawrence's phrase. "Happiness makes no story" is one of those faculty-room strictures that must be hedged, fudged, trimmed, and qualified—with "usuallys" and "generally speakings" and "for the most parts"—to be valid; accepted literally, it reduces fiction from an all-encompassing glory to a nasty game.

Happiness in stories usually, generally speaking, for the most part springs from a contrast with unhappiness. Conversely, unhappiness in fiction is rarely unrelieved. Pessimistic writers are comical—Beckett, Kafka—and writers who have been hurt terribly by life—Poe—turn their terror into unreality and amazement.

Perhaps it's the transition from pain to joy and back that interests fiction most; perhaps the story is not in one state or the other, but in the movement from state to state—the border crossing. The story is about how, when we were hurting in one situation, we packed up and left, and how we eluded capture at the border, and what we found on the other side, and what we missed when we looked back.

INSTITUTIONS AS SUBJECTS

The twelve subjects mentioned above are open-ended. That is, they don't have predetermined time limits or spatial boundaries. A character's growth to adulthood may happen overnight or may take a generation; it may all occur in a bedroom, or it may require a world tour. There are other subjects that are space- or time-limited. They describe human institutions or processes that are set off from the rest of the world, such as:

- a journey, pilgrimage, or quest
- a prison sentence
- a hospital stay
- a job

- a school or school year
- a military tour of duty
- a mission or case (such as a legal or medical case)
- an exploration or discovery

More broadly:

- a career
- a life span

The story ends when the time limit or institutional boundary is reached. Put your characters on a boat in San Francisco and when they reach Hong Kong, the story is over, right? Start the action with the first day of school in September and end with the last day in May or June.

No, not that simple. The institution or process isn't the story; it's the framework within which the story develops. In order to have a story, you must use the framework differently from the way previous writers have used it. *One Flew Over the Cuckoo's Nest* doesn't begin when McMurphy enters the hospital and end when he leaves; it begins when he enters and ends when his fate is decided—and when Chief Broom leaves; and the leaving involves far more than the chronological expiration of a commitment. Between entrance and exit, a story has been enacted that could only have occurred on this institutional stage and that changes our ideas about what the institution itself is. The story reshapes the framework within which it's set.

FINDING YOUR SUBJECTS

Thus far in this chapter, I've answered the question, "What is there to write about?" But that isn't the most important question. The most important question is, "What should *I* write about?" Finding a subject is a personal quest. (Some writers have made the quest for a subject the subject of stories; but as with all subjects, once it's been repeated too often, it gets stale.) If you're looking for a technical exercise in craftsmanship, you can choose any of the above subjects at random, but if you're looking for a life's work, a way to write, a place in literature, you'll have to work toward it by feel. This may take years, even decades. Along the way, you may make many wrong turns, and you had better forgive yourself for them instead of blaming yourself and getting discouraged.

No one, including yourself, can identify your true subject beforehand. Writers sometimes resist their own best subjects: Flaubert was quite dubious, at first, when a friend proposed the idea for *Madame Bovary*. This proves that listening to suggestions can pay off. It also pays to heed the news, "Elizabeth Bowen did a story like that already." In such a case, you'd be shrewd to read the story and concoct a new variation. Beware, however, of the doubter who says, "That's just not your subject" or "Other people wouldn't be interested." Is he or she more creative than you and more well-versed in the subject? How does he or she know what you can do before you've done it? Even if the resulting story is flawed, you can probably learn more from writing it than from not writing it.

It's worthwhile for beginning writers, especially, to explore a variety of subjects and styles in order to develop a feel for the boundaries of their territory, the limits of their powers. In the process, they will inevitably attempt many subjects that aren't right for them. But they may also expand their powers and learn how to write things they didn't think they could. Established professional writers are less likely to experiment in this way because it means a loss of time and money, but that doesn't mean they wouldn't benefit from it.

After all, what you thought was your true subject may only have been your subject at one point in your life. You are changing, and two years later, having already dealt with that subject, you're no longer interested in it.

On the other hand, after telling yourself, "I don't want to write about this subject any more; I've already done it," and thrashing about, trying to escape in ten different directions, you may learn that it really is your subject after all, and you have no choice but to write about it again and again, all your life, trying to make each attempt more successful than the last. That doesn't mean the thrashing was fruitless. Perhaps an unsuccessful attempt to write a horror story has helped free a realist's imagination, so the next time she writes a placid study of suburban marriage it will have more depth and drama than before. Writers are not pack mules. Straying is part of the job description, and a useful guideline for all creative work is "Instinct first, judgment later."

There's no denying that from the reader's and publisher's point of view, some subjects contain more inherent drama than others. Subjects involving visible action are more inherently interesting to more people than quiet subjects involving the inner life. This is not necessarily a good thing, nor does it mean that you must now write sea stories instead of living-room stories. The kind of fiction you *should* write is the kind you *can* and *must* write, and it may take you most of your life to find out what that is.

WAITING FOR A SUBJECT

For many people, thinking of subjects is the hardest part of writing. What to do if you can't think of an idea?

There are two diametrically opposed approaches. The first is this: Don't write, for now. Take a break. Recharge your batteries. Spend a day, a week, a year, however long your psyche tells you, looking at the world around you, observing, perhaps taking notes and perhaps not. Some writers go in cycles: they need to spend a period of time taking in material, digesting it in their subconscious minds, and only then do they feel ready to give it out in the form of fiction. (In cases of people who come to writing late in life, their entire youth has been spent taking in material; the second halves of their lives are devoted to processing it.) Some people feel they can only write when their inner voices speak to them; they may slack off for six months, then pour forth pages in a Kerouacky torrent.

The outside world views such writers as undisciplined; writing textbooks tend to coax students into writing every day no matter what their mood; but rigid discipline doesn't work for everyone, and the writers of those textbooks may be too influenced by the fact that student writers often have classroom schedules that dictate their output. If you have to turn a story in next week, then you'd better get to work no matter how you feel, but that doesn't mean working to a deadline is necessarily the best rhythm for you as an individual. For some people, cranking out two pages a day is all too easy, whether those pages are alive or dead. What they really need is free time in which to open their senses receptively.

This is especially true of writers who have already established good work habits and have written a lot over the course of the years. Professionals get anxious at the thought of going a day without scribbling something on paper. If they wrote page 301 of their current novel on Tuesday, they have to write page 302 on Wednesday or they'll turn crabby and make life miserable for their loved ones. A vacation, a sabbatical, may be the prescribed activity for such people.

If you choose the timeout approach, get as much physical and mental rest as you can, but while you're relaxing, try to increase your powers of observation. Simply keeping your eyes and ears open is the most basic writing exercise there is, and one of the most productive. Try to notice everything around you, letting nothing escape you. Concentrate on some object that's so familiar you hardly even see it anymore—perhaps your own face in the mirror. Stare at landscapes for longer than you're used to doing, so that you memorize the way they look and sound and smell. Visit new places and gather impressions. Eavesdrop on conversations. Sometimes let your attention be unfocused, taking in everything at once. At other times, focus on one object—an ant walking through a forest of lawn grass—and see it as a whole in relation to its environment.

Sometimes, you might want to codify your observations in words. Walking down the street, you might write descriptions in your head: "I passed Zito's Bakery, where the scent of warm bread tumbled out the doorway, past the gray plastic milk crate where the old man sat, onto the sun-scorched sidewalk." But at times, it's best simply to look, to experience pure reality without putting a screen of words between you and it. You will learn about the world, and later you will have plenty of opportunity to put it into words. Goethe said, "It is better to think than to do, better to feel than to think, but best of all simply to look." Of course, Goethe did a lot of thinking, feeling, and doing, for which the looking was preparation.

The disadvantage of this approach is that it does not fit very well into a semester schedule.

The second approach is this: "Write every day no matter how you feel." Writers who have not yet established solid work habits can benefit greatly from this method. If you don't have a subject, there are random and semirandom methods you can use to find one:

- Read the newspaper. *Crime and Punishment* and *Madame Bovary* originated in news stories, as have many modern bestsellers, such as Judith Rossner's *Looking for Mr. Goodbar*. Articles about crime are especially fertile sources. Once you've found an article that inspires you, feel free to change any and all facts in it.

- First think of a title, then invent a plot and characters to go with it. The title can be almost any intriguing combination of simple words; a famous one, the subject of a short-story anthology edited by George Garrett, is "The Girl in the Black Raincoat." Some random suggestions along similar lines: "The Man With the Gray Ponytail," "The Laughing Woman," "The Feminist's Son." If you can't think of a title, borrow a title another author has used and invent a totally new story around it. (Titles aren't copyrightable.)

- Think of a place you have always wanted to go and a kind of job or activity you have always wanted to perform. Write a story about doing that activity in that place.

- Choose a friend or relative. Change this person's appearance, profession, and gender, as well as any personality traits you think might be affected by those basic changes; then use him or her as your main character. Think of the worst possible thing that could happen to that person, and write a story about it.

- Get a clean sheet of paper and write the words, "Once there was" at the beginning. Then write whatever pops into your head. Keep your pencil moving, no matter what, until the page is filled with narrative.

- Give yourself a work quota and deadline, such as "I must write a page in the next hour." If you don't meet it, reset it a little lower for the next session. Once you've declared that a work session has begun, keep going until the deadline, even if you are staring at a blank screen. Consider a session successful even if it does not produce any written words. It is a warm-up for future sessions.

When the keep-writing-anyway approach leads you onto false trails, just throw away your scribbling and start over again. Eventually you will hit on a subject that has legs, as the saying goes. If you practice consistently, you will get into the habit not only of turning out words at a brisk pace, but of finding ideas whenever you need them. The quality of the ideas, too, will improve with practice. You will be able to call upon yourself and get a good response.

You never have to decide whether you are a keep-writing-anyway person or a take-time-out person. You can use both approaches in the same project, even on the same day.

Do It

1. Write a story about your family's life before you were born.

2. Write a story about your own death. Describe when and where it happens and who is present. Write it so that your death shows the reader something about your life. (It doesn't have to be what you really think your life and death will be like.)

3. Open a history book to a random page. Write a story about a historical figure or event mentioned on that page.

4. Write a title on a slip of paper and hand it to a friend or classmate, who will do the same for you. Then each of you should plan a story to go with your partner's title.

5. Think of an object, then invest a character who is involved with that object in some way—someone who needs the object, fears it, desires it, hates it, owns it, creates it, destroys it, finds it, loses it. Plan a story about that emotional involvement.

Writer's Bookshelf

The Bible

has provided more writers with material than any other book in western civilization. William Faulkner's Absalom, Absalom!, *John Steinbeck's* East of Eden, *Thomas Mann's* Joseph and his Brothers, *and innumerable other fiction works are reworkings of biblical motifs.*

Chronicles of England, Scotland, and Ireland by Raphael Holinshed (1578, revised 1587)

was Shakespeare's source for the history plays, Macbeth, Cymbeline, *and* King Lear. *Mortal writers, too, have profited from reading history as a source of subject matter.*

On Writer's Block by Victoria Nelson (1993)

is a prescription for what to do when you can't think of something to write about—or when you can, but can't bring yourself to do it. It also goes beyond the limits indicated in its title to examine the wider range of writerly emotions.

de l'Amour by Stendhal (1822; translated as *Love* by Gilbert and Suzanne Sale, 1957, in the Penguin paperback edition),

a collection of essays and aphorisms, is a witty and still-illuminating study of the eternal subject by the novelist and crush-sufferer extraordinaire.

Chapter 4

Action
Versus Plot

Action is the stuff plot is made of. Plot is an organizational principle; it's the way actions build upon the actions before them and lead to the actions after them.

An action-filled story can be ineptly plotted; a low-key story can be skillfully plotted. To verify this, watch Hollywood action movies. They are filled with murders, robberies, car chases, acts of revenge, and double-crosses, a large percentage of which make no sense. You've probably had the experience of watching an exciting movie and then, five minutes after the lights go on, picking the plot apart: "Why did the villain ransack the office when all he had to do was photocopy one memo from the desk? How come the detectives didn't look for fingerprints on the telephone?" Action films are riddled with holes. Criminals phone their favorite cops and establish personal relationships, warning them about where they're going to strike next. Detectives solve baffling cases on the basis of unfounded hunches, which almost always prove correct. After the jolt, you're left feeling empty and disappointed.

It is a rare action film that doesn't raise issues of this kind. Audiences have become so used to being cheated that they laugh it off: "That's the way movies are." But it's not the way movies have to be, it's just the result of laziness. Or perhaps it's a secret of Hollywood marketing: action movies create a craving for adrenaline and, by leaving the consumer unsatisfied at the end, excite a desire for more movies.

In fiction, bad plotting is more of a drawback, because of the absence of attractive performers and settings to distract the audience. The force behind good plotting is *motivation.* In a well-plotted piece of fiction, things happen because they are the things that the characters, given their individual personalities, choose to do. The characters' choices are either wise or unwise; in either case, they lead to consequences. The chain of consequences is the plot.

Interacting with the force of choice are those of fate and chance. A character contracts a disease or is written out of a parent's will. Such events set up the plot, but what gives the plot its shape and interest is the character's chosen response to the setup. The disease and the lost inheritance have certain results and meanings because of the people they affect. Actions echo off characters.

Characters' choices usually proceed from misunderstanding to understanding. Unwise initial choices lead to complications that test and teach the character, until he or she has learned enough to make wiser choices. Thus character and plot work together to create theme.

Thinking about plot in the absence of character is an artificial, mechanical activity. It can be useful, though, if you're stuck and the characters have gone stale in your mind. Try writing a summary of the plot in one page or less. Start by rehashing what you've already written, then launch yourself without hesitation into what you haven't written yet—what you haven't even planned yet. This is a potentially powerful shortcut, a way to getting into the habit of freeing your imagination. As with most habits, the more you practice, the better you'll get at it. If it works, you've made a breakthrough, and if it doesn't you haven't lost any ground, because there are other and better ways to think about plot.

THINKING ABOUT CHARACTER

The best way to think about plot is by thinking about character. Not, "What should happen next?" but, "What will Louie do next?" Not, "We've put in a chance meeting, then some frustrating misses, now it's time to get the lovers back together through another screwball circumstance," but, "Louie and Stella met at first when Stella dialed a wrong number and got Louie by mistake. Liking his voice, she redialed; they arranged a meeting at a café, but when a bus driving through a puddle drenched Louie's suit, he was late showing up. How can he find Stella when he doesn't know her address or phone number? Is he just going to wait until she calls him back? No, he's bolder than that. Will he show up at the office where she mentioned she worked? No, he's more discreet than that. What he'll do is, he'll return to the café at the same time every afternoon for two weeks."

Think about the characters in specific terms; view them from inside; feel like them. Instead of asking, "What would Louie do next?" ask, "What would I do next if I were Louie?" Even better: "I *am* Louie; what should I do next?" This doesn't mean the character is recognizably based on you. It means that you are able to identify with all your characters, no matter how much or little in common with you they seem to have. Fantasize about yourself in the character's situation; examine the whole range of possible choices you might make. Include choices you wouldn't make in real life, but might if you were a different kind of person. (You *are* a different kind of person, even if you don't show it. Fiction is the place to show it.) Give your characters part of yourself, without making them identical to yourself. In return, your characters will give you part of themselves.

Sometimes you can dwell on your characters without having verbal thoughts about them. If you're at a point in plotting where you can't think of the next event, try repeating your characters' names to yourself like a mantra, visualizing their physical appearance as you do so. You can do it aloud or silently, while sitting alone in a room, while taking a walk, while driving. By repeating their names, you imprint them in your unconscious, where the apparatus of dreaming will go to work creating scenes for them.

Your aim is to concentrate on your characters in a relaxed but focused way until they come to life spontaneously. This is known as *dreaming the scene;* a form of controlled daydreaming. If, for a few minutes, you reach the point where you hardly notice your surroundings and you intensely fantasize about your characters doing and saying things, you have begun to dream the scene. Not every specific scene you fantasize will end up on paper, but all of them will help strengthen your imagination.

Inventing a plot by daydreaming about your characters will give your work a different feel than inventing a plot by thinking, "I've established an initial conflict and one complication; what secondary complication can arise out of it, leading the main character to a crisis point and resolution?" It will help you create something real and alive rather than a counterfeit or a model—carbon-based fiction rather than silicon-based.

FALSE AND TRUE PLOT PATTERNS

Recipes for plotting describe what has already been done; as rules for what to do in the future, they are merely limitations. The rules involve so many loopholes and exceptions and distortions that they lose their meaning. Writers end up making excuses: "True, there are two equally important protagonists in this novel, but they both exemplify the same theme." "I know there doesn't seem to be a clearcut conflict here—the hero simply travels, meeting up with adventures at every point—but the event that *caused* him to set out on his travels was a conflict." "This plot does not develop through a series of complications, but the development is *implied* in this one moment of crisis." "Well, sure, there isn't any definite resolution in this story, but lack of closure is in itself the insight the writer wants to get across."

There is one standardized plot pattern that I think is worth studying. It's the mythological hero motif set forth by Joseph Campbell in *The Hero with A Thousand Faces*. Campbell's all-purpose hero is someone who is set apart from ordinary humanity through miraculous birth or other special qualities, and who undergoes a test in the form of a quest or journey. The quest takes the hero out of the ordinary sphere of human life, often into a new land where different rules apply. Passing through a series of challenges, the hero is helped in the quest by the magic or wisdom of some characters and hindered by other characters. Although the quest seems difficult throughout, when the key is finally found, the challenge is resolved with surprising ease. The hero then acquires a boon—a good thing, such as new knowledge—which he or she brings back to the human community for its benefit.

The conflict-complications-crisis-resolution formulas in writers' manuals are really secular versions of this mythological pattern. Campbell's book is packed with insights, stories, and fascinating bits of knowledge. His belief that all myths follow one structure is disprovable, however, by citing different myths from the ones he uses.

If classic patterns must be taken with a ton of salt, is there anything at all we can say about plotting that is universally, reliably true? It's tempting to say, "In a well-made plot, every event should be causally connected to every other event, with no loose threads," except for the fact that there are great works of literature whose plots are diffuse, digressive, episodic, with events linked only by chronology and not by causation. A loose thread can be the brilliant scene readers remember after they've forgotten everything else about a book. Perhaps we can say, instead, that causation is *usually* the source of plot strength; it's an excellent thing to teach in classrooms, but the most important point about writing is that every writer contributes to the conventions. Every work of fiction expresses both an individual and a culture. The conventions reflect the culture; the departures from convention reflect the individual.

REALISTIC PLOTTING

Here's what I think comes closest to a universal principle of plotting: *Events should arise convincingly from their premises.* Every story starts off with certain givens. They may be realistic: "Raskolnikov is an alienated student who thinks that by killing his landlady he can become a superman." They may be fantastic: "When the planet Krypton, which had a red sun, exploded, the scientist Jor-el sent his son in a rocket to safety; the rocket landed on the yellow-sunned planet Earth, giving the boy superpowers, except for a vulnerability to meteorite fragments of his home planet, called Kryptonite."

Everything that happens in the plot should be consistent with the givens. Nothing should happen that makes us say, "Hey, that isn't what they showed us at the beginning." There may, however, be twists that give the premises enhanced meaning. If Raskolnikov called off his plan and started being nice to his landlady, it would betray the premises of *Crime and Punishment*—but the fact that he feels guilty and repents is an interesting twist that fits in with the given of his philosophical intelligence.

Lapsing from the premises, betraying them, is the major reason why Hollywood movies are as bad as I say they are. A fascinating premise is introduced at the beginning and then is progressively discarded so that more murders and car chases can be crammed in. At the beginning, the murderer preys on father-figures because of his history as a severely abused child; but by the end, you can bet that this very specific psychopathology will be thrown out the window, and the killer will become an all-purpose maniac, a fiend for all seasons who kidnaps store clerks, makes threatening phone calls, blows up police stations, and rolls around in any other kind of filth that happens to be on the producer's floor during the story conference. At the beginning, the hero is an honest cop with limited ideas and a background of drinking and divorce, who wants nothing more than another chance to prove himself; but you can be sure that by the end he will be Superman, invulnerable to bullets, insensitive to pain, and able to anticipate any surprise in advance.

All Hollywood movies are about Superman.

MOVEMENT IN PLOTTING

If your plot is causally based and lacking in loose threads and your premises are followed consistently and convincingly from beginning to end, you have done a craftsmanlike job of plotting, but that doesn't necessarily mean you have written an interesting story. The key to plotting is not shape but movement. A plot is a plot not because its events can be graphed in the form of an ascending curve, but because it *goes* some-where, and the places its goes captivate us.

If you are emotionally involved in your work, you should always be looking forward, eager to find out what's going to appear on your next page, your next scene. You have a good deal of control over it, but if you didn't leave room for spontaneity, for eruptions of the unpredictable from the unconscious, you would lose interest in what you were writing, and your boredom would communicate itself to readers. The writer should be a reader of his or her own work, eager to find out what happens next. A writer must look in many directions at once, but the most important is forward.

Plot momentum requires suspense, and suspense means unanswered questions. Readers can almost glimpse the answers a page, a scene, a chapter ahead. They test possibilities in their mind, but they want you to give them something they haven't anticipated.

You achieve suspense by controlling information. At what point should you tell the readers that the suspect is the long-lost, illegitimate son of the victim? Just before the readers would have guessed it themselves. Throughout the plot, you are issuing little bulletins, teasers, to the readers. "Stay tuned for an important message after these few words!"

If the teasers are subliminal, if readers are made almost aware of them but not quite, allowed almost to guess their meaning before it is pulled away, then they are effective foreshadowing. Solutions to mysteries, answers to questions about characters' identities and fates, surprising turns of plot, deferred explanations of motive—these warrant foreshadowing, for if they're sprung on readers with no preparation, they seem like arbitrary exertions of the author's power, and they deprive the readers of the pleasure of guessing (even if the guess was wrong, even if the readers only noticed in hindsight the opportunity to guess). But if foreshadowing is heavy-handed, your surprises are ruined.

The key to not telegraphing the ending is in not underestimating readers' intelligence. When in doubt, make the hints less obvious. Readers don't need to notice all the foreshadowings the first time around—probably *shouldn't* notice them all. It's enough if, on page 328, when it's revealed that the suspect is actually the victim's illegitimate son, the readers say, "Oh, I remember now! They were the only two who didn't get poison ivy when all the party guests went on a scavenger hunt in the woods!"

Base foreshadowing on tangible facts rather than on stereotypes or loaded impressions: if you claim that the suspect and the victim have an unaccountable, almost telephathic understanding of one another, that's cheating. Foreshadow early: the more pages go by between hint and revelation, the more likely that the hint will skip readers' minds, preserving suspense. Shield your foreshadowings by slipping them into scenes that appear to have other purposes and other consequences—the poison ivy scene might be most memorable to readers as the occasion when the suspect eased the ingenue's itches with calamine lotion.

Unearthed secrets, reversals of expectation, losses and gains move plots forward. Characters turn out to be other than what they seemed. They have hidden pasts that affect the present in unsuspected ways. The powerful lose their power; the weak acquire it. Fortunes collapse, kingdoms crumble, the kitchen servant turns out to be the bravest of knights. Secondary characters often advance the plot by functioning as helpers or hinderers, as Campbell points out.

SUBPLOTS

What about subplots? Two-hundred years ago they were considered necessary; today they're increasingly dispensed with. Short stories and small-cast novels usually lack them altogether. Subplots are the domain of the long novel, and there's no reason to try to *make* a novel longer by adding a subplot you could have done without. A subplot, to be worth the space, should strengthen the primary plot by (1) materially affecting its outcome through a chain of causation, (2) adding crucial information, or at least (3) showing a strong thematic link. The characters of the subplot are usually tied to the characters in a big way: the primary protagonist may be the lover, former lover, future lover, competitor, relative, or business partner of the subplot protagonist. At the very least there is propinquity (closeness in location). The fates of the primary protagonist and subplot protagonist may reflect two harmonizing, or perhaps two counterpointing, aspects of the same society. Perhaps the primary protagonist and the subplot protagonist share a common status—both are fathers of ungrateful children, as in *King Lear*—or a contrast in status—one is an aristocrat and one a revolutionary, as in *A Tale of Two Cities*.

It sometimes works to create parallel plot lines that are equal in importance, as in Tolstoy's *War and Peace* and *Anna Karenina*, where the parallel protagonists are acquaintances—sometimes in-laws—within the same social circles at the same time in Russian history.

Ultimately, though, I tend to think that in plotting, as in love, one good one is all anyone needs.

Do It

1. Give yourself five minutes to invent a plot spontaneously, from scratch. It doesn't have to be a good, tightly knit plot, it just has to

be something that starts with a character and a premise and moves toward and ending. It can be about anything, no matter how ridiculous. Write a summary of it. Chances are, your first attempt will be lousy. The more times you do this exercise, the more you will free your imagination to think up events and ideas without inhibition.

2. Try to write a short story that has no plot at all. If you can, you deserve congratulations, although what you have written may actually be a formless sketch rather than an effective story. If you find that you've written a formless sketch, view it as raw material. Add events, causal connections, and momentum that turn your plotless sketch into a structured story.

3. Write a plot summary for a story or novel you especially like.

4. In a writing group, decide on a premise for a story. It should be statable in one sentence, such as, "An ordinary person wins a lottery" or "Two twins, separated at birth, meet at age twenty." Let each member of the group individually write down a summary of what happens later in the plot, from beginning to end. Try to make your plot unpredictable but believable. Pass your summaries around or read them aloud. If you wish, cull the best ideas from all the summaries into one well-structured plot.

Writer's Bookshelf

Dombey and Son (1848), *Bleak House* (1853), *Great Expectations* (1861), and *Our Mutual Friend* (1865), all by Charles Dickens,
> *are perhaps Dickens' most dazzlingly plotted novels. He's especially good at complicated subplotting.*

The Wild Palms by William Faulkner (1939)
> *is notable for the chapter-by-chapter alternation of two entirely separate plots.*

One Hundred Years of Solitude by Gabriel Garcia Marquez (translated by Gregory Rabassa, 1970)
> stands out among contemporary novels for the sustained momentum—at once viscous and brisk—of its multigenerational narrative. The rise and fall of the Buendia family are the occasions for numerous fantastic events.

The Black Prince (1973), *The Sea, the Sea* (1978), *The Good Apprentice* (1985), *The Message to the Planet* (1989), and *The Green Knight* (1993), all by Iris Murdoch,
> are among the more than twenty enchanting novels by the Oxford philosopher who is the English-speaking world's current champion at handling fast-moving, large-cast plots in an atmosphere of sexy comedy and thematic depth.

W, or Memories of Childhood by Georges Perec (translated by David Bellos, 1988)
> intertwines two divergent plots that actually have a great deal to do with one another: a fantasy about a writer whisked to an island ruled by a tyrant, and a memoir of the writer's childhood as a Jew during the Holocaust.

Chapter 5

Characterization

A fictional character is a human being without a body—a person made entirely of words. Fictional characters inhabit a world of pure language or, to put it another way, pure spirit.

Fictional characters *should be* as complex as living human beings; whether they *can be* is another question. I once heard a writer I respect say that writers should aim to make their characters less complex than real people, because real people are too complicated, self-contradictory, and elusive to provide the illusion of solidity and stability that fictional characters need. Readers, this writer claimed, can only visualize simpler forms.

I almost jumped out of my skin!

It seems to me that if you aren't trying to create real people on the page, you've given up before you've started. Melville made Captain Ahab say, "Strike through the mask!" and that should be every serious writer's motto. Most people, in real life and in fiction, only show us their masks—they do not meet our highest standards—but that doesn't mean we're satisfied with the situation. Our intent is to pierce the mask of social personality and find out what is underneath. What have we learned about the character by page 200 that we would not have guessed on page 10? If the answer is just more details about the character's surface, more examples of how the character deals with specific experiences, it is not enough—at least not on the highest levels of literature. Character should stretch plot and theme; character is what *makes* plot and theme. My goal as a writer is always to go deeper, deeper into the people I have invented; that is the top priority. I don't see the point—call this my personal prejudice—in writing without that motive. Anything else is just playing with words, showing off technique.

DISCOVERING A CHARACTER

Every character should have an inner life, even if you show little of it. In a short story, where there isn't room to actually reveal much about the main character, the work should imply that the character, whom we only meet in one or two scenes, has a past and future extending far beyond the story. A considerable part of the art of fiction consists in leaving the impression that there's more.

In order to come as close as possible to the impossible goal, the writer himself or herself should be continually discovering the character. If the writer knows everything about the character at the beginning—or to put it more accurately, if the writer knows certain things about the character at the beginning and has no intention of going beyond those things—characterization will be constricted. You should believe in your character's potential for growth. After all, you believe in your own, and your characters are part of you.

And you should see the character as a living whole, not as a collection of traits. You don't create a character by fishing around in your bag of tricks and pulling out two parts villainy, one moral twinge, a distinctive speech pattern, and a touch of charm. You don't construct characters, you create them. From their first entrance, they are alive and capable of thought, and they keep becoming more so. The times a writer has to resort to techniques of construction—to asking, "Let's see, should I give this character a limp? a habit of forgetting her clothes at the cleaners? a troubled past as an adopted child?"—are the times when he or she is stuck for inspiration and has to settle for second-best. When things are really going well, the characters come already breathing.

Of course, very few writers—if any—ever succeed at creating characters who are as complex as real people; every day we face the fact that our achievement will not match our ambition; but if you don't aim that high, your achievement will fall even lower. As F. Scott Fitzgerald said, "Begin with an individual and you find that have created a type; begin with a type and you find that you have created—nothing."

My characters are Louie and Stella; they are not "the pseudo-sensitive but pseudo-tough thirtyish middle-class American male" and "the pseudo-tough but pseudo-sensitive thirtyish middle-class American female." Those type-labels might help me focus on them if I ever lose sight of who they are (just as defining myself might help me remember who I am if I ever lose sight of that), but I never accept type-labels as a complete description of Louie and Stella. They have their own individual integrity, which I am discovering in the process of writing about them. They can surprise me. What most interests me about them is not how they are true to my preconceptions, but how they aren't.

Given that characters are made of language rather than protoplasm, there are some things they don't do as well as actual human beings and some things they do better. Physical upkeep such as eating, drinking glasses of water, and going to the bathroom can be skipped altogether unless it makes a causal difference in the plot—for instance, if the glass of water has been poisoned by the heroine's rival. In addition, fictional characters have a much higher pain threshold than physical human beings—in fact, they have no pain threshold. It's very hard to write convincingly about a character's suffering of physical pain. (This doesn't mean it's uninteresting to try.) Fictional characters are continually getting shot, maimed, slashed, and doing much better afterward than a person burdened with a body would do. Fictional characters consume amounts of alcohol that would cause damage to a physical brain or liver and utter eloquent wisdom in the midst of fevered delirium.

Fictional characters have a lower threshold of psychic pain than real people, though. Just about anything makes them suffer transports of sorrow, self-doubt, introspection, or, swinging the other way, joyous celebration of the beauty of life. Any fleshbound person who felt as much emotion as a fictional character would probably not have much time to get any work done—unless he or she was a writer.

In fact, fictional characters don't work nearly as hard as people in our world; they are creatures of leisure. Ninety percent of fiction takes place in the off-hours, when the characters are sitting around chatting, establishing social relations, sizing each other up and—greatest of luxuries—learning about themselves. Whether they're wearing upper-class or lower-class costume, they don't spend many pages counting their money and paying the bills. They are going on dates, going to balls, leaving early and taking cab rides home; they are fox-hunting, hitchhiking, messing around with one another's mates, and going on vacation. As Jane Austen said, "Everything happens at parties." Work is pushed into the shadows in fiction (a condition we fleshly characters could learn from). When work settings are described, they're often window-dressing for romantic intrigue, as in the dairy scenes in *Tess of the D'Urbervilles*. The major exception consists of the kind of work that is adventure: whale-hunting, planet-discovering, spy-chasing, and so on.

It must be fun being a fictional character. Maybe that's why I've spent so much of my life with them. Hoping it would rub off.

FUNDAMENTALS OF CHARACTERIZATION

Whether people are made of flesh or of words, we know them by:

- their names
- their physical appearance
- their personal histories
- what they say
- what others say about them
- how they act in response to specific situations
- how they act habitually
- their thoughts

These are the fundamentals of characterization.

Names

A person's name is an item of cultural information. It is a product of the person's social identity. My paternal great-grandfather's family name was Gornostysky; a generation later it was shortened to Gornosty. When my grandfather immigrated to the United States, Gornosty seemed too hard to pronounce and spell, so he changed it to Cohen, which reflected our family's descent from the priestly caste of ancient Israel, the sons of Aaron. My parents named me Richard because strong-sounding Anglo-Saxon first names were popular among American Jews of the 1950s. A generation earlier, they might have named me Irving or Milton; a generation later, when Hebrew names were again popular among Jewish-American parents, they might have named me Noah or Gideon.

Names also *might* tell you about people's individual personalities. It's often said that people grow up to fit their names. (Those who don't sometimes change their names to fit the way they have grown up.) I don't entirely buy that. When you know that a person's name is Laurie B. Clark, you know almost nothing about her. More distinctive names are likely to contain more information, or at least provide room for guesswork.

For this reason, fictional characters' names tend to be distinctive. Another reason to make your characters' names distinctive is so that readers can remember them. If your characters' names are Bill Smith and Ed Brown, readers are going to have to stop in the midst of the story and ask themselves, "Now which one was which?"

There is a place for simple names in fiction, but the best simple names are ones that become distinctive by repeated association with a memorable character. The most inspired name in English fiction is Tom Jones.

Names don't get any simpler. Under the circumstances—because of who Tom Jones is—the name comes to seem rollicking, adventurous, dashingly heroic. Somehow, it's not the same as calling a character Bill Brown or Ed Smith—I mean Bill Smith or Ed Brown. The inspiration in the name Tom Jones is in making something so simple so memorable.

Many other English novels written around the same time as *Tom Jones* have characters whose names are much less realistic, such as *Peregrine Pickle*. When I tell you that a character's name is Peregrine Pickle, you immediately guess that he is a somewhat silly fellow involved in picaresque adventures. The name serves a purpose, but it's not as deep a purpose as the purpose served by the name Tom Jones. Tom Jones—for many reasons aside from his name—is a real person; Peregrine Pickle is not.

The names of most fictional characters lie somewhere between those two extremes. Another classic title character in a book of the same era, Tristram Shandy, has a name that is not common but not impossibly ridiculous. The name has meaning: "Tristram" harks back to a medieval romantic hero and also means "sad." The name also has tone: we can guess that a book with a title character named Tristram Shandy will be a serious literary comedy.

It's not always a good idea to go overboard in giving your characters resonant names. Henry James was guilty of that, hanging names like Caspar Goodwood and Fanny Assingham on his secondary characters. Knowing Henry, I doubt he intended us to snicker. Often, writers fall into stereotypical patterns in naming characters, such as using hard k and g sounds for tough guys and soft l and s sounds for young women.

Whether or not names reflect personality in real life, they do create impressions in readers' minds. Look over your characters' names to see if you have unintentionally used a pattern that might confuse readers or create inaccurate assumptions. Do you tend to give all your female characters names that end in diminutives? Are your characters' names too obvious, too close to type—have you named your hard-boiled detective Jim Steele? Have you gone to the opposite extreme and named him Gail Bysshe Smedley IV for no reason except a cheap laugh?

Check to see that your characters' names don't clash with each other. Generally speaking, the names of all the characters in a given story should be on the same level of distinctiveness and seriousness unless there's a specific reason for different levels. Bob Smith and Montague Herskotivs don't belong in the same story unless they have very different roles—perhaps Montague is a naive rich boy who is swindled into buying land in Patagonia by the affable but mysterious Bob Smith.

Another way names in a story can clash is by being too similar. If you have called one character Jeff Johnson, you probably don't want to call his best friend Jim Jackson even if you want to be funny. (Be on the lookout for *J* names and names ending in *a*—the most overused forms in America today.)

Use names other writers have not used before unless your intent is to parody or pay homage to a previous author. Henry Fleming has already been taken (in *The Red Badge of Courage*). In paying homage to him Hemingway used the name Frederick Henry.

If you use a common name, try spelling it in one of its less common forms, *if* you feel that suits the character's personality.

With all these issues to think about, and so many names having already been used in fiction, it's hard to come up with new ones. I recommend searching through baby name books for first names. For first and last names, especially ethnic ones, try the Manhattan or Los Angeles phone book. Movie credits, magazine mastheads, bibliographies, and sports rosters are good sources. The trick is not to use a name that's actually *in* the source—after all, you don't want to get sued—but to invent one that might fit into a space between two names that are. For instance, you might find Robert Cohen and Ronald Cohen in the phone book but no Roderick Cohen, so use that one.

When all's said and done, each writer has his or her own style in naming characters. Tolstoy used a lot of aristocratic names that have been called "Hollywood Russian"—dignified, sonorous appellations such as Alexei Vronsky or Natasha Rostov. His rival, Dostoevsky, used more eccentric, jagged-sounding names such as Nyetochka Nyezvanova or Smerdyakov, which often have satirical meanings in Russian. From the names alone, you can guess whose characters take more baths.

The bottom line is, a character's name should be memorable and individual, whether it's got one syllable or five, whether it's serious or comic, meaningful or arbitrary.

Physical Appearance

Someone ought to do a study of the way readers visualize fictional characters. It's a clear impression composed mostly of gaps. It's a mental image but not nearly as precise as a photograph. Perhaps it's more like the way a blind person feels a face than like the way a sighted person sees it. It's not so much a specific portrait as a region of resemblance. The physical appearance of a character could be compared to the location of an electron: impossible to pinpoint exactly, yet undeniably *there,* within a range of probabilities that are useful for calculations.

The physical appearance of a character is often more a matter of tone, atmosphere, emotion than of sensory detail. When I read about Hans Castorp—who occupies seven-hundred pages of one of the greatest of all novels, *The Magic Mountain*—I have a definite impression of him as a physical presence lying in a hospital bed and lounging at a hotel table; but I wouldn't recognize him if I passed him on the street.

It's important for both reader and writer to form a clear mental image of the character, but the image can be created with very few details. Emily Dickinson said that in order to create a prairie, all she needed was a clover, one bee, and reverie. This principle applies to fictional characters. If you can create a vivid picture of the character with one or two details, that's better than half a page cataloguing the character's facial features. I'm not going to write:

> Louie was a man of medium height, perhaps five-ten and three-quarters, with glossy, chestnut-brown hair parted on the left, two-thirds of the way down his scalp, from which an occasional flake of translucent yet ostentatious dandruff made its way toward a square, bony shoulder encased in a purple-and-rose paisley oxford shirt. The skull was round, the skin brightly tanned and clear, save for the nub of a skin tag embedded within the declivity of a chicken pox scar just to the side of his left eye: mallow-pink in color, deepening to bashful carnation when he picked at it. What most struck one were the eyebrows: inverted Vs, the hairs at their bases making a fringe from which a single frolicsome follicle sometimes detached itself and floated on the sclera of the eye, like a child's vinyl raft adrift on a lake. Louie's forehead was Mediterranean, broad and bony, his ears finely formed, and his cheeks hung in sedate but athletic pouches on either side of his short, broad nose. His eyes glinted as luminously as a dark brown Buick gleaming in the sun on an August afternoon— say three-fifteen, a Saturday, mostly sunny with a ten percent chance of showers. . . .

If you retain a clear mental image of Louie from those padded phrases and shopworn adjectives, you're a better reader than most. I'd prefer to describe him this way:

> With his bright orange tan and pouchy cheeks, Louie looked like a jack-o-lantern that's still sitting on the porch a week after Halloween.

One sentence. One image, two details. In general, in describing anything—a character, an object, a landscape—one detail is better than two, if it's a detail that creates a vivid mental picture.

You would never be able to recognize a photograph of Louie based on my one-sentence description, but you might very well have a *feeling* for the way he looks. The feeling is related to his personality—he's a slouching pumpkin, he's likable, he's a bit past his peak. By describing him physically, I have begun to round out, so to speak, Louie's characterization.

I prefer to describe all my characters physically in a sentence or two. Oddly, this is most important for minor characters. If a character isn't going to do or say very much and isn't going to reveal complex depths of personality, you can at least do him the kindness of saying what he looks like. If the character only reappears at infrequent intervals, you might want to refresh the reader's memory with an abridged description each time: "tan, round-faced Louie." Homer did that when he used epithets such as "gray-eyed Athena"; modern writers vary their wordings for each reappearance.

Some authors give very little physical description or none at all. When that approach works, it's a sign that the characterization has been effective in other respects. Paradoxically, the fully developed main characters are the ones who need the least physical description. You get a picture of them from what they say and do and think, not from how they look. This is especially true of first-person narrators. They are usually looking outward at the world and at other characters, not in a mirror. I doubt if there's a single physical description of Jake Barnes in *The Sun Also Rises,* but he's one of the memorable figures in twentieth-century literature.

The historical trend is toward less physical description of characters, both because so much of it has been written in the past, and because selective physical description makes characters into sex objects.

Clothing is an aspect of physical appearance—an aspect that gives information about social status and historical setting. If you're not going deeply into those aspects of life, you can do away with descriptions of clothing altogether. As with facial features and physique, one or two clothing details are generally better than five or six. Instead of listing Stella's garments from top to toe, I'll just say she's wearing a charcoal-gray derby with a feather in its band. The color of the feather can be left up to the reader.

Personal Histories

I haven't decided yet whether to include the following paragraph in my characterization of Stella:

> Personal relationships were a realm of mystery for Stella. Growing up in her mother's cabin in northern Wisconsin, she had learned to icefish when the temperature was ten below and to spearfish in the summer with the Menominee kids from down the road; she knew how to start a balky snowmobile and how to light a campfire in a cold rain. Once, an older boy had pulled her out of the water when she'd crashed through

thin ice while skating. But she and the boy were too embarrassed to linger—even on an average day, much less a day of heroism—though they'd lived a quarter-mile apart all their lives. The things you talked about weren't interesting and the things that were interesting you didn't talk about—unless you had some beer in you, but by the time you were old enough for that, the clamps had been put on tight. It didn't help that the mortgage on the cabin was paid for by Stella's mother's romance novels, which she mailed off to New York at the rate of one every three weeks. Stella's reading of these instruction manuals for future governesses ensured that when she left for the big city, she was prepared to find a world of gallant, heartbroken young stockbrokers who needed only her kiss to be healed, rather than a world of shallows-dwellers who were only in a good mood when they were manipulating someone. She came fully prepared to meet her true love through a wrong number and to believe that when he didn't show up for their first date it was because a taxi ran him over, not because he thought she wasn't worth it.

It's possible to build a characterization without background information, just as it's possible to live a fulfilled life without dwelling on the past; but as in life, an understanding of the past can help us understand the present. So the crucial question in deciding whether to include the above capsule biography is, "Does it increase our understanding of Stella?" By definition, it adds information we didn't otherwise have, but does the information make her a fuller character or does it merely add extraneous details, reinforcing character traits that would be adequately developed in her present actions? If it's consistent with what we already know of Stella, is it so consistent it's redundant? If it's inconsistent, is it the kind of provocative inconsistency that adds a believable extra layer to the character, or does it simply seem to clash?

Another factor in the decision is whether the description is interesting enough to warrant the space it takes up. (The same principle holds for descriptions of objects, landscapes, and so forth.) Two-hundred and eighty-one words is a lot when you're stopping the action in midscene. Consider the effects on the material around it. While reading the capsule biography, has the reader lost the thread of whatever came before? It's possible to write a long introductory description for every character, every setting, every prop, but the result may be a glacial pace.

Background information doesn't have to be given in a single Turgenevan lump, of course. (In *Home of the Gentry,* Turgenev's characterizations exist mainly in the form of extremely well-written capsule bios.) I could have Stella reveal information about herself bit by bit, in conversations and in scattered single lines of exposition. There, the naturalness of the presentation is the key. Characters telling about their past over coffee, or looking in the mirror and remembering their childhoods, can seem artificial; the reader is all too aware that the writer is just trying to put over some information.

Whether you include characters' histories in your finished text or not, it's probably better that you have a mental picture of what those histories are. I might never write a word about Stella's north-woods childhood, but if I know about it, it will color what I have her do and say in her New York adulthood: it will affect her speech pattern, her tastes, her values as expressed in her reactions to people. Some writers write capsule biographies of characters strictly for their notes. It's smart preparation. The danger is that it can lead to a kind of stick-figure psychologizing, in which character traits are simplistically attributed to traumas—you know, like, "Ever since that time she fell through the ice, Stella was afraid of new experiences—as if any solid ground she tried to step on might crack beneath her." This can be caused by treating the biographical notes as if they were the true locus of characterization. The characterization in the text becomes an unachieved attempt to duplicate what's been planned in the notes: "Gee, I said she fell through the ice, so I better put in a scene showing how it affected her psyche."

The characterization that counts is in the text, not the notes. If your portrayal of a character evolves past what you planned, and if that evolution invalidates a note you made for the characterization, there's no need to feel guilty. You probably made other notes that are still valid; check them to make sure you didn't leave out anything you still want to include.

The presence or absence of background information can in itself be an element of characterization. Othello tells us a good deal about his origins, his military career, and his courtship of Desdemona, and it makes us feel sympathy for him even though he commits murder; in the same play and sometimes the same scenes, we learn absolutely nothing about Iago's background, and that contributes to the depth of his enigmatic villainy. How much did Shakespeare know about Iago's past history? I wouldn't be surprised if the answer were "Nothing at all." The guy was incredibly slick. But lesser writers may have to use crutches that Shakespeare could forgo.

What They Say

More than by any other method, we get to know people by talking to them. We know them by what they say, how they say it, and what they don't say.

For the most part, people do not simply announce their character traits. People are devious, and self-disclosure is mostly a matter of indirection. If a character says, "I'm a secure, self-confident person," we do not conclude that he's a secure, self-confident person. We might conclude that he's a person who's trying to talk himself into being secure and self-confident, and trying to talk the world into believing it. We might conclude that he's actually quite insecure and lacking in confidence.

If we want to make a character say things that reveal him as secure and self-confident, we'll have to think up something else. We'll have him say things that *sound* secure and self-confident, in both important and unimportant situations. He sounds secure and self-confident when he's facing down an enemy and when he's deciding what shirt to wear. We might even have him make a self-deprecating joke, on the theory that it takes inner self-confidence to be outwardly modest. (We might do that if we had already, by other means, established his basic security and self-confidence, or if we wanted to create an initial impression of insecurity and later overturn it.)

Sometimes, the things characters say reflect their authentic feelings, but often not. If a character says, "I like Joe even though he got a better grade than me on the test," we have to judge, on the basis of previous evidence, whether the statement is true or not. If it's true, we probably decide that the speaker is a noble, decent, generous soul: a conclusion that might have to be revised on later evidence. If we decide that the speaker is lying, that leads to a different conclusion. In characterization through dialogue, falsehoods lead to complexity.

Mostly, people reveal their personalities without intending to. If two of your characters are having a conversation and Character A continually interrupts the other with witticisms at Character B's expense and never lets a statement go by without rebutting it, that says something about Character A's personality, which she is probably not aware of.

What a character doesn't say can also provide clues. If Character B doesn't warn Character A that Character C is going to rat on her to the teacher, then we know something about Character B as well as about Character C.

Many people are reluctant to talk about things they feel deeply, whether it's love or anger or ambition or frustration. Many people feel it's impolite to say certain things, such as curse words. Many people can't apologize. Many people can't ask for help. Many people can't admit they don't understand something. There are people who can't say "I can't" and people who can't say "I can." All these traits are part of characterization.

What's more, everyone says the same things in different ways. Every human being has an individual speech style, a verbal fingerprint. The technical term for this is *idiolect:* the speech pattern of an individual at one particular period in his or her life. (Our idiolects change as we move from childhood through adolescence and adulthood, from job to job, town to town, social class to social class, and toward new knowledge.) Speech pattern consists of vocabulary, word choice, favorite phrases, intonation, gesture, pauses, syntax, grammar. On the planet Earth, there are more than five-billion ways of saying "I can" and "I can't."

Ideally, every character has his or her own individual speech pattern. It's hard to achieve because, in the final analysis, all the characters are you. They all speak in your speech style. You can partially overcome this limitation by playing the characters' voices in your head and consciously varying them. Stretch your speech style to uncover the phrases that you haven't uttered in daily life, but have heard or thought of—or haven't even thought of until your art asked you to. A good writer is far more than a mimic, but this is where a gift for mimicry comes in handy.

Be subtle about it. Develop a stereotype alarm. If your Southern characters go around saying things like, "Ah do declare, thank yuh, ma'am, and y'all have a fahn tahm at th' bahbecue, y'heah?" the result will probably be unintentionally funny. If your characters have major social differences from others—if one is a Southern sheriff and another is a British duchess—the way to deal with it is by not settling for the obvious. Find difference within a narrower range. After you have established the broad, social definitions of your characters, work deeper down into their personal uniqueness. At a convention of five-hundred Southern sheriffs, each one will have his or her own idiolect. Although you'll only be writing about one of them, imagine him or her talking to the others; it will help you understand the character's individuality.

The Southern sheriff you write about, of course, will be the Southern sheriff who sounds most like you. There is a family resemblance among all a writer's characters. But that's not a flaw; it's part of what makes style.

What Others Say about Them

Character Q moves to a new town when her parents are transferred across the country by their corporation. The first person to befriend her in her new environment is Character P, who suggests they go out for a movie and a burger. The next day, Character P is accosted by the members of her clique, eager to know about Character Q: "What's she *like*?" Character P delivers the resounding judgment: "She's *weird*."

Do you, as the reader, conclude that (1) Character Q is weird, (2) Character P is weird, (3) they are both weird, or (4) neither is weird?

The answer, obviously, is that you need more information. You need to know, specifically, what Character Q said or did that made Character P call her weird. You need to know what the clique's standards of weirdness are. You need to know what connotations the word *weird* holds for them: is weirdness a quality they approve of? You need to know who Character P is: how trustworthy is she, how intelligent, how conformist, how sensitive?

If Character P says, "She's *weird*. She likes classical music. And her parents won't let her get a job—they want her to study," we immediately have more information from which to evaluate both Character Q and Character P. This information, too, is provisional and subject to amendment. Later on, we might discover that Character Q has been raised in a strict upbringing from which she longs to escape; secretly, she wants to be a cheerleader. Meanwhile, Character P secretly hates her clique, but fears their disapproval; therefore, in order to seem cool, she exaggerated Character Q's weirdness.

In life and in fiction, we learn a lot about people from the things others say about them. In both contexts, we need to corroborate the testimony or we risk forming wrong conclusions based on rumor, prejudice, malice, emotionalism, or misperception.

In a way, fictional characters are like courtroom witnesses. They are under oath to describe what they know—but the jury has to determine to what extent their testimony is accurate and truthful. The way to do this is to compare one witness's version with another's. When enough facts are collected from enough viewpoints, a picture of events can be formed. The picture might have some gaps, some parts might be in clearer focus than others, but it's enough to convince a jury.

At the beginning of *Hamlet,* two sentries have seen a ghost. They tell this to their captain, Horatio, who tells it to his best friend, Hamlet. Are the sentries, nervously waiting for the ghost's reappearance, telling the truth? Did they really see something? Was what they saw a ghost? At the outset, we don't know. The sentries' actions and words tell us that they are genuinely frightened. They have no reason to lie—in fact, they could get in serious trouble for raising a false alarm. They're sincere, but whether they really saw anything or not, and what it was, is something that can only be clarified by Hamlet's later experiences.

In any case, as Shakespeare demonstrated numerous times, starting a play by having one character tell a second character about a third character can be a very effective way of stimulating an audience's interest. It gives us enough information to make us want more.

Characters are continually testifying about other characters. It is the reader's job to evaluate the testimony and the writer's job to make sure that it can be evaluated properly. Some people are more trustworthy than others. The writer provides clues to how trustworthy a particular character is through:

- *external evidence*—whether the facts bear out the character's statements, and
- *internal evidence*—whether the character's claims sound full and authentic or partial and self-serving.

But no one is completely trustworthy or completely untrustworthy. The *kind of information* and the *context* affect how we evaluate the testimony.

The most trustworthy things characters say about other characters are factual statements that don't affect our opinion of the characters. If Character P reports about Character Q, "She just moved here from across the country," there's little reason for anyone to doubt it. The factual statements of observant characters are a major source of information in fiction.

Somewhat less trustworthy are eyewitness statements that do affect our opinion of the characters. If Character P says, "She kept me waiting half an hour for no reason," the statement deserves open-minded consideration. Character P had to wait for Character Q—that much is reasonably believable. But was it really half an hour or is P exaggerating? Was there really no reason or did Character Q's parents keep her in order to ask where she was going and whom she was going with?

Less trustworthy still are evaluative statements: "She's weird." We not only don't know how to evaluate the facts, we don't know what the facts are.

Then there are statements of personal emotion: "I like her"; "I don't love him"; "I don't care if I never see him again." Sometimes these are absolutely true—but only at the moment, for time will pass and wounds will be healed and characters will form new opinions of each other. At other times, such statements are misleading even at the moment they're uttered. The person who says, "I don't care if I never see him again," is fantasizing that she will run into him around the next corner.

The subtleties of psychological fiction arise from the following truths:

- No one is objective.
- Every action has a selfish reason.
- Honest, well-intentioned people sometimes distort.
- People don't know what they themselves think and feel or why they do things, and when they know, they're hesitant to reveal it.
- People rarely find out what others really think of them, and when they do, it throws them.

Playing around with the uncertainties of perception and with imperfectly reliable opinion and gossip is one of the fun things about writing fiction, but there's been a cynical tendency in modern fiction to overdo the untrustworthiness of characters. In a contemporary novel, when we hear a character saying, "I did my job faithfully," we can bet the character is either a liar or a simpleton.

William Faulkner's *As I Lay Dying* and *The Sound and The Fury* and Ryunosuke Akutagawa's *Rashomon* (and the Akira Kurosawa movie based on it) are classic examples of fiction in which a group of characters alternately describe the same set of actions, so that each character gives testimony about the others. Edith Wharton and Henry James are two great American novelists who habitually use webs of gossip as a means of portraiture.

How They Act in Response to Specific Situations

Character C and Character K are having a power lunch, sipping vegetable juice and nibbling sourdough bread and trying not to get any crumbs on their pinstriped suits, when, during a discussion of their business deal, Character K makes an idle but odious joke about Character C's ethnic group. We have just learned something about Character K. In addition, we will learn something about Character C depending on whether he (1) ignores the remark, (2) punches Character K in the face in the middle of the crowded restaurant, deal or no deal, or (3) tells Character K forthrightly but calmly that the joke expresses a pernicious stereotype and has hurt his feelings.

All of us are tested from time to time, and how we respond to a test not only illustrates our character but affects it. Whether Character C chooses response (1), (2), or (3) not only shows something about him, it gives him feedback about himself. He will think about his response; he may feel proud of himself or ashamed and regretful; and this thinking will in turn affect his future behavior. It may affect his future behavior to such an extent that we feel justified in saying that it has shaped the development of his personality. Character C's choice of response also affects other characters' opinions of him—Character K and people K talks to. C will see a new reflection of himself in the way K and others treat him and gossip about him; this will affect C's future choice of response in similar situations.

And if Character C sometimes chooses response (1), sometimes response (2), and sometimes response (3), depending on how he happens to feel that day and why, and on how he calculates the effect of his response and how he feels about Character K, then C is truly a complex character. And if you can show that on the page and make it all believable and make it all fit into a story that has shape and weight and momentum, then you are a writer.

Most fiction shows characters in critical situations. This is especially true of short stories, which often take place entirely at the crisis point. We can assume that a character's behavior in a critical situation says something about his or her personality. We can't assume that his or her behavior in a critical situation is consistent with his or her everyday behavior. It may be more interesting if it isn't.

Generally speaking, even when an entire story takes place in a critical situation, we do learn something about the character that goes beyond the immediate. Perhaps there is a flashback to an earlier event, perhaps the character recalls a previous action that didn't match a present action, perhaps the character speaks a line of seemingly offhand dialogue that hints at a broader repertoire of feelings and behaviors. A small amount of such information can go a long way. A sentence or two of background can add dimension, affecting the way readers interpret the critical situation.

How They Act Habitually

> When Stella had to be away from Louie, she would phone him every night, and they would talk—talk endlessly, it seemed, about what they had done that day and what they had seen and how they wished they were together. Then she would read him a paragraph from the copy of *Remembrance of Things Past* that she always kept in her luggage. Over the course of the years, they would read the entire work aloud to each other: over the phone, in airport terminals, in waiting rooms, in bed. Most of the time, it was Stella who read. She couldn't tell whether Louie truly enjoyed the novel—there were long minutes when she read into silence on the other end of the phone—but the fact that he listened was enough.

We have just learned something about Stella and about her relationship with Louie.

Repeated, habitual actions form a large part of how we get to know people—and ourselves—in real life and a larger part than is usually appreciated of how we get to know characters in fiction. The fact that Eddie Haskell, on *Leave It to Beaver,* is always sickeningly polite to parents and nasty to younger children is the key to his characterization. (If, in a critical situation, he acted differently, that would give him another dimension.) The fact that Othello, in Shakespeare's play, is habitually tender and loving to his young wife Desdemona, except in the critical situation, when he becomes murderously jealous, is the key to his.

Multigenerational sagas, especially ones of rural life such as Willa Cather's *O, Pioneers!* and Knut Hamsun's *Growth of the Soil,* usually contain a great deal of habitual action punctuated by moments of crisis.

Their Thoughts

In real life, we know only our own thoughts, unless we are psychotherapists, hypnotists, priests, or the confidants of exceptionally self-revealing people. In fiction, we can know the thoughts of everyone involved in a scene, or of only some people involved, or of only one person involved, or of none of them. The writer's choice of which characters' thoughts to show, if any, and how to show them, is crucial, and it's a matter of feel rather than of rules. I believe that concise writing is usually preferable to verbose writing and that it's usually better to convey meaning through action than through thought.

There are many works of fiction in which no characters' thoughts are revealed. There are many works of fiction narrated by first-person narrators who don't even reveal their own thoughts. If Character C punches Character K in the face, there's no need for him to add, "I hated K at that moment." It's obvious. On the other hand, if he thinks, "Oddly, I felt no personal hatred for K at that moment; I acted automatically, on principle, out of pure righteous retaliation for an insult to the honor of Ethnic Group J," that adds an extra layer to what the action alone shows and is worth including. Then again, perhaps C's lack of personal animosity toward K can be revealed through an action—perhaps, after punching K, he stretches out a hand to pick him up and says, "All right, how about that deal?" Or perhaps you want to leave C's feelings mysterious; we will have to infer, based on later scenes, the extent of personal hatred; we may never be able to settle the question firmly.

DEVELOPING INTERESTING CHARACTERS

So far, this chapter has talked about the how of characterization—how we learn about people. Frankly, I'm more interested in *what* we learn about them. If your characters are bores, what does it matter how skillfully you delineate them?

Fortunately there is no such thing as a boring person. (This belief—and it may be merely a belief—is what makes me a writer in the first place.) People who seem to be boring are only those who don't reveal themselves sufficiently. They're afraid to show themselves or they're satisfied with shallow interactions. In fiction, when characters don't reveal themselves sufficiently, it's because the writer has not seen deeply into their souls. In fiction, shallow interaction is not satisfactory.

We all know some people who, we imagine, would make particularly interesting characters. Some have led adventurous lives. Some have pioneered in their work. Some have overcome challenges or survived misfortune. Some seem especially wise or especially foolish. Some suffer from emotional problems. Some are simply eccentric. Most writers are attracted to such characters, and rightly so. All else being equal, it's desirable that your characters should have traits that are immediately, outwardly interesting. There's no denying that it's easier to write about a criminal than about a librarian.

But the librarian may be a criminal—at least in his or her own mind—and the criminal may yearn for a life of predictable calm.

If you could understand the librarian thoroughly, observe all his actions and see into his thoughts, you would find him endlessly complex. If you were able to observe all the criminal's actions and see into her thoughts, you might discover that her crimes, once you know how they were committed, were quite banal—the kind of thing you'd seen on TV a hundred times before. The really interesting things about the criminal, once you saw deeply into her, might be the unobvious things, the things that made her an ordinary person like you.

There has never been a human being whose personality was completely revealed in all its details, completely understandable to itself and others. As anthropologist Lyall Watson said, "If the brain were so simple we could understand it, we would be so simple we couldn't." What makes people interesting is the search, the attempt at revelation, the real or illusory progress.

One reason the search is always incomplete is that people change. How consistent are the people you know? How consistent are you? Human behavior is not predictable. We are fields of possibility. We shift, we are subject to vague and unforeseen influences, and even when we believe we know one another, we can surprise. Our values and goals change from year to year, from one phase of life to another; our moods change by the minute. Memory influences our behavior, but sometimes we let go of the past, rebel against it, deliberately do what it taught us not to. We belong to groups; we take part of our identities from the fact that we are male or female, young or old, factory workers or artists or teachers or whatever—but each of us is different from every other member of the group. We change over time as a response to experience: we grow. The growth is rarely a straight line; it is jagged, it surges forward, slips back, and fitfully falters toward the point it had already reached.

Most people feel they have an inner core that persists from birth to death. The neurologist Oliver Sacks, in his book *Migraine,* says our feeling of having a stable, continuous self is based on three things: the stability of our body-image (we look the same to ourselves, even as we change fashions or grow), the stability of our outward perceptions (the world looks the same, and we see it from a single point of view), and the stability of our perception of time (it keeps going forward, second after second, without a break). If any two of these factors become disordered, Sacks says, we feel our egos dissolving.

The feeling of having a stable identity may or may not be warranted, but characterization in fiction has been based on it. Too much reliance on the core, however, can make for skimpy, static characterization. A character is not an unalterable outline. Even cartoon characters, who look exactly the same from frame to frame, occasionally have to show new sides or risk losing their audience.

There are writers' manuals that divide characters into categories, round and flat, dynamic and static. The round, dynamic ones, usually major characters, are many-sided and capable of change; the flat, static ones, usually minor characters, are relatively simple and do not change during the course of the work; each time they reappear, they are the same; their sameness, in fact, is what we recognize about them.

That kind of textbook gets me so steamed!

It tells you to aim for mediocrity. It diminishes the art of fiction.

You do not have to *try* to create a flat, static character, any more than you have to *try* to become a fallible human being. What you have to try is to become a better person; and what you have to aim for in your characters is to make them fuller, rounder, more complex people, whether they are onstage for one line or for five-hundred pages. In Shakespeare and Tolstoy, all the characters seem alive no matter how briefly we are acquainted with them. One of Tolstoy's corpses, it has been said, is more alive than the average writer's protagonist. Their life is in what Tolstoy knows about them, and the lives of the sentries in *Hamlet* are in their language. We can imagine that if we had more time to spend with them, there would be a lot to find out about them.

While keeping the sense of a central core, try also to show the mutability of human character. After C punches K, he may feel he is not the same person he was before he swung his fist. He would not have predicted that he would do it. If this new development surprises the reader *and is believable,* it is successful characterization. It is not successful characterization if it seems to have no foundation in anything Character C has thought or done before—if it surprises the reader on the basis of seeming fake.

In other words, changes in characters have a history. History can't be predicted in advance but can be understood in hindsight. We can say, "Yeah, I believe C did that because he's the kind of person who did this and that and because at the beginning of the book he said such and such." C's choices have reasons. He may have had other reasons for other options, but we can believe that he made the choice he did.

It is not necessary for a writer to spell out a character's every motivation. A story doesn't have to answer all the questions it raises, but it should raise provocative ones and should give the impression that interesting answers are possible to find.

There is always a fringe of mystery in any human being, whether in the flesh or on paper. You cannot describe a character completely no matter how hard you strive—and therefore you might as well strive for as much as you can achieve.

WHERE TO FIND CHARACTERS

Where are characters found? Two places: out there and in here.

And they are both the same place. Search for characters in the world around you—take notes on real people; record factual details of speech, clothing, behavior; render them as faithfully as you can in print—and your characters will still only be versions of yourself. A character is not just a collection of traits, it is a representation of a mind, and the mind is yours.

This does away with the question, "Should I write about myself?" The answer is, "You can't do otherwise." Therefore, you don't have to write autobiographical fiction in order to express yourself. You will be expressing yourself just as much if you write about the imaginary lives of strangers you see on the bus or read about in the news.

There's nothing *wrong* with writing autobiographical fiction. Do it if that's your personal inclination. Writing about one's own experiences can be an especially valuable exercise for apprentices: it provides a preexisting subject on which to strengthen their skills. Among university-trained writers today, there seems to be a prejudice against autobiographical fiction: some writers seem to do contortions in order to write about anything *but* themselves. Often, the result is technically proficient fiction that lacks soul. I get the feeling that some writers have been taught, wrongly, that their own lives aren't interesting enough to write about.

Turgenev said that writers must cut the umbilical cord that connects them to their material. In other words, if you are inspired at the outset by events from your own life, you must step back and look at them with a writer's cool eye, cutting away what is merely local or incidental, adding imaginative elements, reshaping, reprocessing your fleeting and fragile life into an object with an independent, enduring existence. I try to heed that advice as much as possible, but I'm not sure I want a world in which every writer heeded it all the time. What about *Sons and Lovers*? What about *You Can't Go Home Again*? If you told D. H. Lawrence or Thomas Wolfe to cut the umbilical cord that tied them to their material, they'd laugh in your face. The whole *point* of their art was that they were tied to their material by bonds of blood that fed them and kept them alive.

I worry that too many young writers use theories such as Turgenev's as excuses to run away from themselves. American culture doesn't train us in self-examination; many of us are instinctively afraid of or embarrassed by it. I worry that contemporary American fiction gives too much credit to authorial distance and not enough to feeling. I worry that teachers of writing, hoping for student stories in which imagination powerfully transforms facts, instead get stories that seem made-up, posed, correct, "literary" in the pejorative sense of the word.

I would rather read the unguarded, spontaneous truth of how a human being has lived and what she has felt than the trumped-up conflicts of masks, in stories that read as if they've been contrived to please an editor or a professor.

Gertrude Stein once said that the real life story of Ernest Hemingway, if he had told it honestly, would have been more interesting than any of his novels. This insight is part of what made Stein a brilliant innovator of fiction. Only an awareness of the limits of fiction can lead a writer to stretch those limits. Only an understanding of the depth and fascination of real human beings can lead a writer to invent great characters.

But you can only write down as many fictional people, and as many traits, as you can find within you. I've often thought that writing is a mild form of multiple-personality disorder: we have people in our heads, speaking in different tones and expressing opposite views and moving toward divergent goals. The more of these little folk you can find inside your head, the more characters you can create. Many good writers work with a set of five or six characters who reappear in story after story under different names, in different settings. Greater writers might have a dozen or two.

Imagine yourself leading alternate lives. Explore its branchings onto paths other than the one it actually took; see who you would have become and met. Think of the social categories you belong to, then imagine different individuals in those categories. Conversely, think of yourself belonging to different categories.

Hear voices in your head.

CHANGING REAL PEOPLE

If you write about a character who blatantly resembles you and whose experiences are your own, you will probably also be writing about real people—relatives, friends, enemies—but you will be seeing them through your own prism. *It is strongly recommended that you change the external facts about those people so that they can't be identified!* Even if they started out as real, make them fictional. Change their hair color, their jobs, their residences, their sex—change whatever you can. Of course, change their names. Perhaps you will keep a core of insight into their personalities, but because the insight now applies to two people—the fictional character and the real model—it is on its way to seeming universal. Or perhaps you'll change so many of the externals that the internal core will evolve into something different. Voilá—you have invented a completely new character.

The surest technique for inventing characters is to create composites. You can take part of a character's personality from yourself and part from someone else. You can take the entire inner life from yourself and the externals from someone else. You can take part from one sibling or friend and part from another. You can take part from a famous person and part from a nonfamous person. You can take part from reality and part from imagination. You can build a composite character from two people, three, or more.

The creation of a composite character can often be reduced to a simple premise: "I'll use X's sweetness and Y's ambition to create Character Z." A simple grafting of X onto Y is good enough to start with. Better still, treat it flexibly: X is ambitious, too, in a different way from Y, and their two styles of ambition combine to create something new. Blurring the boundaries, you've discovered aspects of the character that weren't included in the initial premise. A composite of X and Y does not have to be a mere pasting-together of discrete traits. Think of it as creating a third individual by combining the genes of the parents.

Readers can rarely tell whether a character is based on a real person, purely invented, or a composite. The real question, of course, is whether the character is convincingly alive and interesting.

CREATING SUCCESSFUL CHARACTERS

What makes a successful fictional character? I would like to suggest a couple of guidelines:

- The reader remembers the character after finishing the story.
- The reader can extend the character beyond the story, imagining how the character would act and speak in other circumstances.

Plus a "bonus guideline," harder to meet:

- The character is still believable when acting out of character—when, in response to specific situations (which may be major challenges or small, odd moments), he or she does what wouldn't be expected, and it adds to our previous conception of the character rather than contradicting it.

How to achieve those goals? Best to create a sharp outline first and progressively shade it in. The most memorable fictional characters have strong foundations in physical appearance, speech patterns, jobs or skills, or the basic facts of life history. Sharp outlining is the minimal criterion for good characterization. Given this foundation, the nuances of personality can be explored: unpredictable details, differences from other similar characters, inner struggles and waverings. Huck Finn's first-person adolescent voice and poor-white culture are his foundation; his ethical conflicts contribute shading, as do his personal relations with Tom Sawyer, Jim, his aunt, and his father.

Many writers establish a character's outline at the beginning and never advance beyond it. This happens when plot mechanics are favored over characterization. The writer is willing to make the characters do unbelievable things in order to give the reader a jolt. It's as if the writer checked off a series of character traits at the beginning, from a handy list, and then didn't think about it anymore. It's as if the writer kept goosing the reader forward with one of those electric-shock buzzers you can buy from a novelty store.

Good writers are always thinking about characterization. They are always trying to learn more about the people they have set in motion. They put themselves in their characters' places and ask, as the theater director Stanislavsky advised his actors to ask, "Who am I? Why am I here? Where did I come from? Where am I going?"

Another useful set of questions to ask about a character is "How does she see herself? How do others see her?"

Planning our characterizations and seeing them through in the course of a work, we go through the same process as in getting to know our friends in real life. At first we know only a few big, superficial things—how they look, how their voices sound, what their interests are—and perhaps we have a simplistic, capsule impression of their personalities ("She's vivacious, but she has a cutting sense of humor . . ."). The more we hang around with them or analyze them in their absence, the more we find. We can never say we know them completely, but by showing us their uncertainties and uncharted feelings, they earn our love.

Do It

1. Write a one-page character sketch of yourself. Reread it and keep revising it, trying to increase its depth and truthfulness, eliminating anything that is self-serving or evasive. Show it to no one.

2. Write a character sketch describing what you would be like if you were of the opposite sex.

3. Write a character sketch of what you would have been like if you had been raised in a different family or a different culture, or if you had a very different physical appearance.

4. Write a sketch of yourself twenty or more years from now; or write about an older relative when he or she was young.

5. Select one or two partners and create a composite character based on all of you. Use this method: Without previous discussion, have each member of the group write a separate sketch of the composite character. Then read the sketches aloud or exchange them for silent reading. Discuss the similarities and differences among your versions and assemble them into a master sketch.

6. Write a story about identical twins, showing their differences as well as similarities.

7. Choose a character from a published work by another writer. Write a story in which that character lives in your community. Alternatively, write about that character at a different stage of life from the one shown in the published work.

8. Write a story about someone you dislike, so that your readers come to understand that person's motivations. Consider writing the story from the first-person point of view of the main character.

Writer's Bookshelf

Emma by Jane Austen (1815)
is the consummate portrait of the inner life of a thoughtful but flawed human being by a writer who is both detached and sympathetic.

An American Romance by John Casey (1977),
a novel about the interlocking love lives and up-and-down careers of the members of a theater group in Iowa, contains at least one psychological insight per paragraph and some of the most fully realized characters in modern American fiction.

David Copperfield by Charles Dickens (1850)

is a touchstone for sharply outlined characterization. For that matter, so is everything by Dickens.

Middlemarch by George Eliot (1872),

the masterpiece of the most serious Victorian novelist, is at its best in the first couple of hundred pages, where the personality of the intellectual heroine, Dorothea Brooke, and her unhappy marriage to the dry scholar Casaubon are dissected.

Something Happened by Joseph Heller (1974)

repelled some readers and critics because of its exhaustive, psychoanalytic exploration of an unattractive narrator, the self-loathing, self-serving, self-justifying advertising executive Bob Slocum. It belongs on this list for those very same qualities.

What Maisie Knew by Henry James (1897)

is a rigorous, compassionate study of the inner life of a young girl caught up in her parents' divorce. All of James' major novels are recommended for their psychological richness and nuance, especially The Portrait of a Lady *(1881) and* The Ambassadors *(1903).*

The Red and the Black by Stendhal (1830)

is ancestral to modern psychological fiction. Its protagonist, Julien Sorel, is a shrewd and contradictory young social climber, and Stendhal takes him apart with the greatest conceivable insight and irony. The same author's The Charterhouse of Parma *(1838) is even more incisive, though its perceptions are spread among several characters rather than concentrated on a single memorable antihero.*

Chapter 6

Dialogue

Talking is what fictional characters do best. When a fictional character eats, fights, makes love, or climbs Mount Everest, the words on the page are only a description of eating, fighting, lovemaking, or mountain-climbing, but when a fictional character talks, the words on the page are authentic dialogue. A fictional character cannot really bleed but can really communicate.

I can't have a sword fight with Hamlet. My sword would cut through a piece of paper rather than through flesh; it would have no effect on Hamlet, and of course Hamlet can't really pick up a sword and attack me the way he attacks Laertes in the play. But I can hear Hamlet's lines in my mind when I read, or in my ears when an actor speaks them, and they'll have as much meaning for me as for the other characters. They'll have *more* meaning for me than for the other characters. And if I forget Hamlet's exact words, I can look at the play; I don't have to scratch my head and think, "Now what was that he said again?" Dialogue is the only area in which characters can compete with fleshly people and win.

No wonder there's so much talk in fiction. A great many modern novels could be retitled, "People Going from Room to Room, Talking." Whenever a writer describes a character *doing* something, there's a certain sleight of hand involved, which allows the reader to disbelieve. If a writer tells me, "My main character, the bravest teenager in eighteen universes, single-handedly saved the planet Canthus from utter destruction," I, as a skeptical reader, tend to think, "Oh really?" It's easy for writers to describe characters doing extraordinary things; there's no sweat involved; there's an element of cheating about it. But when Hamlet says, "What a piece of work is man! how noble in reason! how infinite in faculty! in form and moving how express and admirable! in action how like an angel! in apprehension how like a god!" that's exactly what he's saying, and no one could say it better. Hamlet's swordsmanship may be a little hard to believe, but his words are the real thing. For characters, talk is action; it is life's peak experience. Or as the poet and novelist Kelly Cherry has put it, "Fiction is *about* talk."

CHOOSING DIALOGUE

To write good dialogue, then, do you simply let your characters gab freely and wittily for as long as you can keep thinking up clever lines and hope the reader is entertained?

No. Quite the opposite. The reason fictional characters talk so well is that their talk is so carefully chosen. They don't just open their mouths and see what comes out, the way we all do at times in real life. Real conversations are first drafts. Written dialogue is revised. In a first draft, you can let your characters say whatever comes into their heads, but in the final draft, you might keep less than half of it.

Most fictional conversations are shorter than their equivalents in real life. A one-page fictional conversation contains about twenty speeches and takes of couple of minutes of real time. Most passages of dialogue do not go longer than that without changing scene. The conversation you have with your best friend on the bus or in the lunchroom, on the other hand, is probably longer. A written transcript of it would go on for pages and pages, with long stretches that could easily be crossed out without affecting the meaning of the conversation as a whole. To turn it into dialogue, you'd take a pencil to that transcript and cross out 50 to 90 percent of it, leaving only the lines that revealed important truths about you and your friend.

Real people have their own reasons for talking, and fictional characters have their own reasons for talking, but fictional characters also have their authors' reasons for talking. Every time you write a line of dialogue, you should have some ulterior motive. You should be slipping the reader a note under the table. It might be a note about the character: "Isn't this person dishonest?" (or conceited, or modest, or whatever). Or a note about the plot: "This character doesn't know it, but he's headed for trouble." Or a note about the bass-line of ideas that pulses underneath your story: "Look at how people deceive themselves!"

There is no idle chatter in good fiction.

For this reason, revision is especially important in writing dialogue. The better your ear for dialogue, the more likely you are to let your characters blab on. Use your gift—but edit the results. Try to make your characters say what they have to in one or two sentences rather than four or five.

Here is the difference between conversation and dialogue:

Conversation

Louie: Hi!

Stella: Hi!

Louie: How are you?

Stella: I'm okay, how are you?

Louie: Okay, I guess. Hey, welcome back.

Stella: Thank you.

Louie: Yes, welcome back. So how was your flight?

Stella: What? Oh, my flight. Long. There was this guy, like, this guy sitting next to me, I don't know. What he was trying to do, you know. Talked to me the whole way? He would just talk about anything he happened to see in front of him, like, uh, the seat trays. You know the trays on the back of the seats that they serve you food on in airplanes? What do you call—

Louie: Seat-back trays, I think they call it. Is that the technical term?

Stella: I don't know, I would just call in the seat—seat tray, dinner tray, something. So how was traffic getting to the airport?

Louie: Not bad. Um, how was Paris?

Stella: What, didn't you get my postcard?

Louie: Which one? I got one.

Stella: I wrote you one. That's the one I wrote you.

Louie: Only one?

Stella: Paris was great. But it's so expensive.

Louie: (under his breath) Only one postcard.

Stella: Like if you're an American you buy your plane ticket, get over there, and you find out you can hardly afford to eat! Or— listen—what are you looking at?—I went into this fast-food place and it was just as expensive as a real restaurant, because they're just learning about fast food; it's like a new adventure for them. They love a lot of American stuff, you know, but they just don't do it right. Like they don't know about ketchup. Or else they do know about it but they don't believe you're actually supposed to put it on your hamburger.

Louie: *Le ketchup.* Or would it be *la ketchup*? Hey, love the earrings.

Stella: Thanks. Should see how much they cost.

Louie: Eh. How much is the franc worth nowadays?

[And so on—forever.]

The Same Conversation Compressed into Dialogue

Stella: Oh, what a flight! There was this guy sitting next to me trying to make clever conversation about the seat trays. Seat trays! What did he think he could accomplish?

Louie: He probably thought he would get to talk to you. (Pause.) I missed you. (Pause.) "I missed you too."

What makes one line part of the central core of the dialogue, while another line is excess weight that can be cut? What's the talk in fiction for?

Dialogue is Characterization

Suppose Louie, reading a restaurant menu, says, "Stuffed eggplant! I don't know—I've never tried eggplant before." Reading that line, we think, "This guy is afraid to try new things." We know the author put in that line so we could generalize about Louie.

If Stella, sitting across the table from Louie, says, "You're afraid to eat eggplant?" it enhances characterization two ways: by showing her opinion of Louie (with which we may agree or disagree) and by showing who *she* is. I can alter Stella's personality on the spot depending on whether I have her say, "You're afraid to eat eggplant?" or "If you order the eggplant and don't like it, I'll trade" or "The first time someone offered me sushi I almost gagged" or any of a million other possible responses. In rough drafts I might want to try various replies; for the final draft I'd choose the one that was most believable, most revealing, and most in tune with the way I see Stella.

Dialogue Is Information

It fills us in on things that happened in the past. If Louie says, "I haven't eaten eggplant since my brother was blinded in one eye by a stuffed eggplant thrown during a wrestling-team banquet," we have learned some important information that affected Louie's view of life.

Dialogue Is Foreshadowing

If Stella says, "You're afraid to eat eggplant?" and Louie replies, "Hey, I eat what I want and I don't eat what I don't want. You got a problem with that?" we know we can look forward to some interesting conflicts between Louie and Stella in future scenes.

Dialogue Is Description

If Louie says, "Mm, that eggplant looks good with tomato sauce and melted cheese on top!" we form a mental picture of the mouth-watering stuffed vegetable. Fiction writers often use this technique to describe something relatively minor in an offhand way. For playwrights, it's a very important technique, because a playwright can't put a written description on the stage—it has to go in the characters' mouths. This is why characters in plays are always uttering corny exclamations like, "Here comes Edsel running through the rain! And he's—he's smiling!"

Dialogue Lets the Writer Test Ideas

At some point in his life, Shakespeare had an idea about how wonderful humankind is. Maybe he thought of it at the very moment he put the words in Hamlet's mouth, or maybe he thought of it years before, scribbled it in his notebook, and dug it up when he found a place to use it in a play. At any rate, by putting the idea in a character's mouth, Shakespeare expressed it without having to take responsibility for it. If his friend Ben Jonson met him at the tavern and said, "Yo, Will! Whence cometh this jive about noble in reason and infinite in faculty?" Shakespeare could tell him, "I didn't say it, my character did." By putting a number of opinions in the mouths of a number of characters, a writer can explore all sides of an issue without being pinned down to a single position. (That's not cheating. The best writers, such as Shakespeare and Chekhov, do it most, because they see life from the most points of view. Great writers usually do not have a single character speak for them directly.) This gives the writer the reputation of being wise.

Dialogue Does Several Things at Once

It works on characterization *and* plot *and* theme. It slips us a note saying, "This character is not as heroic as he wants to seem, and he's going to be killed later, and isn't life tragic?"—and it does so by having the character make a seemingly unrelated comment about anything from humans to eggplants. This makes written dialogue compact, condensed, and concise, despite the fact that fictional characters sometimes wax eloquent. (In real life, instead of Hamlet's speech, you might say, "Gee, people are wonderful." That's shorter. But in order to convey as much *meaning* as Hamlet's speech, you'd have to talk for ages.) When one line of dialogue serves two or three purposes at once, it's a sign of strong writing. If you write a passage of dialogue that does not do that, you could probably find a way to cut it and say the same thing in less space.

Dialogue is more than conversation. And dialogue is less than conversation. It is greater in quality, smaller in quantity. It contains far more information per word than real talk. Dialogue also tends to stick to its subject rather than wandering as we do in real life. Fictional characters don't talk for hours just for the sake of passing time or making acquaintance. Dialogue in print also has fewer "tics" than real speech—less hemming and hawing, fewer "like, you knows," fewer sentences that go off track or end in shrugs or laughs. It's okay to include speech tics for characterization or to make the lines sound realistic, but you only have to do a little of it for the reader to get the point.

DEVELOPING AN EAR FOR DIALOGUE

How can you develop the ability to write good dialogue? There's a one-word answer: *Listen.*

Listen to people talking. Listen to the conversation at the next table in the restaurant. Listen to your brother and sister arguing. Listen to as many different kinds of people as possible. Listen to yourself. Train yourself to observe the differences in vocabulary, tone, rhythm, and gesture that constitute idiolect. Notice the difference, for instance, between the way your English instructor greets you in the morning and the way your best friend does. Some people are raised to believe that eavesdropping is rude; in order to become a writer, it is absolutely necessary to get over this.

Develop your speech-memory: after you've had, or heard, an interesting conversation, go to a quiet place and replay it, until you feel you could write it from memory. Keeping a notebook of quotes can be an excellent aid.

Above all, listen to the speech of *real* people. Don't try to learn to write dialogue by imitating the dialogue on television or in books. Your dialogue shouldn't sound like some other writer's dialogue, it should sound like your own.

After you have written a passage of dialogue, read it over. Read it aloud in order to hear whether it sounds like real people talking. (If you're shy like me, you may read silently to yourself.) Time how long it takes to read. Chances are, your first draft of any passage of dialogue will contain a large percentage of lines that don't contribute much to characterization, plot, or theme. Delete those lines. If an otherwise expendable line contains a clever, useful phrase that you want to keep, try to transfer the good part into, or next to, a more important line. If, while trimming, you think of new lines of dialogue, add them, but be prepared to subtract them later if you find that they aren't as brilliant and useful as you first thought. After paring away all the unnecessary lines—I mean *all* the unnecessary lines— reread. Pretend you are sharpening a blade. Keep doing it until your words can cut through anything.

A NOTE ABOUT SPEECH TAGS

Those little phrases that identify the speakers in dialogue are called *speech tags*. Keep them simple. It's perfectly okay always to use "said" and "asked" instead of "he retorted insincerely" or "she exclaimed from the upper right corner of her month." Fancy speech tags risk sounding old-fashioned and pretentious. When possible, do without speech tags altogether. The main reason to use speech tags is to help the reader remember who is saying what. (Sometimes you might also want to throw in a speech tag for reasons of pace or rhythm.) Readers can usually keep track of the sequence of speakers for several lines without needing a speech tag as reminder. If your characters have distinct, individual speech styles, the reader can often tell who's talking on the basis of the words alone.

In order to decide when to use a speech tag, simply read the dialogue and ask yourself, "Is the speaker's identity clear?" Add a speech tag to each line for which the answer to that question is "No."

Do It

1. Think back to an interesting conversation you've had or heard, and write it down as exactly as you can. If you don't recall the exact words, write the most realistic version you can. Then turn this conversation into tight, well-crafted dialogue by crossing out every unnecessary line and adding lines that strengthen characterization and meaning.

2. Have a five-minute conversation with a partner on a topic that interests you both. Then, separately, each of you write down the conversation as exactly as your memory allows. Compare your versions. The differences between them are likely to show you something about individual speech styles and individual interpreta-tions of events—in other words, about characterization.

3. Write a dialogue in which two characters discuss a third character, who is not present. Using only the dialogue, try to create three distinct characters. (You might want to write one-paragraph descriptions of the characters before or after writing the dialogue.

How much of the information in your descriptions can be gleaned from the dialogue? Try to polish the dialogue so that it says as much as possible.)

Writer's Bookshelf

Chilly Scenes of Winter by Ann Beattie (1976),
the first novel by this cool and skillful contemporary American, is notable for the on-target yuppie conversations that take up most of its pages. Beattie's short stories, too, are enriched by her accurate notation of the way middle-class Americans, for the past couple of decades, have talked.

JR by William Gaddis (1975)
is a huge, multileveled compendium of American dialogue from various socioeconomic niches, especially the business world.

The Maltese Falcon by Dashiell Hammett (1930)
is a treasury of hard-boiled speech. In the same author's The Thin Man *(1934), the tough-guy lyricism is overlaid with a ritzy tone for the more well-heeled joes and janes.*

The Sun Also Rises by Ernest Hemingway (1926)
contains much of the best dialogue ever written.

Real Life Funnies by Stan Mack
is a weekly comic strip in which all dialogue is guaranteed factual. Syndicated in the Village Voice *and other "alternative" newspapers, it's a treat for eavesdroppers, though in recent years Mack has tended to focus too much on characters who are Manhattan media types. The strip has been collected into book form.*

Clockers by Richard Price (1992)
takes us into the realm of crack dealers and cops. Price is perennially, and deservedly, praised for his tape-recorder ear and his careful research into his subjects.

Chapter 7

How to Describe Things

Storytelling is a form of virtual reality that was invented tens of thousands of years ago, before there were microchips. When you hear or read a story, you enter a fantasy world in which you are both an observer and, by identifying with the characters, a participant. It is a sensory experience: you see and hear the action, the characters, their surroundings . . . sort of.

The "sort of" is important. Literary virtual reality is less complete than electronic virtual reality. As a reader you are not totally immersed in the fantasy world of the story; not for a moment do you actually believe you are in the landscape. Reading a story is having one foot in one world and one foot in another. But the incompleteness of the illusion creates important advantages. Literary virtual reality does not try to fool you. It allows you to move from world to world in a completely fluid way and in your own sequence, at times straddling both worlds at once, at times entering the fantasy more fully, at times stepping back and evaluating the experience. It allows you to revise and recreate your image of the fantasy world as often and as thoroughly as you want; and your version of the fantasy world will be your own creation, different from every other reader's version of it, rather than a standardized, mass-produced one. Literary virtual reality stimulates thought rather than sensation. It leaves your intellect intact—in fact, strengthens it.

And literary virtual reality is made of language, which can be beautiful.

A VIRTUAL REALITY WITH WORDS

The writer's job is to build a virtual reality using words. When you describe a lake, a tree, a boat in your fiction, you are trying to create a picture of a lake, a tree, a boat in the reader's mind. The words you use to achieve this may, in addition, form pleasant or impressive combinations of sounds, but forming pleasant or impressive combinations of sounds is not the primary function. The primary function of description is the mental picture.

Creating a mental picture in the reader's mind can be done by surprisingly simple means. It doesn't require ornate phrases or vivid descriptive words. (Those things are counterproductive more than half the time.) It doesn't require originality or cleverness. It doesn't require you to write "vermilion" when you mean "red." (Do you have a clear mental picture of what vermilion looks like, as opposed to, say, cinnabar or cochineal?) All it requires is a basic, concrete vocabulary plus an understanding of how you yourself form mental pictures when you read.

The words are the easy part. The hard, important part is the vision. If you can see what you want to describe, you can describe it. Writing your vision down in the plainest, clearest, most ordinary words will do. Indeed, a great deal of the revision process in writing descriptions consists of making them simpler.

Often, one word is enough. When I write "lake," a picture of a lake appears in your mind. It is not a photographic reproduction of a specific lake, but photographic images are not needed in fiction. The fuzzy logic of the image offers advantages. It makes the reader creative, encouraging him or her to adjust the picture to suit the unfolding story.

How specific you want the description of the lake to be depends on the role of the lake in your story and on your personal style. I've just decided that Louie and Stella should vacation beside a lake during their first summer together. How shall I describe the lake?

One approach, as I've suggested, is just to say "lake":

> That summer, Louie and Stella spent hours each day sitting on the grass at the edge of the lake. The sky was almost always blue. Swimmers dove off the old wooden dock and swam fifty yards out to the float. You couldn't hear traffic; you couldn't even hear a raised voice. Standing ankle-deep in the water, Stella watched minnows chase each other around her foot.

That creates a clear mental picture, yet the word "lake" has not been modified in any way. We don't know how big the lake is, whether the water is gray or green, whether the shoreline is smooth or jagged and how developed it is. We have not used any adjectives for the lake—it is not tranquil, limpid, pearlescent, or any such stuff—nor have we strained for some high-toned noun or figure of speech that we could use instead of "lake." It is not a tarn, a shimmering, lacustrine body, or the liquid, light-filled eye of the land—it is just a lake. That is all it has to be. And each time we mention it, we will use the same four-letter word: lake, lake, lake, lake, lake.

Details about the appearance of the lake are provided by describing the surrounding objects: dock, float, swimmers, sky, minnows, silence. Yet each of these things, in itself, is described in the same very simple way, with a minimum of adjectives. I have not dressed the lake up with words. I have not stretched a layer of verbal gauze between the scene and the reader. The impact of the description has nothing to do with how cleverly I have translated the lake into language; it has to do entirely with how clearly I have visualized the lake.

My point is not that this is the only way to describe things; my point is that it is often a good enough way. It is so effective, so often that many great writers, such as Chekhov, Georges Simenon, and Jean Rhys, have relied on it exclusively.

There will be other occasions when I want to describe Louie and Stella's lake more elaborately. This is partly related to Louie's and Stella's own feelings about the lake. Are these people nature lovers? What do they notice about the lake? Do they take frequent walks around its shoreline, observing birds and trees? Do they canoe or swim in its waters, noticing the sunlight on the ripples and the fish darting below? Is their awareness of nature increased by staying at the lake? Or are they hopeless urbanites for whom the lake is a decorative but meaningless picture, in front of which they conduct exactly the same discussions they would in an apartment? In this last case, the repeated use of the bare word "lake" would appropriately imply that Louie's and Stella's consciousness of their natural surroundings is minimal and undetailed.

If, on the other hand, their previously dormant consciousness of nature is being aroused for the first time while they are at the lake, I might want to include specific details that impress them, such as the fact that fish jump in hot weather or that the rocks on the bottom are slippery with algae. The description conveys the character's discovery. If they become experienced lake-dwellers who know the environment inside out, I might want to research many details of plant and animal and insect species to bring myself up to their level of awareness.

CHOOSING WORDS

We can say something similar about choosing the right word to describe an object. Stella is looking at a tree. Is it just a tree or is it a conifer? Is it just a conifer or is it a Norway spruce? The answer is, *what is it for Stella?* Does she care about the difference between one tree and another? Is the mere fact of something's being a *tree* the important fact for this citified, nature-starved person, or does she possess a keen knowledge of and feeling of kinship with other species?

Description is a function of characterization.

And just as fundamentally: *What is it for the reader? What is it for the writer?* In the context of the story, with a given setting and a given set of people and ideas and a given author's frame of mind, is it important that a certain tree is a Norway spruce or is "tree" enough?

All else being equal, it's best to keep the language plain. Sounding educated is an ignorant reason for using a word. Simple words, gracefully combined, usually sound better than fancy ones anyway.

The title is *A Tree Grows in Brooklyn.* It isn't *An Ailanthus Grows in Brooklyn*—although there are ailanthus trees by the thousands in that profuse borough.

Stephen Crane, in one of the most famous descriptive lines in American literature, didn't write, "The crimson sun was pasted in the sky like a wafer." He wrote, "The red sun was pasted in the sky like a wafer."

Now, it may be that a certain area of Louie and Stella's lake—let's say the place where an underground spring bubbles up into a pool and then flows into the lake—plays an important part in their story, as the setting of a key scene. This is the place where Louie, hunkering down in the muddy grass and tearing up thistles from nervousness, first declares that he loves her. In that case, you'll probably want to describe the area in some detail.

Description is a function of plot.

In deciding which details to describe, it doesn't hurt to think of yourself as a movie camera cutting from shot to shot. You have begun with an establishing shot, a broad panorama, of the lake as a whole. For the scene of Louie's declaration, you cut to close-ups of the bubbling spring, the water flowing into the lake, the thistle plant being torn by its roots. The words can be quite simple; what makes the description is the choice of shot.

This camera analogy only works partially, however. Word-pictures are not the same as photographic pictures: they don't show physical images of the objects to our eyes. Words have sounds, words have rhythms, words have connotations and the sounds, rhythms, and connotations color the picture. It's nice to think of language as a transparent medium through which we can see objects clearly and without distortion, but that isn't true. The term *transparent* is itself a metaphor, a figurative comparison. We don't literally see through words: they're opaque marks on a page. But the word *transparent,* by comparing language to something clear such as water or air, helps us understand the role language plays in forming pictures.

Figurative comparisons—similes, metaphors, and the like—play a big role in descriptions. ("Play a big role" is a metaphor. Almost everything is a metaphor if you look.) Use them when they're original and helpful: when they contribute to a clearer mental picture of the thing you're describing, and at the same time give the reader a pleasant surprise. You're likely to think of similes and metaphors throughout your writing, and it's important to develop a feel for when they're genuinely vivid and fresh and appealing and when they're stale, corny, and pretentious. Also, look at the visual image your figurative comparison adds to the scene: Is it one you want? Does its presence in the reader's mind clarify the description or cloud it?

In American writing today there's a tendency to applaud the clever comparison. We tend to believe that metaphor is the most important aspect of poetic language (which is true for most modern American poets but not for all poetry in all cultures—not true of Pushkin, the greatest Russian poet, to name one). We tend to assume that by linking an object in a scene to an object in the author's consciousness, we increase the meaning of the scene. A thematic connection, we think, justifies an image. "Hm, so the lake is an eye! What he's saying is that objects in a landscape are not really out there but are products of human perception, and it must contain religious symbolism, too—the eye of God, get it?—and, wait!, it also shows that the relationship between Louie and Stella is a product of the male 'gaze' or 'look'!"

I have to admit that I share this tendency. I love clever comparisons when I think of them myself and when I read them in the work of other writers. But a puritanical part of me wonders whether that kind of imagery really does help. If we compare a lake to an eye, do we see the lake more vividly? Or do we see a jumbled combination lake and eye? Are we, as writers and readers, coming closer to or into more intimate contact with the object described, or are we running away from it to some other object we happen to have thought of through a quirk of association? I sometimes think that in modern literature too much emphasis has been placed on seeing things as other things and not enough on seeing things as themselves. Too much "a lake is an eye is a God" and not enough "a lake is a lake is a lake." It takes a great deal of self-training to see a landscape as what it simply is; perhaps more than to see it as a kaleido-scope of comparisons.

Comparing a lake to an eye is old and pseudo-poetic and lends a pretentious tone to the description, and it makes me visualize a huge, inhuman eye lying spread across the landscape; it adds an inappropriate touch of surrealism to the simple love story of Louie and Stella. I want to get that eye off the land, not put it on.

The best figurative comparisons are those that add afresh to the sensory image, the mood, and the meaning at one stroke. Stephen Crane's wafer image is the classic example. It's surprisingly exact: the sun really does look flat at times, especially in hazy sunsets when it's big and red. We have probably noticed the phenomenon at times without thinking much about it; Crane brings it forcefully to our attention. He sharpens the sensory image for us in an accurate, original way, and that's the first criterion of a good figurative comparison. Second, the image of a big, flat-looking red sun in a hazy sky at sunset enhances a mood of lurid melancholy or doom, and that's appropriate for Crane's intentions in the scene. Third, the image of a wafer contains thematic connotations having to do with the Eucharist in Christianity, thus giving critics something to mull over between faculty meetings. (To tell the truth, the religious overtones in that description are probably a bit too obvious, even for 1895, but it's a close call, and the simile has enough strengths to overcome the drawback. The tendency to sprinkle facile religious imag-ery over every scene—and to claim Christ or Buddha figurehood for characters who haven't earned that stature—is a temptation many writers should resist.)

Crane's wafer image makes the sun look more like a sun, in sensory as well as ideational terms; my eye image makes the lake look less like a lake. That is the test. Does a particular detail, word, or image actually clarify your mental picture of the object, or is it just there for its own sake? If the latter, cross it out.

Writers use figurative comparisons at different rates and in different ways. Some use two per sentence, others, two per novel. If you want to develop the knack of thinking up figurative comparisons, it's a matter of opening your mind to what's already there. You can learn to do that through exercise. Look at an object: for instance, an inner tube hung around a piling in the lake. In one or two minutes, think of as many comparisons as you can. Do it rapidly, not stopping to determine whether your comparisons are any good or not. (Most comparisons are not very good. The trick is to find *one* that works. Readers will never know about the ten you didn't use.) The inner tube is a quoit on a ring; it's a ring on a finger; it's a space station docking; it's a donut on a muffin stand; it's a hollow mind settling around a prejudice; it's a bird lighting on a nest; it's a plane landing; it's a boat at anchor; it's a swimmer treading water; it's a toy in a bathtub; it's nodding at the water like a lonely person recalling past regrets. I thought of those in about as much time as it took to type them, and most of them are ordinary at best. But they were good exercise. Eventually, you become able to think of them more freely, and you think of better ones.

Once you have thought of them, you must winnow them, keeping only the ones that add power and vividness. Be ruthless with your own clever ideas. Force yourself to reject many, perhaps most, of them. They are probably not as clever as you first think. Few things are more painful for a writer, rereading his own published work, than an image he used to think was brilliant and now knows is not.

In my own writing, I use a principle that guides me toward effective descriptions: a principle of factual reporting. I learned it by reading Tolstoy's description of wounded soldiers in a field hospital in *War and Peace*. Each sentence, I realized, reported a fact. Here's a passage:

> In the long room, brightly lit by the sun which poured in
> through the large windows, the sick and wounded lay in two
> rows with their heads to the walls, leaving a passage down the
> middle. Most of them were unconscious and paid no attention
> to the visitors. The others raised themselves or lifted their thin
> yellow faces, and all gazed intently at Rostov with the same
> expression of hope that help had come, and of reproach and
> envy of another's health. Rostov stepped into the middle of
> the ward, and looking through the open doors of the two
> adjoining rooms on both sides saw the same spectacle. He
> stood still, silently looking round. He had never expected
> anything like this. Close to his feet, almost across the empty
> space down the middle, a sick man lay on the bare floor, a
> Cossack probably, to judge by the way his hair was cut. The
> man was lying on his back, with his huge arms and legs
> outstretched. His face was purplish-red, his eyes were rolled
> back so that only the whites were visible, and the veins in his
> bare legs and arms, which were still red, stood out like cords.
> He was beating the back of his head against the floor, hoarsely
> muttering some word which he repeated over and over again.
> Rostov tried to hear what he was saying and made out the
> word he kept repeating. It was, "drink—drink—a drink!"

> Rostov looked round in search of someone who would lay the sick man back in his place and give him water.

The description goes on for a full page, showing us everything Rostov sees in the ward. Each sentence adds specific information to the picture. There are no sentences that merely repeat previous details in different words. Not every fact is physical—"He hadn't expected anything like this" is a psychological fact, but a fact nonetheless. A mood is created, but it is created solely through the transmission of information. As a result, the scene—like most of Tolstoy's work—achieves an overpowering conviction of truth.

There is something journalistic about this direct, reportorial approach, but something beautiful as well. Each detail is beautiful not because of how its phrases are turned, but because it illuminates a piece of reality.

This kind of fact-reporting clarifies the reader's mental picture in another way as well: by separating images from one another. To make details sharp and memorable, it's wise to give each one its own moment of the reader's time. Jumbling a lot of images in one clause or sentence tends to blur them in the mind. When each detail is separated from the others, the reader can focus on it attentively; it doesn't get submerged in the word-soup. This is why simple sentences tend to create more vivid pictures than complex sentences. Compare these two descriptions:

> The lake, at which Louie and Stella had arrived the previous afternoon when the setting bronze sun lit the window of the cottage on the far shore, was now, in the breeze of early morning, a pale watercolor, shivering fragilely in the wake of a small motorboat that buzzed across the open water.

> Yesterday afternoon, the sun was bronzing the window of the cottage on the far shore. Now, in the morning breeze, a motorboat buzzed across the open water. The lake shivered, pale, fragile.

In the second example, sunset and morning are separated grammatically by being placed in two sentences. This keeps them distinct in the reader's mind. Cluttering details have also been removed. In particular, I cut the phrase about the boat's wake. It has become unnecessary because of the revised placement of images. When the shivering of the water came first, in Example 1, an explanation was necessary: the water is shivering because of a boat's wake. But when, in Example 2, the motorboat buzzes by first, we are prepared, on the basis of what we know about motorboats, to see a mental picture of its wake. When the water shivers in the next sentence, we know why without being told. The wake is already an implicit part of the mental picture.

That's one reason why it only takes a few details to render a scene: the reader's mind can fill in the rest, if the writer knows how to imply it.

Paragraphing is also a way to keep images separate. Paragraphing creates a border; it says, "Here, one thing ends and the next thing begins." It also creates a brief pause in the reader's pace, allowing time to absorb or dwell on the picture. If the descriptions in a story can be compared to snapshots in an album, then each paragraph is a new snapshot.

CREATING ATMOSPHERE

So far, I've discussed description almost entirely in terms of physical sensation, but there's more to it than that. In written fiction, as opposed to on the screen, a description is not just sensory data. The same landscape, accurately and simply described by ten different writers, would look ten different ways. Description is as subjective as every other part of fiction writing. Description is the writer's mind imposed on the outside world.

Sensory data plus individual consciousness equals atmosphere. Suppose you want to describe a river in the central African forest. Hippos and alligators; sandbanks; heat; silence; shoals and channels. How that river looks depends on how you feel about it. Perhaps you live in that forest— it is familiar to you, you know it, it is home; you respect the animals' territory, but you don't fear them, nor is there anything ominous or menacing about the atmosphere of the place. Or perhaps you are an American who has always wanted to travel to Africa: the river is a magical place full of half-glimpsed, exciting sounds and sights. Or perhaps you are Joseph Conrad, a great prose stylist living in the age of European imperialism: to you, an African forest river is a place of brooding danger and menace, even of symbolic evil. Your description (in "Heart of Darkness") combines sensory data with glints of your consciousness, your attitude, to create a highly charged atmosphere that is not nearly as objective as it tries to seem:

> An empty stream, a great silence, an impenetrable forest.
> The air was warm, thick, heavy, sluggish. There was no joy in
> the brilliance of sunshine. The long stretches of waterway ran
> on, deserted, into the gloom of overshadowed distances. . . .
> The broadening water flowed through a mob of wooded
> islands; you lost your way on that river as you would in a
> desert, and butted all day long against shoals, trying to find
> the channel, till you thought yourself bewitched and cut off

forever from everything you had known once—somewhere—
far away—in another existence perhaps.

Technically, everything in this description fits in with our definition of
fact-reporting: every phrase adds either a physical detail or a psychological fact. There are so many sensory details in this brief passage, indeed,
that some of them are conveyed in short, telegraphic bursts: "An empty
stream, a great silence, an impenetrable forest." Nine words, three
sensory details. However, notice how much editorializing there is in the
passage. The choice of adjectives and nouns—"impenetrable," "thick,
heavy, sluggish," "mob"—tilts the description in the direction of gloom,
when other synonyms might have produced a different effect. "There was
no joy in the brilliance of sunshine" is a psychological fact (for the author)
and does convey sensory information, but it also reinforces the gloomy
atmosphere. So does the description of losing one's way, of spending all
day searching for the right channel, of feeling bewitched; so does the
comparison to a desert. This is superb use of language to express the
author's frame of mind through physical description. As the Nigerian
novelist Chinua Achebe has noted, however, the frame of mind is one of
unconscious racism.

Conrad and Crane are perhaps the two greatest masters of impression-
istic description in English-language fiction. They build their scenes like
painters covering the canvas with dab after dab of carefully chosen color,
arranging the details in the order in which they might strike the observer's
eye. Crane's style is swift, Conrad's slow. Hemingway's dry, concise
descriptions are more like a post-Impressionist such as Cézanne, building
a scene out of flat, geometric areas of color. A writer whose nature
descriptions are as concise as Hemingway's but livelier, with a breathless,
off-the-cuff feel, is D. H. Lawrence—his flower descriptions are the best
in English. Lawrence violates my principle of fact-reporting, using
repetition for rhythmic effect without conveying new information—and
I'm not about to argue with him. My favorite among all writers of
descriptive prose is Colette. Her rendering of plants, flowers, animals,
and faces is beyond compare. Colette has a gift for simile and metaphor,
but ultimately the beauty of her phrases arises from the accuracy of her
vision: her ability to see objects with sympathetic clarity, making us feel
that no one before her had ever paid them enough attention. In *The
Vagabond*, Colette described the writing process as follows:

> To write is to sit and stare, hypnotized, at the reflection of
> the window in the silver inkstand, to feel the divine fever
> mounting to one's cheeks and forehead while the hand that
> writes grows blissfully numb upon the paper. It also means
> idle hours curled up in the hollow of the divan, and then the

orgy of inspiration from which one emerges stupefied and aching all over, but already recompensed and laden with treasures that one unloads slowly on to the virgin page in the little round pool of light under the lamp.

To write is to pour one's innermost self passionately upon the tempting paper, at such frantic speed that sometimes one's hand struggles and rebels, overdriven by the impatient god who guides it—and to find, next day, in place of the golden bough that bloomed miraculously in that dazzling hour, a withered bramble and a stunted flower.

To write is the joy and torment of the idle. Oh, to write! From time to time I feel a need, sharp as thirst in summer, to note and to describe. And then I take up my pen again and attempt the perilous and elusive task of seizing and pinning down, under its flexible double-pointed nib, the many-hued, fugitive, thrilling adjective. . . . The attack does not last long; it is but the itching of an old scar.

Do It

1. Without looking, make a list of every object in your bedroom. Add to the list as you remember more things. Next time you are in your room, look around and notice which objects you forgot. Add them to your list in a separate column.

   For writers, as for spies, it is important to notice and remember as much of your surroundings as possible. This exercise is very useful for training your powers of observation. Try remembering details at a friend's house, in a subway car, a store or public building, a vacation spot—wherever you find yourself wanting to feel like a writer but lacking pen and paper.

2. Describe the physical appearance of your best friend, from memory. You might want to do this in two different ways: first, write a paragraph including every detail you can visualize of your friend's appearance; then, write a paragraph in which you convey an impression of your friend's appearance using no more than three details. You may include clothing as part of the description. You might want to write a description of your own physical appearance using the same techniques.

3. Describe an imaginary place. You might want to do this with a partner or two, discussing what the place is like and writing separate descriptions. One partner might want to draw the imaginary place as a prewriting activity.

4. Describe a place or thing you love, without using any adjectives.

Writer's Bookshelf

A Farewell to Arms by Ernest Hemingway (1929)

has landscape descriptions that are models of image separation: every object gets its own clause, its own frame of the film. Chapter 1 and the first half of Chapter 2 are particularly fine.

Tristes Tropiques by Claude Lévi-Strauss (1955; translated by John and Doreen Weightman, 1974)

is an anthropological classic that happens to contain the world's longest description of a sunset: six pages in Chapter 7.

Letters on Cézanne by Rainier Maria Rilke (1952)—

one of the twentieth century's greatest poets reaches for the heights of gorgeous prose. Dig the differentiations among shades of blue, as well as other nuances of color and light.

Modern Painters, vols. I–V, by John Ruskin (1843–1860)

is the first, and most florid, work by the Victorian art critic and social reformer who may be the most gifted prose stylist in English. On the pretext of describing landscape paintings, he indulges in virtuoso word-painting of clouds, sea, sky, and the like. Ruskin is best sampled in anthologies, such as The Genius of John Ruskin, *edited by John D. Rosenberg (1963, revised 1979).*

The Hunting Sketches by Ivan S. Turgenev (1852)

is a cornucopia of the kind of purple prose they just don't write anymore: coruscating sunrises, ethereal pale lilac hues, and so on. It's also a genial scrapbook of characters and a landmark in both the history of the short story and the history of Russia. The 1962 Bernard Gilbert Guerney translation best captures the descriptive lushness; other translations have different titles, such as A Sportsman's Sketches.

Chapter 8

Narration and Dramatization

There are two ways to render a scene: you can narrate it or dramatize it. This is narration:

> Finally, after Louie had waited at the airport for hours, the correct arrival time was posted on the board.

This is dramatization:

> Louie looked at his watch. Three-fifteen. He'd been here since eleven-thirty; that made almost four hours. Three and three-quarters. Every few minutes, the readout on the arrivals board changed; first it had said, "Flight 4043, from Paris, arriving 12:15," then the number had changed to "1:35," then "2:40," and now it simply said, "Delayed."
>
> A flight crew walked by in uniform, one of the flight attendants running ahead, laughing, his wheeled cart rattling behind him.
>
> "Well, *those* people are gonna get out of here this afternoon," said the gray-haired man who was also waiting for the Paris plane.
>
> "Hey, look!" Louie said, leaning forward in the hard plastic chair. "They're putting up a new arrival time!"

And so on. You get the picture. Dramatization is the full-fledged rendering of a scene in its particulars: the speeches, the gestures, the moment-by-moment changes that make us feel we are watching the action unfold in real time. Narration is a summary.

WHEN TO DRAMATIZE

The example of dramatization, above, could have been greatly expanded: I could have written pages about how Louie arrived at the airport, and what he did during all those hours when he was waiting. In theory, I could have written a large book dramatizing every action, word, and thought of Louie's and of everyone he observed during that period.

The problem is, that wouldn't be dramatic. It would be excruciating, because the events themselves are boring.

Hence we arrive at a great principle:

- Dramatize when it makes things more dramatic.

There are scenes that benefit from being rendered in detail for a number of pages, and there are scenes that gain dramatic intensity from being compressed. Underdramatization and overdramatization are equally common failings among apprentice writers, but overdramatization at least gives you practice in scene construction.

Should you dramatize the loud moments of life and summarize the soft ones? Definitely not: dramatic doesn't necessarily mean big or violent. Whether ten pages of a whale hunt are more compelling than ten pages of tea on the Countess' lawn is largely, though not entirely, a matter of what the writer finds in each. (The smart money is on the whale hunt, but the smart money has never seen Henry James steaming down the stretch.) You wouldn't want to shrink the climactic chase into two lines that the reader couldn't savor; however, at an earlier point, you might summarize how the captain got his ivory leg.

Big upheavals are often precisely the ones that can be effectively narrated in summary form:

> Twenty years earlier, Stella's brother had been killed when the train he was riding in derailed.

Intense moments of personal interaction and communication are often most effective when dramatized. By doing so, you can expose the nuances of emotion and of psychological revelation in each line of dialogue, each small gesture:

> "I don't like trains," Stella said.

"Trains? Why not?" A laugh wanted to begin in Louie's throat.

"I don't want to talk about it. I shouldn't have said anything." She looked at him. "You shouldn't laugh at people when they're telling you their fears."

"I wasn't laughing." He laughed.

Similarly, when Stella's plane arrives and she and Louie have a crucial conversation that hints much about their relationship, we'll want to dramatize. We won't write, "The plane arrived, and Louie and Stella had a crucial conversation that hinted much about their relationship." Readers will want to know exactly what they said to one another, both because what they said is interesting and because hearing the characters' exact words will allow readers to form their own interpretations.

Our decision not to dramatize the hours of Louie's waiting has to do with causation: nothing happens during those hours that makes any difference to what he and Stella talk about later. The fact of his waiting may make a difference by putting him in an irritated mood, but that fact is adequately conveyed by the one-sentence narration.

The decision not to dramatize Louie's waiting also has to do with pace. A dramatized event occupies more space and takes more time to read than the same event narrated. Is it important for readers to live in the scene, or will they get just as much out of a brief summary? This is a judgment call, which writers make for every scene they write. Often, the decision hap-pens instinctively—you find yourself writing the scene, and it's interesting and worthwhile, or you find yourself condensing seven years of a char-acter's life into the line, "Seven years passed," in order to skip over a stag-nant period and get to the exciting part. If the decision doesn't come easily in a given scene, it's often worthwhile to dramatize in the first draft, sub-stituting a brief narration in later drafts if the full-fledged scene doesn't seem worth the space.

By altering the pace of a story, you alter time. A cup of coffee might stretch out for five pages; a chunk of years can pass in a phrase. When you dramatize a long scene, you are putting a claim on the reader's time and giving that scene a larger percentage of the story than if you had narrated it. Try to see the scene from a reader's point of view to decide whether to do so.

WHAT TO DRAMATIZE

Narrating an important event briefly can create a majestic, mysterious effect. In the Bible, the creation of the universe from the void is narrated in a single sentence. Most of the great Bible stories—the life and death of Jesus, the fall of humankind, the tales of David and Bathsheba, Daniel in the lion's den, Jonah and the whale, and many more—are narrated rather than dramatized, with the exception of a line or two of dialogue here and there. This may be partly a result of the fact that the Bible stories are quite ancient, but Homer's stories are also ancient and are much more fully dramatized. Nowhere in the Bible is there the kind of microscopic description and scene-rendering we find in the battle scenes in the *Iliad* or the scene of Odysseus meeting Nausicaa in the *Odyssey*. (Compare the battle of Jericho with the former and the story of Solomon and Sheba with the latter.)

Both the Homeric approach and the biblical approach are powerful and "right." Homer is telling us, "These people—Odysseus, Hector, Achilles, and the rest—are affected by the gods of Olympus, but primarily they are human beings like you. I want you to feel that you know them intimately." The Bible is telling us, "These people—David, Saul, Jonah, and the rest—are human beings like you, but primarily they are creatures of God, and this is what happens when God's creatures obey or disobey His laws." We don't have to know exactly what was on David's mind in order to feel the moral weight of his encounter with Bathsheba and her husband Uriah. We can guess, we can interpret, we can write commentaries, but everything necessary for our commentaries is present in the compressed narrative.

The decision to dramatize or not arises from the function of the event in the work as a whole.

Imagine if the stories in the Bible were fully dramatized in the style of a modern psychological novel. The book would fill several shelves. It would bog down in the mundanities of how David felt when he got up on the morning of his battle with Goliath, how hard and rocky the ground where he slept was, and what the giant looked like. In contrast, the swiftness, the compactness, of biblical tales adds tremendously to their power as moral illustrations.

Most fiction writers nowadays deal, most of the time, in the details of psychological relationships rather than in parables of universal importance, and this is one reason why most writers today rely more on dramatization than on narration. Narration is risky: if you say something flat-out, it had better be convincing.

A modern writer who took that risk and succeeded, relying mostly on narration in his short stories, was Franz Kafka. His stories' impact is in their symbolism rather than in the personalities of his characters. Kafka's predecessor, Heinrich von Kleist, used an entirely narrational style in stories of macabre melodrama in which the events are so bizarre that merely telling them, one after another in swift succession, produces a hair-raising effect.

Most contemporary writers, especially writers of realism, seem to follow the principle, "Dramatize unless there's good reason not to." They dramatize all significant scenes and narrate, or skip over, transitions. Often they dramatize the immediate action and narrate the flashbacks. This is a sound, basic strategy, but as with all principles of writing, it is far from absolute. And deviating from the principle just for the sake of doing something different can sometimes be quite effective.

SHOWING VERSUS TELLING

The issue of narration versus dramatization brings us to the famous phrase, "Show, don't tell." This is an important dictum that should be part of every writer's education, but there are a couple of teensy quibbles that inevitably come up in relation to it:

1. What does it mean?

2. Is it true?

"Show, don't tell" could be paraphrased as, "Be concrete, not abstract" or "Illustrate, don't explain." According to this principle, if you want to demonstrate that your character is angry, for instance, you don't say, "She was angry." You show her acting angry, speaking angrily, perhaps thinking angry thoughts. Thus the reader draws his or her own conclusion about the character's anger, without being told straight out. The word *angry* probably won't even be used in such a scene, but the impression of anger will be clear. A picture has been drawn rather than an idea directly stated. This is especially valid for conveying themes. If you want to express the idea that love is usually a form of madness and friendship is usually a pretense, you don't say, "Love is usually a form of madness and friendship is usually a pretense." You show characters experiencing love and friendship in ways that lead the reader to draw conclusions about madness and pretense.

Another way of paraphrasing "Show, don't tell" might be, "Write sensory descriptions rather than flat statements." This encourages you to find new ways of describing things, avoiding clichés. For instance, instead of saying, "My sneakers got dirty during the ballgame," you might say, "I came home from the ballgame with a crust of half-dry mud around the edges of my sneakers." The phrase "got dirty" is a summary statement of fact, while "a crust of half-dry mud around the edges of my sneakers" is a visual picture. It's easier and more natural for the reader to infer the idea "dirty sneakers" from the image "half-dry mud around the edges of my sneakers" than to form a mental picture of mud from the phrase "dirty sneakers."

When applied sensitively and judiciously, "Show, don't tell" can produce lively, immediate writing. The trouble is, it's so easy for students to apply the principle injudiciously. I've seen too many writing textbooks in which the impression was given, purposely or not, that student writers should always glop up their descriptions with purple prose—portentous, hokey adjectives and figures of speech—and should never simply state a fact; that they should never just say, "The sun set" but should instead say, "The great orange ball of the sun descended upon the horizon in a burst of magmalike flame."

That kind of overblown description is garbage. It is stale, trite, turgid—how shall I put this?—pulpy, pseudo-literary, low-rent prose, the kind of writing that people who don't know anything think is "vivid description."

As I have shown (or told?) in Chapter 7, vivid description has a great deal to do with the simple statement of facts, the clear outlining of pictures. The important point is that the facts themselves should be vivid and fresh. *That* is true showing. Showing does not mean that it is taboo ever to say anything directly.

This pulpy, misguided form of showing particularly annoys me in descriptions of characters' emotions. Many student writers think they can never just write, " 'No,' she said angrily," because they would be telling rather than showing that the character is angry. As a result of this needless inhibition, they end up writing, " 'No,' she shouted, eyes bulging, capillaries reddening, cheeks turning purple as they filled with air." Their characters come to seem like a weird species of humanoids who perpetually go around with exaggerated facial expressions and hand gestures, eyes that are always in motion, hands that saw the air ceaselessly, and voices that never speak in an ordinary, neutral tone.

It is perfectly all right to write "she said angrily," even if it is technically telling rather than showing. The phrase "she said angrily" is not original, but it is serviceable: readers know what to make of it and they don't mind. If you can dream up a more original way of showing that the character is angry, great, but if not, don't bog readers down in stale, cornball descriptive phrases just for the sake of showing.

The "show, don't tell" philosophy was first enunciated by newspaper editors during the green-eyeshade era, urging their reporters to include vivid scenes in news stories. The reader didn't want to learn in the abstract that a fatal fire had occurred on Main Street; he or she wanted to know that the flames reached three stories high and that two elderly residents of a rear apartment were trapped by smoke, dying of smoke inhalation before firefighters could reach them.

It's a pretty good principle for some kinds of journalism. I'm sure that more concreteness was needed, and appreciated, in small-town newspaper writing a hundred years ago. Even in that field, however, it's hardly an ironclad rule. If tank troops are massing along the Israeli-Syrian border, I want to know it, as information; I don't want to wade through descriptions of tank tracks raising clouds of dust as the multi-ton behemoths groan their way over poorly paved roads before I can reach a tangible fact.

Keep in mind that the dictum "show, don't tell" was originally a way of making prose cleaner, swifter, more concise, not a way of padding it with gloppy, pointless modifiers; of nailing down facts, not hiding them.

There's something anti-intellectual about "show, don't tell" (and its companion phrase, William Carlos Williams' "No ideas but in things"). The assumption seems to be that readers don't want anything explained to them: they're too impatient, and they just won't get it. This is underestimating the readers' intelligence. Our readers are smart, and we must treat them as such. Writers of comic books respect their audience's intelligence nowadays; for print fiction writers not to is wrong even on the most crass commercial grounds.

Let's say a history teacher tries to teach his classes about the Civil War by having them read a chapter in a textbook and supplementing it with a lecture based on his own reading. For a week, he tells them what happened in the North and in the South, at Shiloh and Bull Run and Gettysburg and Vicksburg, but they don't seem interested, and when he pulls a pop quiz, he discovers that they don't remember anything he told them. What does he do next? He comes in with a blue Union cap and a gray Rebel cap and keeps exchanging them on his head as he reads aloud from the letters of ordinary soldiers, the memoirs of generals, and the speeches of Abraham Lincoln and Jefferson Davis. He passes around a book of Matthew Brady's photographs of Civil War soldiers on the battlefield. At last he has shown the lesson rather than merely telling it.

Well, there's no doubt that hearing the participants' words and seeing the photographs makes the subject more interesting and lively, but it's also true that this method conveys less information per unit of time than the telling method. Furthermore, even through most of the class didn't like the telling lessons, there were two or three who got it just fine, and they're disgusted by the teacher's hat-wearing antics. They feel they're being spoon-fed.

As fiction writers, our audience is those two or three people. Surveys have shown that only 3 to 5 percent of the American population buys books regularly; the audience for serious fiction is only a fraction of that. Our readers are not frightened by abstractions. They are capable of making up their own abstractions. Indeed, that's why they prefer concrete illustration over abstract explanation most of the time: they want to be allowed to draw their own inferences. However, if you have an idea that's original and thoughtful and provocative, they want to hear it.

The problem is, so many writers have ideas that they think are original, thoughtful, and provocative but that are really old, simple-minded, and dull. The standard for an abstract idea worth stating in a book is much higher than the standard for one worth thinking about in private. In private, it's quite all right—it may even change my life for the better—if I think, "Love is the answer," but if I am Paddy Chayevsky writing that line in *Altered States,* it's a wincing cliché.

Many of the great writers have written thematic passages in telling style rather than showing style, for the valid reason that they had important, profound things to say. Shakespeare said outright, "Most friendship is feigning, / Most loving mere folly." That's as deep as you can get, though it's not original.

There are two reasons he could get away with it, while you could not get away with, "Love is usually a form of madness and friendship is usually a pretense":

1. He said it beautifully. That is *always* a justification for *anything* in literature. (And notice how simple his way of saying it beautifully is.)

2. He was in the midst of showing it, too. As a playwright, Shakespeare was an expert on conveying abstract ideas through concrete action. His lines on love and friendship are part of a song lyric that is sung during the action of a funny, engaging plot involving characters whose loving is very clearly folly and whose friendship very clearly feigning. If those wonderful two lines weren't in the play, the theme would be just as evident on the basis of what happens onstage. It just so happens that Shakespeare also came up with a lovely way of saying the idea outright and found a place where it fit.

Every work of fiction shows some things and tells others. No matter how much is said explicitly, there is always another layer whose presence the reader must infer. Kafka, in his narrational way, tells his stories outright, but doesn't tell us one word about their meaning. His meanings are shown in concrete form in his plots. The Book of Ecclesiastes, which tells a great many profound thoughts outright, shows the growth of a philosopher's mind. Conversely, in the works of the minimalist writers of the 1970s and 1980s, who tried to push scene-rendering to the limit of photographic super-realism and never to make a generalization, you can find a surprising number of flat statements about character's personalities and histories, often smuggled into dialogue as if the quotation marks were a kind of protection. In Henry James, whose motto was, "Dramatize, dramatize, dramatize," you can find more mulling-over of abstractions than in almost any other writer.

"Show, don't tell" is most valid as a strategy when events, characters, or props are presented as clues from which the reader is expected to draw conclusions. One reason writers mishandle this strategy is that they focus on the putting-in aspects rather than the taking-out aspects. "Show, don't tell" is a strategy of implication, not of overelaboration.

Ron Wallace of the University of Wisconsin once wisely suggested age forty as the threshold after which writers should be allowed to tell what they know instead of just showing it.

TRANSITIONS

And now, without further transition, I'll discuss transitions. Keep them brief. Do without them whenever possible.

Transitions are the switching-points between scenes. They usually involve a change in setting: moving from place to place or going forward or backward in time. Sometimes we follow one character or group of characters from scene to scene: "He dressed hurriedly and ran out the front door, hailing a cab on the run. Twelve-and-a-half minutes later, he was downtown." At other times, we switch our attention from one character in one setting to another character in another setting: "Meanwhile, back at the ranch. . . ."

Transitions are among the mechanical, unglamorous aspects of writing. They are easy to get bogged down in. Often they are more worrisome than they need be. Virginia Woolf once complained that she had spent an entire morning's work getting her characters down a flight of stairs.

Fortunately, a historical change has taken place in the style of fiction: readers do not expect as many transitions as they used to. Movies and television, and especially commercials and rock videos, have taught audiences how to move from scene to scene, character to character, topic to topic, instantaneously, leaving quick cuts where transitions used to be. The same change has occurred in printed fiction. There is an increasing tendency to plunge readers into scenes *in medias res*—right into the action, without introduction. Changes in location, gaps in time, are often signalled nowadays by a skipped space—no words at all. That makes for swift pacing and economical prose.

There are still times when it feels necessary to give the reader a bit of information about where and when a scene takes place: "Two hours later, Louie was at the airport." Sometimes, however, that feeling can be mistaken. If I simply show Louie at the airport, readers will understand where he is.

Beginning writers often feel uncertain about how much of a routine action to describe. If Louie is traveling from his apartment to the airport, do you have to show the cab ride? If you show the cab ride, do you have to mention that he opens and shuts the door of the cab? If you show him opening and shutting the door, do you have to describe the coolness of the chrome handle and the comfortable way his hand fits around it? If you didn't draw the line somewhere, you could spend two-hundred pages describing Louie's cab ride to the airport.

The thing to remember is that readers already know what these routine or transitional actions are like. They assume the character has performed them, without being told. They don't *want* to read them. They know that someone who is waiting in an airport has arrived there somehow. (And the waiting itself may be an unnecessary transition.)

If I happen to think of something significant, original, or compelling that happens to Louie during his cab ride, I might include it—but I might not. Even though it's interesting, it might not be relevant to the ongoing drama of Louie and Stella. It might be distracting. Maybe I ought to set it aside and write a whole other story about it. And even if it's relevant, maybe I can transfer it to a nontransitional scene. For instance, let's say that in a conversation with the cabbie, Louie indirectly reveals his insecurity. I could probably have him reveal the same thing in a preexisting, more central conversation with Stella.

Keeping transitions in creative writing to a minimum is quite a different strategy from what American students usually learn in composition courses. Textbooks for such courses usually bear down hard on the subject of transitions, giving lists of recommended transitional words and phrases and urging students to use them often to make sure readers follow their arguments. The model paragraphs in such textbooks are usually tied to the paragraphs before and after them by verbal knots: "As we have just seen," "And so, in conclusion, let's turn to the question of. . . ."

It's like the overprotective parent who makes his or her child wear a winter coat when the temperature is above freezing.

The result is overdressed, padded, stiff, pedestrian, clumsy, toddling prose. The writer holds the reader's hand and says, "And now we're going to discuss *this* topic . . . and, as you can see, we have just discussed *that* topic. . . ."

I can think of two justifications for the transition-heavy approach:

1. Transitions are more necessary in expository or persuasive prose than in fiction, and the former categories are what students read and write more of.

2. Even though transitions should probably not be used as often as the composition textbooks say, understanding their use trains students in basic thinking skills such as cause-effect relationships and chronological organization. In other words, what the textbooks claim to be teaching—good writing—is not what they're really teaching. They're really teaching something much more elementary—clear thinking.

Nevertheless, they overdo it to an extreme.

It is ridiculous to suppose that the same students who watch rock videos and commercials, understanding the messages without any transitions at all, need constant written warnings about the subjects they are about to encounter and wrap-ups of the subjects they have just encountered. It is not only an insult to their intelligence, it is a gross miscalculation of their tastes and is totally out of touch with contemporary American culture. No wonder so many students think of literature as stodgy and old-fashioned.

Do It

1. Read a handful of short stories or skim some you have already read, and notice the proportions of narration, passages of dramatization, and transitions. If the stories are in books or magazines that you own, you might wish to highlight each type of passage in a different color or style.

2. Look over old stories that you have written and notice how you have used narration, dramatization, and transitions. Think about how you might use them more effectively in future work.

3. Do Exercise 2 with a partner, each reading and critiquing the use of narration, dramatization, and transition in the other's work.

4. Write a short story using no transitions at all. Read it over and decide whether the lack of transitions creates confusion at any points. If so, write economical transitions at those points.

5. Write a short story entirely in narration. Save that draft, then write another version of the same story relying entirely or mostly on dramatization. You may find yourself wanting to create a hybrid of the two.

6. Tell a story aloud to a friend, relative, or yourself. (It might be a condensed version of a published story you have read.) Most oral storytelling relies mainly on narration. Try to include some dramatization and detailed description in your storytelling.

Writer's Bookshelf

Literary Criticism by Henry James (2 vols., Library of America edition, 1984)
> *includes James' prefaces to the New York edition of his novels, which expound upon the technical choices involved in composing the works.*

The Craft of Fiction by Percy Lubbock (1921)
> *is a classic treatise by a disciple of James. Lubbock is the one who coined the phrase "loose, baggy monsters" to describe big, sprawling nineteenth-century novels that lacked form.*

The Dramatic Experience by J. L. Styan (1965)
> *teaches readers how to see a play by reading it: how to summon actions, gestures, and sounds from printed words. For the reader who is also a writer, this can lead to insights into the craft of dramatization. Styan's* Shakespeare's Stagecraft *(1971) follows the same approach and can greatly enhance one's appreciation of the plays.*

Chapter 9

Point of View and Narrative Distance

For about a century, point of view has been the big playground for experimentation in fiction. As a result, writers have a great deal more latitude than they used to in choosing which point of view to tell a story from. It's no longer true that you have to choose a single point of view and stick to it or that you can't shift viewpoints within a story. The demand for consistency in point of view has jumped to a higher level of abstraction: rather than a single, unchanging point of view, contemporary taste asks for a consistent, or at least defensible, *pattern* of points of view. If you're writing about a family, for instance, you don't have to choose one family member to be your first-person narrator throughout; you can shift from Mom to Dad to Buddy to Sis; but you wouldn't devote a chapter or section to the first-person point of view of the family cat unless the cat had previously been established as an active agent whose consciousness made a difference to readers' perceptions of the drama.

Because point of view was being renovated at the time, and because it could be talked about as a technique—and anything analyzed as a technique enjoys more prestige in our society than anything discoursed upon free-form—it has been overemphasized in academic approaches to narrative. In the day-by-day practice of writing, deciding on a point of view is one of those decisions that can affect the texture of an entire work, but making this decision is usually quick and hard to do wrong.

POINT OF VIEW

There is no mystery about point of view. There are basically two of them: first person ("I") and third person ("he, she"). There is rarely a reason to use anything else, and your choice is generally a matter of instinct. The chances are that before you set a word down on paper, while the swirling gases of your imagination are still coalescing into characters and a story line, some sentences will arise spontaneously in your mind—the first or last sentence of a story, perhaps, or a key sentence from a crucial later scene: "Stella and Louie joined hands and walked toward the sunset. 'Wait a minute,' Louie said, and went to answer the phone—a call that our hero did not realize would affect the entire course of his life."

Most stories come prearmed with a point of view. There is some angle of narration that naturally fits—in this case, I want to give equal treatment to both lovers, to show each in scenes without the other, and to preserve objectivity in observing their actions. I didn't think of the reasons first; I didn't muse, "Hm, how can I best preserve objectivity while treating both Louie and Stella equally when together and in occasional separate scenes? Aha, I know! The third person!" No, I *felt* that the third person was right for these characters and their story; the technical reasons are just a rationalization of what my instinct already knew. If I had felt that I wanted to narrate the story from Stella's first-person viewpoint, I could have come up with reasons for that, too. (Working in the other direction—starting with a rationale and trying to match a strategy to it—is a time-consuming error many academically trained writers fall into. It's thinking like a computer instead of like an artist.) Ideally, a story's point of view is a natural outgrowth of its material, rather than an artifice imposed from outside.

THIRD-PERSON VARIANTS

It's usually said that there are two variants of the third person: the omniscient and the limited. In the omniscient, the narrator knows everything that's going on in the story and may switch from one character's third-person viewpoint to another's in order to illuminate the action more clearly. An omniscient narrator may enter the thoughts of all the characters, enter one or two chief characters' minds while politely refraining from entering the minds of minor characters, or stick to characters' observable behaviors, declining to presume to state what any character thinks.

In the limited third person, the author chooses one character as the viewpoint character and shows only what that character knows, only what that character can observe. Thus the limited third person has the intense, individual focus of the first person, but the main character is called "he" or "she" rather than "I." The limited third person can be very effective in psychological fiction. It allows you to probe a character's mind and show that character's worldview while maintaining a distance, as if you were a therapist discussing your character's case. It lacks both the advantages and the disadvantages of narrating in a character's voice for the duration of a story or novel; it allows the narrator to step back discreetly at times to observe the character from outside.

There are certainly cases of strictly omniscient narration and of strictly limited narration in fiction, but it's important to realize that there are also blendings: the categories blur at the center. They aren't two separate species that can't mate; they are two varieties of the same species and can give rise to infinite individualities, which are more interesting than the pure types.

If you are writing from the omniscient viewpoint, it doesn't oblige you to give equal time to every character; there may very well be a protagonist who deserves 75 percent of the attention. If you are writing from the limited viewpoint of a single protagonist, it doesn't mean that you can never present background information in a flashback that doesn't involve the protagonist, or that every time you describe a room you have to use that tiresome formula, "Louie glanced around at the room," or that the other characters must be opaque mysteries. You can switch from the limited third-person viewpoint of one character to the limited third-person viewpoint of another character—what might be called a rotating omniscience, as in Hemingway's "The Short Happy Life of Francis Macomber." You can stay within the protagonist's limited point of view when that character is onstage, then move to wide-angle omniscience for scenes involving other characters. You can do anything that works. What works is whatever persuades readers—whatever has so much life and strength that it makes readers forget to say, "You can't do that."

Scope, scale, and context influence a work's point of view. Suppose I write a five-page story, from the limited third-person viewpoint of the character, about a woman walking through a forest. Then suppose, however, that I insert those five pages into a spy novel in which the woman meets her contact in the forest for an exchange of secret information, with consequences involving dozens of other characters around the world. The novel is narrated from the omniscient point of view, though I haven't changed a word in the five inserted pages.

FIRST-PERSON NARRATION

Working in the first person puts a constraint on you: the narrative can only reveal information the narrator could believably know about. It can't show scenes at which the narrator wasn't present, unless the narrator learns about them somehow—hears about the events from another character, reads a letter describing the scene, uses telepathy, and so on. There are a million ways of getting around the restrictions of first-person narrative, but they can seem corny and artificial if overdone. Some writers simply cheat and have the first-person narrator describe events he or she had no way of learning about, but this is not recommended unless you are Herman Melville *and* you are writing *Moby Dick*.

The constraints of first-person narration can be used to the writer's advantage to create suspense. If the narrator is a detective trying to crack a murder case, she (and the reader) uncovers the clues piecemeal, by interviewing one witness at a time; she can't jump ahead, as an omniscient narrator could, and peek at the culprit in his hideout. In contrast, if you're writing a work in which it's important to show events the narrator couldn't possibly know about—for instance, a political thriller with simultaneous scenes in Washington, Moscow, and Beijing—that may be enough reason not to use the first person.

First-person narration also adds interesting kinks to characterization. All the secondary characters are viewed through the prism of the narrator's mind, which by definition produces some distortions. The reader must then ask, "How trustworthy is the narrator?" Untrustworthy or partially trustworthy narrators have become a staple of twentieth-century fiction. Perhaps the narrator states the correct facts about the other characters but systematically misinterprets their motives; perhaps the narrator is totally wacko and claims the other characters did things they didn't do; more commonly, the narrator's interpretations, like most people's in real life, are spotty and must be evaluated through clue-comparison and common sense. The narrator's self-characterization must also be evaluated in the same fashion. Most people present themselves in a flattering light, blaming others for things that go wrong; some overemphasize their flaws, wallowing in self-blame. Reading between the lines of a first-person narrative to discover what the characters are "really" like is one of the significant pleasures of psychological fiction.

If a first-person narrator knows enough, and is self-effacing enough, he can function as an omniscient narrator. The omniscient first-person narrator is an old device, best used by Dostoevsky in *The Devils*. The narrator is putatively a character but has no active role; he exists only to narrate what happens to the other characters. He may or may not have a name and a personality; he very likely has a tone and some implicit opinions; he is by nature observant, garrulous, and an incorrigible gossip and snoop who is always running around entering other people's homes, making sure to be wherever anything interesting is occurring—or at least to hear about it in retrospect from another character, perhaps at an inn or soiree. This kinky little point of view was delightful in nineteenth-century novels set in provincial towns where everyone knew everyone else. On one hand, it verged on Melvillean cheating; on the other, it verged on omniscient authorial comment à la Anthony Trollope. A sign of the decline in literary sophistication since then is that when Iris Murdoch used the device a hundred years later, in *The Philosopher's Pupil*, she felt compelled to explain it within the novel.

SECOND-PERSON NARRATION

There's another point of view that must be mentioned briefly, though it's mainly used for novelty: the second person ("you"). Every once in a while, a writer uses the second person with extraordinary skill, and then it becomes briefly fashionable, with diminishing returns for every succes-sive user. Actually there are two distinct forms of the second person: the second-person declarative, as in Jay McInerney's *Bright Lights, Big City*, and the second-person imperative, as in Lorrie Moore's *Self-Help*.

The second-person declarative simply shows the actions of a character who is called "you":

> You decide to use the second person in your next story. You start typing your first sentence; it is, "You meet while you're out for a walk."

The second-person imperative tells the character what to do; it is addressed to the character, but the word "you" is often implicit:

> Decide to use the second person in your next story. Start typing your first sentence; it is, "Meet while you're out for a walk."

The big advantage of the second person is that it cajoles the reader into identifying with the point-of-view character; that generally works best if the reader *already* identifies with the character. The big disadvantage is that it's inherently gimmicky.

A CONSISTENT POINT OF VIEW

Whatever point or points of view you choose, you need to use some basic care to maintain consistency. At the most rudimentary level, if you're writing a short story in the omniscient third person, it's a sign of amateurism if you suddenly switch to the first person and if the switch is not part of a consciously created pattern. At the highest level, if you're Virginia Woolf and you're writing *The Waves,* you establish a set of six major characters and periodically switch from one character's limited third-person viewpoint to another's, as well as inserting passages of lyrical description from an omniscient viewpoint.

Maintaining consistency requires simple attentiveness. It's a mechanical operation: you look over what you've written and fix any places where the point of view strays from your scheme.

This book is written consistently in the first, second, and third persons.

All narrative points of view ultimately are disguises. The constructed narrator conveys, directly or indirectly, the worldview of someone else—the author. In *War and Peace,* we can hear Tolstoy's indignant, bearded mutterings behind the omniscient narrator whom he calls "the human mind." A disguise is a way of sneaking something in.

FINDING THE BEST POINT OF VIEW

As I've indicated, the choice of viewpoint often suggests itself along with the initial inspiration for a work. What if it doesn't? Here are some guidelines.

When in doubt, try the most flexible third-person viewpoint you feel comfortable with. Set your default at "omniscient" and change it only if another viewpoint seems significantly more attractive or illuminating or original. The wider the scope of your subject—the more characters in your cast, the more time and space you cover—the more likely it is that the omniscient third person is best. If you're writing about a relatively small group of people, such as a family, and a set of actions in which one member of the group is most interesting or most deeply affected, it often feels natural to write from that character's limited third-person point of view. A shifting first-person point of view is often very successful in dealing with a group of people who each see the same action from a different standpoint, contributing to a mosaic of mind-sets, opinions, prejudices, and observations; it's also used often in multigeneration novels, where the narrators form a descent lineage.

Using a single first-person narrator takes us more deeply into one mind than any other form of narration. Not only is it effective when the character is a likable person, but it can make an unsavory character likable, or at least understandable. It's an old truth that very few people think themselves evil or misguided, even if they appear that way to everyone else; the first-person viewpoint gives an opportunity to explore a character's reasons for unwise or wicked actions.

It's often good to use the first person when the narrator has a distinct way of speaking and thinking—a distinct personal voice, to use a trite phrase. Obvious examples are Huckleberry Finn and Holden Caulfield. When a character undergoes a series of trials that wouldn't be as exciting if observed from outside, that's also a time to use the first person—and again, *The Adventures of Huckleberry Finn* and its descendant, *The Catcher in the Rye,* are examples. Of course, if your protagonist is going to die at the end, that's a reason not to use him or her as the first-person narrator unless you have some brilliant gimmick for using a deceased narrator.

Most of the time, the first-person narrator is the protagonist; at times, however, using a secondary character as narrator can dramatically revamp a story. This is especially true when the narrator is an observant but bland person whose tale relates the impact of a more charismatic person. The classic examples are *The Great Gatsby, All the King's Men,* and *One Flew Over the Cuckoo's Nest.* It is conceivable that those novels could have been narrated, respectively, by Jay Gatsby, Willie Stark, and McMurphy, or by an omniscient narrator, but those characters are not introspective and might have seemed dull if we were allowed to know their thoughts directly. The choices of Nick Carraway, Jack Burden, and Chief Broom Bromden were inspired, opening up those novels to much greater possibilities for depth and detachment while maintaining a personal voice and turning bland secondary characters into fascinating central ones.

Changing your mind about point of view during the writing process—not in the final text—can sometimes lead to illuminations about the meaning of your work; it can lead you to see a story where you had trouble seeing one before. For instance, I might have initially written about Louie and Stella from Louie's first-person viewpoint; then, one sunny afternoon, I saw a sign in the sky, with flaming letters in 36-point Palatino, telling me, "This isn't Louie's story. It's both of theirs!" Thus enlightened, I returned to the beginning and rewrote from the third-person point of view. Most writing experiences, however, are not like that.

If you're persistently unable to choose from among possible points of view for a story, it probably means that none of them is ideal but that some or all of them would serve adequately. You might write a few pages one way and a few the other, read them, and decide; if you can't decide by yourself, consult a friend or teacher. If that doesn't reduce your anxiety, you've probably been successfully looking for a way to block yourself rather than unsuccessfully weighing points of view. As a last resort, flip a coin and pick one.

I believe that the cases in which choice of viewpoint makes or breaks a work of fiction are exceptional and that the choice is usually a rough and ready one. There are many great works of fiction that would have been equally great given a different point of view. You pick what's at hand and what feels right, and you go with it, and it's almost always the basic first person or third person.

One of the illusions fiction creates is that the author's choices had an inevitable rightness about them. The reality, however, is that there are innumerable ways of describing any given object or handling any given scene. Of those ways, many may be weak, unconvincing, or unskillful, but many may be good. It's self-evident that if you assigned a million competent writers to describe the same scene, you'd get a million different competent versions of the scene; why then can't one writer imagine many equally effective ways of handling a scene? Our job, after all, is to be universally imaginative.

Even in defining a single word, there is more than one way. Look up the same word in five dictionaries, and you will find five different definitions; you may prefer one of them, but it's likely that one or more of the others will be equally adequate to define the word. If there's no ideal definition for a single word, how can there be an ideal rendering for a scene, a story, a novel?

Another reason for doubting the existence of a single, correct point of view for any given work of fiction is that, in my observation, relatively few works suffer from point-of-view problems. The range of quality in published fiction runs from the sublime to the abysmal. There are a lot of published works in which the characterizations are thin, the plots are sloppy, the ideas are shallow, the descriptions are lame, the dialogue is stilted—they are published because books get published for nonliterary reasons (see Chapter 20). If choosing the wrong point of view were a major sticking point for writers, we would see a lot of published works in which the point of view seemed faulty. But we don't. We see an occasional work in which the choice of point of view seems inspired and a great many in which the choice seems okay, good enough. If *A Farewell to Arms* had been narrated in the third person instead of the first, I don't think it would have made any difference in the book's quality. On the other hand, narrating *The Sun Also Rises* from Jake's first-person viewpoint was absolutely essential. He suffered a war wound that had a devastating but invisible effect on him; he didn't talk about it, scarcely even thought about it consciously. The effects of the wound on Jake's characterization are present all throughout the novel, but primarily between the lines; a third-person narrator couldn't have revealed them, because we detect them in Jake's tone and in his indirect thoughts on other subjects.

In few works of fiction does the choice of a standard point of view set our teeth on edge. It's merely something that's there and accepted. I have heard of cases where a story or novel, after being repeatedly rejected, sold after the author changed its point of view, but I have a hunch that's because the person buying the manuscript was the person advising the change or was influenced by the person advising the change. The contact, not the technique, made the sale. As a manuscript reader, I rejected thousands of manuscripts for all kinds of reasons, but I don't remember rejecting any for faulty point of view.

Seeking the ideal point of view—or any other technical ideal in art—can be an incentive to keep working, but that doesn't mean the ideal exists. Cézanne painted the same mountain over and over, longing for its ideal realization, always discontented with what he'd previously done; as a result, he produced dozens of great pictures of that mountain, though he never achieved his self-imposed ideal.

NARRATIVE DISTANCE

What interests me more than the choice of point of view is the flexibility available *within* a point of view. Once you've said, "I'm going to use the third-person omniscient" or "I'm going to use the first person," innumerable moment-by-moment choices of viewpoint still await you. We can think of these as choices of camera angle or of narrative distance. This point will become clear if you think of yourself, once again, as directing a movie. Movies are almost always in the third person; they see all their characters from outside. (Virtual reality, like real life, is always in the first person.) This fact, however, gives the director very little guidance as to where to set up the camera for any given scene. Should it be a long shot, a close shot, a close-up; should it show this character or that one? These are point-of-view questions, and the fiction writer faces them, too. Let's say I'm writing the scene in which Stella calls a wrong number and reaches Louie. My choice of what to describe is a choice of angle and distance. Should I focus tight on Louie, describing the furrowing of his brow, his hand twirling the phone cord? Or should I do a medium shot of his room, describing the light coming through the window and the presence of an onlooker, his mother, who is waiting to be driven to the supermarket? How about a split screen, moving back and forth from Louie adorably twirling his cord to Stella adorably twirling *her* cord?

Choices of this kind become more visible when you're working on a panoramic scale, such as in a battle scene. At times, you'll want to show the whole thing from a distance; at other times you'll close in on one character's face.

The same process occurs in first-person narrative. To begin with, there's the question of choosing what the narrator notices—where her glances alight. Does she notice so much about every scene that she functions practically as an omniscient narrator, or does she describe things partially? These choices affect characterization: we learn something about the narrator if she doesn't comment on people's physical appearance, or if she does; or if she emphasizes other people's actions and keeps hers in the background, or vice versa.

More subtly, perhaps, first-person narrative can be placed at various distances from its narrator. How can this be, since the narration comes from within? Well, the withinness of the first person is, like everything else in fiction, an illusion; the only place it's "within" is the writer's mind. Let's say I'm writing a first-person story about the excitement of making my first cup of coffee in the morning. I can place the narrative at a distance from myself by showing only the external actions:

> I poured the beans into the grinder; it ground for ten seconds. I opened the plastic cap and poured the aromatic grounds into the filter cone.

There's nothing in that narration that couldn't have been narrated by an observer, nothing of the character's thoughts or attitudes. I can bring the narrative a bit closer to the character by adding hints of emotional coloration:

> I poured the beans into the grinder. Ten seconds of hideous noise later, I uncapped the sweet-smelling grounds. I poured them into the filter cone.

That gives the reader a stronger feeling of being inside the narrator's head. We can increase intimacy by adding thoughts and gestures:

> I poured the beans into the grinder—the grinder that, I remembered, she and I had bought together. After ten seconds of hideous noise, I uncapped the sweet-smelling grounds and thought of her chestnut-colored, herbal-scented hair. Sniffing deeply, I poured the coffee into the filter cone.

Tags such as "I thought" and "I remembered" slow the pace, however, and maintain a sense of formal distance between the narrator and the reader or between the narrator and his own thoughts. It's more stylish to do without them. A way of further closing the narrative distance is to add glints of thought, in the form of sentence fragments, illuminating digressions, chips of lyrical description:

> I poured the beans into the grinder. Ten seconds of hideous noise—sweet-smelling grounds! A deep sniff, then the pouring into the filter cone: a sifting like hourglass sands, a chestnut scent like auburn hair.

The hourglass image shows the narrator's preoccupation with mortality; the lyrical tone gives the flavor of his thought without narrating any specific thoughts. Stream of consciousness, by relating thoughts in the mind's own words, brings the narrative closer still:

> Pouring the beans into the grinder. Ten seconds of hideous noise—sweet-smelling grounds! The grinder we bought together, when we were together. Her hair scented with herbal conditioner. A deep sniff of auburn coffee powder, and it pours into the filter cone like hourglass sands.

We could close the distance to the utmost by expanding the above short paragraph into a long interior monologue in which the narrator's observations of the coffee-grinding process and memories of a bygone love blossom into rambling ideas on a dozen subjects, jumbled together in run-on sentences.

The narrative distance you choose in any given passage (for it can shift during the course of a work) depends on your personal style and on what you want to reveal about the narrator. It also depends on how much space you want to devote to the passage, for the closer the narrative comes to the narrator, the more words the narrator is tempted to use. Stream of consciousness takes up space. Conciseness is a virtue. There is also much merit in leaving things implied when possible rather than expressing them.

The prevailing style in contemporary American fiction favors narrative distance: a cool, detached tone, thoughts and feelings that are implied rather than expressed, and flamboyant technical devices that place a gate between the reader and the character. For example, if a love story is narrated as a collage of phone messages, E-mail transcripts, postcards, and office memos, it tends to create a sense of distance even though the characters are expressing their emotions candidly and colloquially. As a result, we're more likely to admire the author's cleverness than to feel anything. There are times when maintaining that kind of detachment works very well, but there are insurmountable limits to what it can reveal about a character. My own personal preference—my keenest desire when I write first-person fiction—is exactly the opposite: to close the distance between reader and character as much as possible—to maximize the illusion that the narrative is within the narrator, while balancing that with the demands of telling the story.

You trade away certain virtues when you zoom in tight on your narrator and others when you move back. It's up to you to decide which technique will best serve any piece of writing.

Do It

1. Write two versions of the same story, from two different points of view. This can be done by a pair of writers, each producing one version.

2. Write a story that shifts point of view gracefully. (This, too, can be done by a pair of writers, each choosing one point of view and writing those sections of the story.) Then try writing a different version of it, using a single, consistent point of view.

3. Rewrite a story by another writer, using a different point of view. You might want to study the use of point of view in a number of stories, looking for places where you feel it is particularly effective or particularly ineffective. Then, rewrite passages in order to test your impressions.

4. Film students sometimes write shot sequences for the films they study. A shot sequence is simply a numbered list of every camera shot in a film (or a portion of a film), labeling the shot's type and briefly describing its contents; for example, "37. Closeup—Rich bites his lip, glowering with romantic cynicism." Do the literary equivalent of this for a short story—either one you've read or one you've written—by writing a numbered and labeled description of what happens in each passage. The definition of a "passage" may vary with the context: it might be a single descriptive paragraph, or a stretch of dialogue, or a transitional sentence, or anything you feel constitutes a single "camera shot." Label the passages in a way that seems fitting to you; examples might be "Dialogue," "Description—Panorama," "Description—Close-up," "Narration," "Exposition," "Flashback," "Stream of Consciousness." Label the shifts in point of view and narrative distance; for omniscient narratives, specify when the narrative enters a character's point of view and when it bespeaks an impersonal, external narrator.

Writer's Bookshelf

Wuthering Heights by Emily Brontë (1847)

anticipates modern uses of the shifting narrator. Some sections of this gothic masterpiece are narrated by Mr. Lockwood, the tenant at *Wuthering Heights*, but he turns most of the heavy labor over to his housekeeper, Mrs. Dean.

Lord Jim by Joseph Conrad (1900)

uses a "frame device": the first few pages describe a group of friends sitting around telling tales, and the rest of the novel is the tale one of them, a man named Marlow, tells. As a result, almost every paragraph in the novel begins with quotation marks, and when a character speaks, double quotation marks are required. This cumbersome device works superbly in Conrad's hands; he also used Marlow in Heart of Darkness *(1899) and* Youth *(1989).*

As I Lay Dying by William Faulkner (1930)

consists of sixty-one chapters using the alternating first-person viewpoints of fifteen characters. This *tour de force was written in six weeks during Faulkner's spare time while he was employed at a boiler factory.*

The Good Soldier by Ford Madox Ford (1915)

cunningly manipulates a first-person narrator who is a wealthy, cultured fool and whose observations of his own and others' actions are suspect. The author never comments, but can be seen standing ironically behind the narrator on every page.

Chronicles of Barsetshire by Anthony Trollope (1855–1867)

is a six-volume saga that made its author's reputation and is still probably his most enjoyable and solid achievement. The novels are The Warden *(1855),* Barchester Towers *(1857),* Doctor Thorne *(1858),* Framley Parsonage *(1861),* The Small House at Allington *(1864), and* The Last Chronicle of Barset *(1867). Trollope is known for his use of an omniscient point of view in which the narrator often breaks in to comment on the action, even stating which characters he likes and dislikes. Modern critics have sneered at Trollope for the supposed artlessness and clumsiness of this technique; but if it's so artless and clumsy, why does he almost always use the device at points where it increases the reader's interest, and how does he manage to keep up suspense when he blabs about his endings beforehand?*

Chapter 10

Style, Voice, Tone

Style? 'Tis a slippery fish, which wriggleth in the palm and slippeth away, with a fin-slap of water in your face as bye-your-leave; 'tis the invisible serpent of the lake, which all tell tales of and none hath seen, till you, foolish mariner, row past human vision in the depth of midnight and smite Leviathan with the broadside of an oar: the wood snaps with a crack as of lightning felling a Highland oak; the monster raiseth a maelstrom that doth whirl the skiff from under you, a stormy half-league from shore with naught to get you home but chutzpah.

Whose style is that?

Not mine. I don't write like that. But wait, I wrote that.

I was imitating someone else's style, but I don't know whose. I don't think any previous writer ever wrote like that. It's supposed to be some kind of antique Scottish style, mostly, but it wouldn't pass as the real thing. You might call it, "Robert Louis Stevenson riding the Twelve bus to school."

If it's no one else's, it must be mine. I have to claim this poor, wretched style as my own or it will be orphaned. Nevertheless, it's not my own natural style; I have to strain to write that way.

But writing in my "natural" style requires effort too, although an effort of a different kind. This effort aims at becoming more myself, rather than at mimicking someone else. For instance, in the previous sentence, I first wrote, "It requires an effort aimed at becoming more myself. . . ." I changed it to "This effort aims at . . ." to make it swifter and more active. That alteration is neither more more less extensive than the ones I made when writing the opening paragraph, but it's a way of shaping my natural style, not altering it.

What if I decided that I always wanted to write pastiches of historical styles? Then the first paragraph *would* be in my style. But my style wouldn't be limited to parodies of antique Scottish writers; I could also do pastiches of 1950s Existentialists, Icelandic scops, and whatnot. Some unifying resemblance would mark all those parodies as mine.

This business of style is paradoxical. Style, one's natural, personal way of writing, is achieved through conscious effort.

How conscious the effort has to be is a question that has been much debated. If style is personality, won't it arise without effort? Won't effort actually impair its spontaneity and authenticity?

A partial answer has already been given above. In revising "It requires an effort aimed at becoming more myself . . ." I wasn't betraying my own authenticity in the slightest. I was finding a more graceful way of expressing my authentic self. It was less spontaneous only in the mechanical sense that it was a second attempt rather than a first. (There have been writers, notably Jack Kerouac, for whom spontaneity was so important that they felt it was wrong to revise. The usual result is passages of brilliance separated by longer passages of dullness.)

The fact is, we *do* work on our personalities. I'm a nice guy, but my imperfections trouble me, and I try to overcome them. As I have gone from being a withdrawn, alienated teenager to an uncouth, ambitious young man to a sociable, self-confident professional who is nothing short of Buddhalike in his serenity and universal compassion, I have changed the style of my personality. If I had said, "No, this is me and I'm not going to be any other way," I would be a lot unhappier than I am. Indeed my writing style has probably changed less than my personality has.

In both cases, natural equipment plus self-correction equal style. Style in writing is a writer's habitual way of using words: the verbal expression of personality.

I can't tell you what kind of writing style to develop, but I can suggest a principle or two that I consider to be generally valuable, just as I can't tell you what kind of personality to have, but I can say that it's better to be strong, calm, generous, and decent than weak, panicky, selfish, and rude. There are virtues and vices in life, and I believe there are also virtues and vices in writing.

WRITING VIRTUES

Clarity is a virtue. Some writers are more difficult than others, but I believe that no writer should try to be more difficult than he or she has to be. James and Proust are difficult because they deal with extremely subtle, rarefied abstractions concerning human personality and social relationships: they are as difficult as they have to be, and neither more nor less so. There are things that go on in human life that cannot be accommodated within the compact, externalized he-said-she-said of conventional realistic fiction; Proust found a way to go beyond that and show everything he knew about human life. He wasn't doing it to be difficult; he was doing it because he had so much to show. In his page-long, looping sentences, in which every clause seems to backtrack or comment on some other clause, you can be sure that every clause adds an observation, every word has a function that doesn't duplicate some other word's.

Most writers, if they tried to write as lengthily as Proust, would be overreaching. Not only would they not have enough to say to fulfill the principle of function, but writing so lengthily would not come naturally to them. They would sound as if they were trying to imitate someone else rather than being themselves.

Truth to oneself is another stylistic virtue. I am a turn-of-the-millennium American, and I have to write like one, even if I would rather write like an Elizabethan or a nineteenth-century Russian or an ancient Greek. If I parody one of those historical styles, it's irremediably a parody by a turn-of-the-millennium American and gives more clues to my own identity than to my model's. If you asked a hundred different writers, from a hundred different cultures and eras, to parody Shakespeare, you'd get a hundred different styles.

WRITING VICES

So in a sense it's impossible *not* to be yourself, but the problem is, a lot of writers try their hardest. The pervasive vice of American writers today is the desire to sound "literary." There are many American writers who have mannerisms, several who have trademarks, but few who have styles. In volume after volume of published, critically praised contemporary fiction, writers consistently use more words, and more difficult words, than they need to in order to describe what they are describing. They use more complex technical devices than telling their stories demands, in order to prove their credentials as members of the educated elite.

There are perfectly ordinary middle-of-the-road bestsellers today—the kinds of bestsellers written by people with graduate degrees—

complete with rare diseases, missing children, fatal accidents, and gratu-
itous gore—that use alternating narrative points of view, complex time
sequences, and literary allusions, not as original devices but as obligatory
signs of the "literary" genre.

The problem is social climbing: middle-class Americans trying to
sound as if they are sitting on the Left Bank discussing Texts with Roland
and Jacques, or in a Bloomsbury salon overturning inhibitions with
Virginia and Lytton. The product is writing that smells like chalk dust,
novels that are researched like dissertations—complete with acknowledgments at the beginning—and meant to be filed, not read.

During recent decades there has been a counterreaction in the form of
fiction that self-consciously tried to be real. In story after story, writers
offered tight-lipped snapshots of life among truckers, hairdressers,
shoplifters, and the like, inevitably showing how contaminated by the
mass media the characters were. The characters, however, were probably
less contaminated than their authors. Such stories almost always conde-
scended to their characters rather than treating them with respect and
giving them basic human dignity. The giveaway was in the laugh lines or,
rather, snicker lines that amused audiences at fiction readings. The
deadpan ironic tone showed that the authors were viewing their characters from above rather than from within. Another giveaway was that the
stories appeared in literary quarterlies that were almost never read by the
kind of people the stories were about. The genre was realism, but the
attitude was phony. The subject was nature, human nature, but the credo
was artifice. Why? Because that was what they taught in school.

Henry James was not trying to show how well-educated and sophisticated he was. He didn't have to try, because he was. He did not
deliberately make his prose more complex than it had to be; his most
complex, late style is his natural speaking style—he dictated his last novels
to a stenographer. Earlier in his career, when he wrote by hand, he
worked harder on compressing his prose.

Finding out what works for you always involves a certain amount of
experimenting with what doesn't work. In learning to write, you may
have to overreach, write lame imitations of previous writers, use complicated but stale technical devices, just to strengthen your muscles and find
out what you're capable of doing and whether there's anything you can
do that hasn't been done before. Perfect clarity and truthfulness to oneself
is an ultimate goal, the path to which may lie through years of unsuccessful effort. That kind of effort isn't wasted.

Feedback from editors, teachers, colleagues, friends, spouses, can
shorten the journey. Remember, though, that the people who give you
advice are neither all-knowing nor impartial. They have prejudices,

agendas, personal tastes, and axes to grind. What's more, they probably don't know you as well as you know yourself. They have never seen your unexpressed potential. They have only seen what you have done in the past, not what you might do in the future. Their own personal potential has probably not been fulfilled, for the simple reason that most people's isn't, and thus they may be (a) competitive with you and (b) obtuse. Advice—especially that of editors and teachers—usually amounts to a wish that you would conform and play it safe, not a wish that you would liberate yourself and pioneer.

THE VIRTUE OF SOUNDING GOOD

So far, what I've said in this chapter could be summarized in one sentence: "Be as simple as possible given your purposes." Of course, I've used a lot of sentences to say it. But reducing my message to one sentence would have maximized conciseness at too great a cost in clarity and comprehensiveness. Much of writing consists of balancing virtues; a word that has a function is not a wasted word.

A word used beautifully is not a wasted word, either. Our next and final virtue is the virtue of sounding good. Reading or writing good prose makes me happy; reading or writing bad prose makes me cringe. I used the word "cringe" instead of "miserable" or "sad" or "unhappy" in that sentence because I thought it sounded best. The four-syllable word "miserable," coming at the end of a string of very simple, short words, might have made for an unexpected rhythmic variation and they added a slight sense of intrigue to the statement, but I felt it was too vague. The word "sad" would have sounded sing-songy and made the whole sentence sound simplistic. "Cringe" is a stronger syllable and the image is also more specific. The word "unhappy" was a very distant fourth choice: it would have echoed the word "happy" in a flat-footed way, and it's not a vivid word. Having thought of "cringe," I then had to consider "grimace" and "wince" as well.

This kind of choice will occur in every sentence you ever write. Writing well is a matter of being aware of that fact.

Making prose sound good, and read interestingly, has something to do with the traditional poetic devices of simile and metaphor, alliteration and assonance, but none of these is central to what constitutes good prose. Verbal devices can sometimes give zip to a sentence, but they can just as often make it sound like a failed attempt at being poetic. Particularly eyebrow-raising is prose that rhymes—you know, the kind of prose that sounds like chimes. Even when Nabokov does it, it often makes one want to retch.

THE RHYTHM OF PROSE

Aside from accuracy in word choice, rhythm is the most important element of good prose. The rhythm of good prose is not the strict meter of traditional poetry; when prose does fall into a strict rhythm for more than a clause or two, it tends to sound unintentionally ridiculous, just as rhyming prose does. The rhythm of prose is a flowing cadence similar to, but not always the same as, human speech. Variation is an important part of it: the alternation of long and short sentences, of hard vowels and consonants with soft ones, of simple words and polysyllabic ones. Because it is supple and fluid, good prose can accommodate a greater range of thoughts and feelings than poetry, although poetry is a more intense, exalted, masterly art form.

Prose should *move:* it should create an illusion of forward momentum that carries the reader from point to point. The way to make prose move is to care. Tend carefully to every sentence in every paragraph, every word in every sentence, and every syllable in every word. As in my example above, there are many times when you can choose among synonyms, and the reason to choose one over the other is often a matter of sentence rhythm. Look at how each sentence flows. Where are the pauses for breath, if it is being read aloud, or the eye-pauses, if it is being read silently? Where are the places where a reader would stop to think about the meaning? These are the equivalents of line-breaks in a poem, though they don't necessarily occur at the same places where line-breaks would occur. If, in reading your own work, you find yourself pausing in awkward places or continuing helplessly when your mind wants a pause, it's probably a problem in sentence rhythm.

In the sentence, "Reading or writing good prose makes me happy; reading or writing bad prose makes me cringe," there's a pause at the semicolon and another at the end of the sentence. The punctuation marks serve two functions: as grammatical signs and as controllers of rhythm. This becomes important when punctuation is discretionary, as in placing commas or using a colon versus a dash. The less punctuation, the faster the pace of the sentence.

The sample sentence also contains parallelism—the repetition of "(Gerund phrase) makes me (something)." There's repetition within the repetition, in the phrase "reading or writing (good/bad) prose makes me. . . ." Yet the repetition is not monotonous, as using the word "sad" might have been.

The sound of a sentence should assist its meaning. Sound affects meaning by influencing mood. A short declarative sentence may make a different impression from a long, winding sentence whose overt message is the same. A sentence that builds from a quiet introductory phrase to a surprising climax has a different impact from a sentence that brags its bold message at the beginning and then curves into a subordinate clause. Whether a paragraph is long or short affects readers' emotions. Whether the sentences in a paragraph ascend from least to most important point or descend from most to least important can create suspense, on one hand, or a sense of denouement, on the other.

DEVELOPING YOUR OWN STYLE

If you've absorbed everything in this chapter so far, you've learned some things about what I call "virtuous style," but you haven't learned anything about how to develop your *own* style. You must teach yourself that. You must write, and what you write will be bad—it might be bad for a distressingly long time—before you become capable of writing anything good. You must also read. You must suffer the pain of becoming influenced by better writers, comparing your imitations with their originals and being disheartened, and throwing off their influence—and doing this again and again.

Tone

Once you have found *a* style, make sure it is the right style for your material. If you are writing a farce about life in a university humanities department—an unenviable task—it's not likely that the appropriate style will be hard-boiled and monosyllabic and never reveal the characters' thoughts. That would be alien to the characters' way of life and frame of mind. The tone is likely to be wrong.

Inappropriate tone is a global stylistic flaw that can be surprisingly hard to spot: you can write an entire draft of a book in elegant, accurate prose without realizing that the tone is inappropriately tongue-in-cheek, off-puttingly snide, or misguidedly impersonal (to pick three common flaws). The way to solve this problem is to read long sections of your work, preferably out loud, after you have drafted them. Readers' opinions can also be useful here. Some flexibility of tone is often desirable to prevent monotony—for instance, you might want to throw in a line of ironic relief in an otherwise serious passage—but there is usually one dominant tone in any effective piece. You should be aware of what the tone of your writing is—both the momentary fluctuations and the overall coloration.

Control of tone is a matter of word choice. Be aware of the connotations of words and the impact of rhythms. Saying something in short words and sentences usually produces a different tone from saying the same thing in long ones, but precisely *what* the difference is varies: using long words can make you sound impressively intelligent, folksily witty, or unintentionally funny.

The safest generalization about tone is: *Understatement is inherently more sophisticated than overstatement.* Try to achieve each effect with a minimum of means. Readers pride themselves on being able to pick up signals quickly and hold it against writers who oversell a point. If you are trying to achieve some special tone—telling yourself, for example, "I want to be really suspenseful in this scene where he's walking down the dark street"—reread the passage and see if you can cut some of the loaded words and phrases without losing the effect. Readers have read many previous stories in which characters walk down dark, suspenseful streets, and they're ready to seize the moment, activate their suspense reflexes, without much prompting. Let the tone arise from the action rather than merely the words: if you want the reader to feel suspense, make sure there's really something suspenseful in the situation rather than just a writer trying to give the reader a verbal hot-foot.

The opposite problem—needing more loaded words and phrases— occurs among writers whose tone is chronically flat and needs to be souped up. A uniformly flat tone is likely to sound grim, ironic, or both, but not much else.

Here is a single mundane action described in three different tones:

1. Impersonal
Louie waited at the empty street corner while the light was red. When the light changed, he crossed.

2. Melodramatic
The street corner was empty, but Louie couldn't cross. He couldn't. He felt frozen in place, appallingly, and he didn't know why.

3. Satirical
Citizen Louie waits at the empty street corner, back rigid, eyes fixed on the red light. No jaywalker he! Sure enough, his patience is rewarded: the light turns green, and, looking both ways first, Louie crosses.

Example 1 is simply a report of facts; the only subjectivity involved is in the choice of details, a hidden variable. Example 2 takes us into Louie's consciousness, which is one way of influencing tone. The first sentence uses the word "but" to establish a melodramatic contrast between a previous state and a present, distressing state. "Frozen in place" and "didn't know why" are loaded phrases. The rhythm of short sentences beginning with "He" lends a melodramatic tone, as does the appalling adverb. In Example 3, the present tense, though you'd think it would add immediacy, is actually a distancing device inviting us to look down on the character. The satirical tone results from the fact that someone, a personal narrator not an impersonal one, is speaking ironically about Louie, making fun of him.

Voice

This brings me to that favorite buzzword of publicist and publishers—*voice*. Example 3 has a strong, though snotty, narrative voice. The word *voice* is sloppily used sometimes as a synonym for *style* and sometimes as synecdoche for *writer*. "Here is a powerful new voice of our generation," an ad will say. Writers sometimes use the word in relation to themselves: "I am searching for my true voice," or even, "I have found my true voice," although I assure you that anyone who has really found her true voice is not likely to announce the discovery through buzzwords and clichés.

I'm always suspicious of the claim that a writer has found his or her "true voice." It's just a high-falutin' way of saying that the writer has found an effective way to write within a given story or novel. The next time the writer tries to use that "true voice" in a follow-up work, the voice might be hoarse from the exertion of repeating what has worked in the past. If there's anything we know about voices, it's that they change. To find one's "true voice" can mean you've arrived, but to become too attached to it might mean you're stalled at the entrance.

The word *voice* diminishes writers by making it seem that their work is primarily a vocal performance, as if they were opera singers or ventriloquists, putting pretty sounds into the mouths of characters who are puppets to be manipulated. It's yet another manifestation of the undue dominance of the performing arts over the creative arts in our day.

Writers are not performers. We do not write with our voices; we write with our minds. We can't perform as thrillingly as actors or musicians, but there are things we can do, in private and silence, that no one else can.

Another usage of the word *voice* connotes advocacy or message. It often refers to a writer's background or ideology: one writer is the voice of western Iowa, another is the voice of lower Manhattan's Alphabet City, and so on. "At last the long-suppressed voices of Avenues A, B, C, and D are being heard!" *Mouthpiece* or *advocate* sounds suspect, *message* sounds drippy, but *voice* sounds swank.

Used properly, the word *voice* refers to a specific aspect of style, the aspect that makes the words on the page sound like those of a human being talking, with a personality. Voice is at the juncture of style, characterization, and tone. If you try hard enough you can find a voice in almost any piece of writing, no matter how impersonal—if only to say that it's written in an impersonal voice. At that point, voice blends indistinguishably into style. Many works of literature, however, have immediately recognizable, individual-istic voices that make the reader feel that the writer is communicating directly with him or her, one-to-one. I'm trying to write as if I were talking to you. I could write another way, with a less distinctive voice but still in my own style.

The most meaningful use of the term *voice* refers to characters rather than to authors. As I said in Chapter 5, every character should have his or her own individual speech pattern. When a character is a first-person narrator, we find the character's tone of voice in the narrative as well as the dialogue. When several first-person narrators alternate in one book, as in *The Sound and The Fury,* and *As I Lay Dying,* we can see how the writer has developed a different voice for each one.

Voice can also be attributed to third-person narrators, giving them a kind of shadow existence that falls short of characterization. This helps literary critics by enabling them to infer the presence of attitudes, emotions, and values in invisible narrators. In the fourth section of *The Sound and The Fury,* we hear the voice of an omniscient third-person narrator, and in the Appendix, which was written many years after the body of the novel, we hear a different omniscient voice.

Faulkner's voice is not the voice of Benjy, Quentin, or Jason, but all three of those voices came out of him and contribute to what we call his style. Perhaps the fourth section of the novel represents Faulkner's voice as a man in his early thirties, while the Appendix contains the voice of Faulkner in his late forties, but we can't assume that either of these is his "true" voice, since we know he was supremely capable of altering his voice to suit an occasion. Nor can we claim that any single voice in these works represents Faulkner's true personal style. A writer's style might be represented as a Venn diagram in which each intersecting circle is one of the narrative voices he or she has used. The midpoint at which all the circles intersect represents the writer's most habitual personal stylistic traits—a voice print that can't be altered no matter how a writer tries to disguise his or her sound. The sum total of all the areas in all the circles, intersecting or not, is the writer's style.

Do It

---

1. What is your style like? Think about it. Then write a short essay in which you discuss your style: its traits, what you like about them, what you might wish to change, how you hope it matures.

2. Do a mathematical analysis of your style. Pick something you have recently written, and include the following variables: average sentence length, average word length (in syllables or letters), longest and shortest sentence lengths, number of adjectives or adverbs per sentence. If you have a computer, you may be able to determine the reading level of your style as well. (Some word-processing software can analyze some of these variables by running a grammar check.) Then write one or more short pieces in which you deliberately try to change your style. Do similar analyses of them. Compare and contrast the analyses of the pieces. Use this knowledge in whatever way you wish, to either alter or reinforce your present style. In a group, analyze one another's writing. You can also analyze the styles of published writers mathematically.

3. Choose a work of fiction you have recently written and are not completely satisfied with. Rewrite it in the simplest style you can achieve. If you feel the work is already too simple, rewrite it in a more complex style instead. How do you feel about the result? What does this tell you about the best style for you?

4. Collaborate on a short story with one other writer. Discuss how the style of the collaboration resembles and differs from your individual styles.

5. Write a page of prose imitating the style of your favorite writer. If you're ambitious, do this for several writers. You might wish to write a story in which you parody several writers in turn.

6. Rewrite a story by one author in the style of another—for example, Eudora Welty's "Why I Live at the P.O." in the style of Poe.

7. Rewrite any classic short story, or a passage from it, in your own style.

Writer's Bookshelf

A totally subjective list of works written in English in the twentieth century whose words have given the list-maker pleasure would include:

The Stories of Ray Bradbury (1980)

"*Earth people left to the strangeness of Mars, the cinnamon dusts and wine airs, to be baked like gingerbread shapes in Martian summers, put into harvested storage by Martian winters.*"

Pilgrim at Tinker Creek by Annie Dillard (1974)

"*The world has locusts, and the world has grasshoppers. I was up to my knees in the world.*"

The Gastronomical Me by M. F. K. Fisher (1943)

"*I tell about myself, and how I ate bread on a lasting hillside, or drank red wine in a room now blown to bits, and it happens without my willing it that I am telling too about the people with me then, and their other deeper needs for love and happiness.*"

Tender Is the Night by F. Scott Fitzgerald (1934)

"*On the pleasant shore of the French Riviera, about half way between Marseilles and the Italian border, stands a large, proud, rose-colored hotel.*"

A Walker in the City by Alfred Kazin (1951)

"*When we went home, taking the road past the cemetery, with the lights of Jamaica Avenue spread out before us, it was hard to think of them as something apart, they were searching out so many new things in me.*"

Sea and Sardinia by D. H. Lawrence (1921)

"*There are heaps of pale yellow lemons under the trees. They look like pale, primrose-smouldering fires.*"

Lectures in America by Gertrude Stein (1935)

"*No matter how often what happened had happened any time any one told anything there was no repetition.*"

Portrait of the Artist as a Young Dog by Dylan Thomas (1955)

> *"In the middle of the night I woke from a dream full of whips and lariats as long as serpents, and runaway coaches on mountain passes, and wide, windy gallops over cactus fields, and I heard the old man in the next room crying, 'Gee-up!' and 'Whoa!' and trotting his tongue on the roof of his mouth."*

Cane by Jean Toomer (1923)

> *"Dear Jesus, do not chain me to myself and set these hills and valleys, heaving with folk-songs, so close to me that I cannot reach them."*

Elvissey by Jack Womack (1993)

> *"Regooding proposed to make all that was long-wrong rainright once more."*

Orlando by Virginia Woolf (1928)

> *"He—for there could be no doubt of his sex, though the fashion of the time did something to disguise it—was in the act of slicing at the head of a Moor which swung from the rafters."*

Chapter 11

Theme

Louie and Stella: Archetypes of the Insignificant

a dissertation submitted for the degree of Doctor of Philosophy
by R. Lawrence Cohen, B.A.

Department of Seemiotics and Applied Polysyllabics
Institute for Serioso Studies
School of Humanities Lite®
University of the Upper Central Midwest at Rubesville, Exit 242A
Campus, About a Mile to the Left and Just Across
from the Fruit Stand
December 1, 1994

. . . And then I woke up. It was just a horrible nightmare; I wasn't really a critic after all, I was a writer.

Always remember that you are not writing a dissertation—and give thanks.

WHAT STORIES MEAN

It is not the job of fiction writers to provide the meaning of their own works of art. Critics will find the meanings, whether they're the meanings you intended or not. If you create, there is nothing you need to explain. Your job is to put the gold in the ground, not to count it.

If you write a good story, it will mean something. The reverse is not automatically true. If you write a meaningful story, it may or may not be a good story—by which I mean it may or may not be alive.

Excessive concentration on making a story mean what you want it to mean can actually limit its meaning and its life. The result will be a robot story, not a living story, a rigid thing, not a flexible one. Let's say that Melville, while writing *Moby Dick,* wanted it to mean: "It's destructive to renounce one's life in order to pursue an obsessive goal." In every scene, Melville made sure to insert some character who exemplified that idea: Ahab pursuing the white whale, Ishmael pursuing peace of mind, Queequeg pursuing personal honor, the ship *Rachel* pursuing its lost crew; each one, like a bowling pin, is duly knocked down in succession. Well, the message is a valid one, but if Melville had written *Moby Dick* that way, doggedly cramming a single message into every scene, making sure that everything meshed, with no contradictions, it would have been a pretty lame book. The way Melville actually wrote it was quite different. He set up a situation and a set of characters, one of whom, Ahab, is destructively pursuing an obsessive goal—and then he put in a lot of other stuff, too. Ahab is not just destructive and unwise, he's also brave and strangely admirable. He is a character, a person, not just an exemplar of an idea. The message about obsessive goals is in there, but so are many other ideas. Some of those ideas may have been ones Melville was aware of; others, he was surely unconscious of. I doubt if Melville could have stated, in a hundred words or less, the exact meaning of the white whale. If he could have, he wouldn't have had to write a whole book on the subject. But he knew it meant something—he knew it meant many things—and he had a general idea of the intellectual region in which those meanings could be found: the region of the symbolism of good and evil. He wrote down the problem; he didn't have to add up the sum.

CREATING MEANING

The process of putting meaning into a story is similar to the process of putting meaning into a dream—something you do every night without planning it. It just happens. It's beyond your control. Trying to control it can be fun—you may tell yourself, before you go to bed, "Tonight I want to dream about my true love"—but it's never completely successful, and the most interesting parts are often the ones you couldn't have anticipated. Afterward, you may want to interpret it. Your interpretation may be more or less sound, but it doesn't affect the creative dreaming process.

The most interesting meanings, in my experience, are the ones I become aware of *after* I have put them in a story. I start out writing a scene in which Louie and Stella argue and make up, argue and make up by the lakeside; then I realize that their cycle of arguments and reconciliations is related to the natural cycles of daytime and nighttime, and of animal life and death, which I have also described in the scene. Ta-da! I have created a theme, but I didn't know it until the second draft. It arose spontaneously out of my unconscious, and for that very reason it contains a sense of life. It's organic, not manufactured. Of course, having recognized the theme's presence when I read my draft, I can fiddle with it in the rewriting. I can underline it by thinking of some other natural cycle to add in my descriptive passages. Or I can understate it by cutting one or two descriptions of natural cycles. Or I can vary the theme by looking for places in the story where I can mention other kinds of cyclic events, not necessarily connected to nature—perhaps economic cycles affecting Louie's and Stella's jobs. Perhaps I can add a contrast by describing some events that are not cyclic, such as Louie's and Stella's aging process.

No matter how I tinker with the thematic contents, however, I am doing it for the purpose of making the story a better story. I'm not doing it for the purpose of making the ultimate comment on the cyclic quality of human life.

Ideas have a role to play in fiction, but they are subordinate to the living, human quality of the characters and action. Ideas are part of the entertainment. If the ideas hamper the story, making the characters less believable and the action less interesting, then it's time to change the ideas. For instance, let's say you want to write a story showing that peace is desirable, and you decide to do it by describing a world at peace. The people in your story are smugly contented, and they go around talking at length about how wonderful peace is. Their ideas are very true, but their story is boring. You have created vehicles for a commendable message, not living human beings.

Let's say you decide to solve the problem by approaching your idea from another angle: instead of showing how wonderful peace is, you'll show how terrible war is. You write a powerful antiwar novel. Your message is very true. It is also a cliché. Your characters are all either good or vile, victims or victimizers, and readers can see right through them.

Better if you start out simply by trying to show what you know about war and peace. Create some people who undergo experiences in war and peace that other writers haven't described before. Loosen the reins: don't try to steer your story into delivering a predetermined message. Your desired meaning will still be in the story; it's part of your outlook on life, and you can't help conveying that. After all, it's true that war is bad and peace is good, so if you write a story on the subject and the story has the ring of truth, it will certainly contain that idea, more subtly than if you had planned it.

Theme is not a container into which you pour a story, trying to make the contents fit. Theme is one of the ingredients you are mixing in. It's a seasoning in the soup. The goal is to make the soup taste good, and you adjust the seasonings accordingly. You don't start out by saying, "I want to cook a soup in which there are two teaspoons of salt." You say, "I want to make a great soup," and in the cooking process you taste how much salt it needs.

Robert Lowell, one of the most intellectually powerful of American poets, used to alter his ideas on the spur of the moment in order to suit the metrical requirements of his verse, according to his biographer, Ian Hamilton. If Lowell was writing a line and found he needed an extra syllable, he might throw in a "not," causing the line to scan, but completely reversing his statement. A lesser poet would have clung to the statement, writing an earnest, clunky-sounding line. Lowell had his priorities straight. Writers should come to their work unprejudiced, willing to receive ideas from it rather than giving preconceived ideas to it.

"Okay, I get the point," you say, "but I have beliefs that are important to me and I want to express them. I believe that men and women should view one another as individual human beings, not as stereotypes. How can I make sure that my story says this while also being 'alive,' as you call it—having three-dimensional characters and interesting events?"

My answer is: if your story really is alive, it will inevitably support your idea, because it will show its characters to be individual human beings rather than stereotypical males and females. In the planning and drafting stages, you may want to be aware of your desire to express the theme of individuality, but there's no need for you to force it into the story. Trust your unconscious to put it in.

"Yeah, but what if my idea is that males and females behave incorrigibly according to type, *not* as individuals?"

In that case, if you write a living story, it will disprove your idea whether you want it to or not—and it will be a more interesting story because of that. It may even achieve the complexity of demonstrating both contradictory ideas at once.

Allow the process of writing to enlarge your ideas. Later, if you read the completed first draft and find you would like a certain idea to be more prominent, you can adjust accordingly.

"How do I 'adjust accordingly?' That's what I'm trying to get you to answer."

Okay, here's the answer. The best way to express any idea in fiction is to embody it in the life of a character or characters. If you want to say that verbal abuse can be as harmful to a child as physical abuse, show a parent verbally abusing a child; then show the personality damage in the way the child interacts, or is afraid to interact, with others. Showing consequences, and letting readers draw conclusions from them, is perhaps the oldest form of thematic development; it is the basis of most fables. (Aesop did not provide explicit morals to his stories; they were tacked on by later editors.)

Using contrasting characters can be very effective. In the child-abuse story, you might want to write about a verbally abused child and his physically abused friend, showing that they both have personality damage, but of different types. You might want to bring in a third friend who is not abused by her parents.

You may or may not want to have your characters talk about, and think about, the idea openly. If they do, they may sound preachy, especially when the subject is one such as child abuse where there is a clear right and wrong. If your subject is more ambiguous, you may want to have the characters discuss various sides of the issue in order to keep from having them be mouthpieces for your ideology. Exemplify ideas through action rather than solely putting them in the mouths of characters. Visualize who your characters are and how they feel, and if they begin to express ideas you hadn't planned on, take it as a good sign. Follow your characters' lead. They express your own unconscious wisdom. You are ultimately in control—you can reverse or delete any ideas you think are harmful to the story's unity—but the more secure your control, the more slack you can afford to give.

The harder a writer tries to express a single unambiguous idea, the more likely it is that he or she will express clichés and stereotypes.

Do It

1. What are your themes? What ideas do you care about? How can you include your ideas in your stories? Try to think about these questions clearly enough so that you could answer them in a short essay or speech.

2. Reread a previous story of yours, approaching it from the standpoint of a reader. What themes do you find in it? Are there any ideas in it that surprise you on rereading? Are there any ideas you hoped to express but didn't express effectively? If you were writing the story today, what would you do differently?

3. Try to write a story that does not contain any ideas. Then, exchange the story with a partner who has done the same. Read one

another's stories and write brief analytical essays stating what themes you find in them.

4. Have a group of writers or students read a story by one of its members and discuss its themes. Whose analyses sound most insightful, the author's or the readers'? What differences are there between the way a writer thinks about a story and the way a reader thinks about the same story?

Writer's Bookshelf

The Critic as Artist: Essays on Books 1920–1970 by Gilbert A. Harrison, ed., with "preliminary ruminations" by H. L. Mencken (1972),
> *is a collection of critical essays on American writers by their colleagues: F. Scott Fitzgerald on Ring Lardner, James Thurber on Fitzgerald, John Updike on Vladimir Nabokov, and so on.*

The Language of the Night: Essays on Fantasy and Science Fiction by Ursula K. Le Guin (1979)
> *collects essays that find serious meaning in popular fiction, by the grande dame of this genre.*

Playing in the Dark: Whiteness and the Literary Imagination by Toni Morrison (1992)
> *is a slim, trenchant, personal volume in which the Nobel Prize-winning African-American novelist examines how white American writers (Twain, Cather, Poe, Melville, and others) have treated darkness and light in symbolic terms.*

Lectures on Literature by Vladimir Nabokov (1980)
> *offers a great modern stylist's idiosyncratic, droll appraisals of a roomful of heavyweights: Austen, Dickens, Flaubert, Stevenson, Proust, Kafka, and Joyce.*

Chapter 12

Fancy Stuff

So far, I've tried to cover the basics of craftsmanship that cut across all forms of storytelling. Characterization, plot, and theme are tools that you need to know how to use regardless of what kind of fiction you write and whether or not you emphasize each one equally in each work.

If you handle these tools skillfully and try to write a good story without any special attention to form, you will end up with a traditional linear narrative, the most common and most adaptable of story types. The traditional linear narrative follows one character or a small group of connected characters, starting at the beginning of the action and proceeding in a straight line to its end. There may be occasional flashbacks along the way to fill the reader in on essential background information, but they are not frequent enough to counteract the sense that the story is a stream flowing continuously forward.

This linear form is the best way to tell a story unless you have some compelling reason for using an alternative form. There is no need to tell yourself, "Gee, this story I've written is just a traditional linear story; what can I do about that?" No need to do anything about it. If you inject nonlinear devices into a work that doesn't call for them, the result might be more flashy, but it's unlikely to be a stronger work of art. Nor is it likely to be more "original" or "experimental," since the nonlinear elements most writers put into their stories nowadays—such as fractured time sequence and shifting point of view—were developed almost a century ago by great innovators such as James Joyce and have been recycled countless times by imitators. At this point, they are just as stale as the traditional linear form, and the novelty having worn off, they often make irritating rather than impressive reading. They divert the reader from the action and characters without providing enough compensation.

It's worth looking at those nonlinear devices, though, and it can be fun to practice them, for two reasons. First, they can still be effective at times: leftovers can be tasty when reheated. Second, studying the innovations of the past might inspire some writer, somewhere, to create the innovations of the future. Perhaps you shouldn't use ostentatious formal devices unless you have a compelling reason, but what's a compelling reason in fiction? If you have an idea and it's attractive and new, that's compelling enough. There are few things more annoying than a stale experiment and few things more exciting than a fresh one.

EXPERIMENTING WITH NONLINEARITY

The fundamental change that occurred in fiction in the early twentieth century was the fracturing of linearity. Experimental narrative did two major things:

- It broke up the chronological sequence.
- It shifted from one character's viewpoint to another's.

These alternative strategies are so broad and basic that they've become part of the updated traditional toolbox.

There are many ways to break up the chronology of a story. You can intersperse a linear plot with a lot of flashbacks, including as many layers of flashback-within-flashback as you like. Or you can establish a double time-track, cutting from present to past and back again; this is done very effectively in John Fowles' *The French Lieutenant's Woman* and even more effectively in the movie based on that book. In works of this kind, the setting in the present often provides the narrator with a base of operations from which to look back and comment upon the past; Gunter Grass does this in *The Tin Drum,* where his narrator, Oskar, writes the story of his life and also tells us about the hospital in which he is writing it. Grass also uses the interesting gimmick of switching from first-person to third-person in the midst of a sentence, although the viewpoint remains that of the same character, Oskar. A complete jumbling of time sequence is accomplished in Joseph Heller's *Catch-22,* where the main clue to chronological sequence is the number of missions the squadron has flown in a given scene. Key plot events such as Snowden's death or Milo's bombing of his own base are also used as clues, for sometimes they are mentioned as having occurred already, sometimes mentioned as fated to occur in the future, and sometimes they take center stage, described in present time (but in the past tense).

The most skillful time-shifter among twentieth-century writers, in my opinion, is someone few people would guess: Georges Simenon, author of hundreds of Maigret mysteries and hundreds of psychological novels. The typical Simenon novel is about an investigation of a crime or bizarre event that upsets the daily routine and needs to be explained, put in perspective so that orderly life can be resumed; the event prompts a character's investigation of his or her own past or the past of someone he or she knows. In the course of investigating the event, interviewing witnesses, researching the locale, and so forth, Simenon's protagonist becomes involved in an intricate web of past events that are narrated in the most fluid, subtly shifting way imaginable. Especially in his psychological novels as opposed to his Maigrets, Simenon was as skilled a literary time-traveler as Proust, but while Proust was the most complicated of stylists, Simenon was the simplest, using a vocabulary of only two thousand words. The amazing thing about Simenon was that he only took ten days to write a novel—a chapter a day plus one day for polishing, mostly cutting. Because of his work habits, I don't think Simenon ever wrote a completely successful, major work of art; but a good handful of his novels come close—especially *The Cat* and *The Little Saint*—and none of the five-hundred is without interest.

A special sort of time-shifting is time-reversal: telling a story backward so that what would usually be the ending is the beginning, and vice versa. This was done by Martin Amis in *Time's Arrow,* and before that by Charles Baxter in *First Light,* and before that by Harold Pinter in *Betrayal,* and before that by Brian Aldiss in *Cryptozoic,* and before that by J. G. Ballard in "Time of Passage." The most obvious pattern is to follow a single character from death to birth. There's nothing inherently innovative about time-reversal anymore, but it can sometimes make a provocative point. *Cryptozoic* is an especially apt use of the device, because it doesn't follow the most obvious pattern, and because time is the book's subject rather than merely its method.

A step beyond shifted chronology is the reshuffleable novel: chapters that are to be read in any order the reader chooses or a variety of orders the author suggests. Julio Cortazar, in *Hopscotch* and *62: A Model Kit,* cornered the mass market in shuffleable fiction. The ultimate pick-up-stix novel is Marc Saporta's 1962 work, *Composition No. 1,* which consists of a boxed set of 150 pages, each containing a single vignette about the novel's main characters. The pages are intended to be reshuffled randomly or in any order the reader wishes to assign. This form of experimentation has in turn led to such glories of literature as the choose-your-own-adventure and the interactive novel.

EXPERIMENTING WITH POINT OF VIEW

If stories can shift around in time, they can also shift around in space by adopting shifting first-person points of view (see Chapter 9). This is not a new device—the biblical *Song of Songs* uses it—but fiction writers avoided it until Faulkner and others opened up its possibilities. There's no doubt that the device is overused in contemporary fiction. Many writers seem to switch first-person points of view simply because they can't find enough to say about one main character, or because they can't handle an omniscient third-person viewpoint, or perhaps because they think it's trendy. There's a tendency to confuse complexity with art. I'm of the other school—I confuse simplicity with art. I think a writer ought to use the minimum number of technical devices necessary to tell a story. That's the literary equivalent of Occam's Razor—the idea in science that the best theory to explain any given phenomenon is the one that contains the fewest propositions. There's no reason to believe that Occam's Razor is an absolute truth, either in literature or in science; it's just a decision-making strategy to hold on to in times of uncertainty.

EXPERIMENTING WITH FORM

Stories can shift not only from time frame to time frame and viewpoint to viewpoint but from form to form. Several of the most interesting works of twentieth-century fiction fall into the category we might loosely call "the novel-as-something-else." Vladimir Nabokov's *Pale Fire* is a novel in the form of a long poem by a fictitious poet, with an introduction, notes, and index by a fictitious critic. Another admirable novel-as-poem is D. M. Thomas' *The White Hotel,* which is also a novel-as-dream and a novel-as-psychoanalysis. Manuel Puig's *Heartbreak Tango* is a novel in the form of a radio soap opera. Steven Millhauser's *Edwin Mullhouse* is a novel in the form of a biography, in this case the biography of a literary child prodigy. Many novels and stories take the form of collages, the most notable of which is John Dos Passos' *U.S.A.* trilogy. A classic kind of novel-as-something-else is the epistolary novel, the novel in letters, which was most popular in the eighteenth century. (Samuel Richardson's *Clarissa* is the longest and greatest example.)

The novel-as-something-else often involves an element of parody. One section of *Ulysses,* for instance, takes the form of a parody catechism. John Barth's *The Sot-Weed Factor* is a twentieth-century-novel-as-eigh-teenth-century-novel, a literary parody. Many of Puig's works parody pop culture in order to comment on the meaning of love.

The most ambitious novel-as-something-else, perhaps, is Georges Perec's *Life: A User's Manual,* which is a novel-as-verbal-equivalent-of-a-painting-of-an-apartment-building. The apartment building in question has ten stories of ten apartments each, making a perfect square of one hundred, and the novel has one hundred chapters, each providing a detailed physical description of one of the apartments while at the same time advancing a clever plot that involves some of the building's tenants, one of whom is painting the picture of which the novel is a description. As if that weren't enough, the narrative moves from apartment to apartment, not in a straight line but in an L pattern, like a knight's move in chess, ending up in the painter's apartment; and it goes without saying that the entire book is a commentary on the nature of art. Perec, one of the truly brilliant and weird writers of recent times, was a founder of Oulipo, a society that revived ancient experimental forms; he tried a different experiment in each of his novels; in one of them, *La Disparition,* he never uses the letter e, and in its sequel, *Les Revenentes,* he never uses any vowel *except* e.

Formal experiments such as Perec's follow strict rules, and once the rule is established, the entire structure of the work is set; what remains is to fill in the details. If the rule is ingenious and the details are competently filled in and the work as a whole resonates with meaning (as *La Disparition* definitely does, because it is about the nature of disappearance, the nature of loss, the nature of language) and if—which is sometimes the hardest thing—the thing is *readable* (which *La Disparition* is, if you read French), then the result is a tour de force. The trouble with tours de force, though, is that, like mystery stories (*La Disparition* is a fine mystery story, by the way), they tend not to improve on rereading. Once you know the key, they feel predictable; their innovation is technical rather than psychological or linguistic.

These formal experiments often involve an element of self-reference, in which a fictional text reminds us that it is a fictional text. (*Metafiction* is, or was, the jargon term for it.) Luigi Pirandello's six characters assault the author who put them onstage; Groucho Marx or Bob Hope looks at the camera and comments to the audience about the on-screen hijinks. Self-referential devices can still be used wittily, even at this late date, but there's nothing intrinsically surprising in the sheer act of noticing that your work of fiction is a work of fiction. All fiction creates an illusion, and no story labeled "realism" corresponds exactly to the sensations labeled "reality." That being the case, it seems to me that the most skillful illusion is the one that makes its readers think, "This is real!"

EXPERIMENTING WITH LANGUAGE

I'm more awed by the few writers who have transformed language, expanding the range of things we can say and the vocabularies we can use rather than just the structures we can play with. James Joyce and Gertrude

Stein are the ultimate exemplars. In *Finnegans Wake,* Joyce invented a new language, a kind of universal idiolect, which we can translate into standard English if we have the patience and devotion. The principle is one of fermentation: just as grape juice is fermented into wine, producing a mysterious and potent substance, so Joyce, by combining pieces of English words, pieces of foreign words, puns, and cultural allusions, creates a multi-leveled, strange, and potent form of verbal intoxication. Stein's technique is very different and at least as original. She created cubist language, the equivalent of the cubist pictures being painted in her era. She takes a standard sentence and simultaneously extends it and breaks it down, using repetition and fragmentation so that her words and phrases become abstract, their sounds and rhythms acquiring a life apart from the real-world objects they represent.

Stein's cubist sentence is also a form of stream of consciousness: her repetitions and fragmentations follow the backtracking, the pauses, the musings that occur whenever anyone reads a standard sentence. For instance, if I read the sentence, "A cat cannot be a bird," the thoughts in my mind might be something like, "A cat cannot be a bird, cat cannot be a bird, because a cat eats a bird, can't be what it eats, it can't, it's a cat, can't be what it's not, it can't be." Take out the commas in order to speed the pace and create ambiguities, and you've got a Steinian sentence: "A cat cannot be a bird cat cannot be a bird because a cat eats a bird can't be what it eats it can't it's a cat can't be what it's not it can't be." In order to decode a Steinian sentence, look for places to insert plausible punctuation, then collapse the backtrackings into standard syntax.

Once an extended, stream-of-consciousness sentence is written out, and we read it, then a higher-order, even more complex sequence of backtrackings and pauses is created in our minds, and if we wrote *that* out . . . and so on, potentially into infinity. Which, I suppose, could be a rule for an experimental novel that germinates from one sentence.

Stream of consciousness is, of course, one of the major additions the twentieth century made to the writer's toolbox. It's impossible to duplicate the human stream of consciousness exactly in words, because the human stream of consciousness is not purely verbal and even the verbal parts of it move more swiftly than words on a page can indicate. In the last section of *Ulysses,* Joyce made the most successful attempt, but Molly Bloom's train of thought is more linear and more orderly than any real person's train of thought. Dorothy Richardson and Virginia Woolf are often mentioned as having practiced stream of consciousness; they use standard grammar rather than Joycean fermented English to follow their characters' thoughts. In *The Waves,* Woolf alternates among the consciousnesses of six interrelated characters, following their whole lives' spans to produce a profound, unified vision of human existence. Another very great novel saturated in the stream of consciousness is Malcolm Lowry's *Under the Volcano*.

Stream of consciousness is a method by which literary experimentation can deepen our understanding of human beings, rather than just tinkering with technique. It's harder to say something new about human beings than to think up a new way of structuring a story or to invent a fantasy world. It's easy to imagine what happens when a winged horse flies across the sky; it's much harder to imagine what happens when a man and a woman sit in a room and talk. Courageous geniuses modernized fiction's formal apparatus—but why? Presumably because traditional form turned out to be smaller than their vision of human life. They did not intend their innovations to become status symbols adorning bourgeois fiction that in other respects—in its melodramatic contrivances and editorially enforced happy endings, its deference to fads and failure to question assumptions—was no different from what they were rebelling against. Maybe it's time for their descendants to work on deepening our vision of human beings and their relationships—especially because human beings and their relationships *are* really changing so much, so suddenly, in the world outside of books.

EXPERIMENTING WITH CHARACTERIZATION

Innovations in characterization are scarce. D. H. Lawrence made some, perhaps intuitively, in *Women in Love* and *The Rainbow* and other works. His characters, though outlined sharply enough to be recognizable objects for Lawrence's tart satire, are not individualized in the traditional sense; they exist more on the levels of spiritual communion and biological longing than on the everyday psychosocial level in between.

An intriguing step toward multidimensional characterization was taken in the late 1980s by Lorrie Moore in *Anagrams* and Philip Roth in *The Counterlife*. In both novels, the main character's traits change from chapter to chapter, sometimes contradicting what has gone before. By comparing and contrasting the altered traits and keeping in mind the traits that remain constant, we can get a glimpse, at the end, of some enigmatic, overarching identity that has been fantasizing it all. Part of the fun is that the character's "true" personality is up to each reader to imagine. In the process, we realize that a human being is like a string of letters (characters) that can be reshuffled into many anagrams.

OTHER EXPERIMENTS

There are other successful literary experiments that do not fall as neatly into labelable categories. Peter Matthiessen's *Far Tortuga* is a favorite of mine, a visual and aural experiment in which, by playing with typography and making a collage of landscape, weather, and speech, the author (and the book's designer) transform a conventional sea story into a solemn encounter with the beautiful. Matthiessen's method was anticipated in a Lowry novella, "Through the Panama," but *Tortuga* is a far more polished work.

The most enduring one-of-a-kind experiment in English fiction was written in 1759. Laurence Sterne's *Tristram Shandy* is a comic novel of nonstop digression and self-reference: the narrator, Tristram, is not born until the end of the third volume, and he uses ample opportunities both before and after his birth to comment on the art of novel-writing, as well as throwing in some squiggles, an all-black page, and so forth.

All the experiments discussed in this chapter now seem as traditional as *Tristram Shandy,* if not more so. Each can be used again by other writers as long as they add some new element of form, language, insight, or, at minimum, subject matter. To repeat an experiment without adding something of one's own is merely to imitate, for in literature unlike in science, experiments don't have to be reconfirmed.

I have not written this chapter so that everyone can grind their material through the old modernist mill, but so that someone, sometime, somehow can go further.

I'd do it myself if I knew how.

Do It

1. Read at least two of the works mentioned by title in this chapter. Discuss them with friends or classmates.

2. Choose any literary form described in this chapter and write a short story using it. Repeat the exercise using as many different forms as you like. Or write a single work that incorporates several different forms in turn.

3. Think of a literary experiment that was not mentioned in this chapter. Write a work of fiction using it. If you can do so in a truly original way, let the world know.

4. Found a literary magazine to encourage experiments by new writers. Recruit contributors and editors to help you.

Writer's Bookshelf

Forty Stories by **Donald Barthelme (1987)**
> *assembles the published short fiction of the most innovative and readable member of the metafiction generation.*

A Barthes Reader by **Roland Barthes (edited by Susan Sontag, 1982)**
> *serves as a handy one-volume introduction to the French stylist and thinker whose literary criticism was his art.*

Complete Dramatic Works by **Samuel Beckett (1986)**
> *contains* Waiting for Godot *(1953),* Endgame *(1957),* All That Fall *(1957),* Krapp's Last Tape *(1958),* Happy Days *(1961),* Rockabye *(1981), and many short plays by the post-Joycean comic absurdist, written in French and translated into English by the author. Beckett's novels are dense but very readable: the first sentence of* Murphy *(1938, published 1957) essentializes one long season of the human soul.*

Petersburg by **Andrei Bely (translated by Robert A. Maguire and John E. Malmstad, 1983)**
> *is the prose masterpiece of Russia's "Silver Age," the declining years of the Czarist Empire at the beginning of the twentieth century. Bely's experiments with language have been compared to Joyce's; the non-Russian-reading audience has to take that assessment on faith.*

Ficciones by **Jorge Luis Borges (translated by Anthony Kerrigan, 1963)**
> *is a short, tricky book of stories, many of which read like scholarly articles by a playful fabulist. Its influence on recent fiction in the western hemisphere has been incalculably large.*

If On A Winter's Night a Traveler. . . by Italo Calvino
(translated by William Weaver, 1981)

   *is a kind of ultimate self-referential novel, a tale about reading tales
   about reading tales, and so on. Calvino's range was wide; each of
   his books presents its own vision of how fiction can be written.*

The Left-Handed Woman by Peter Handke (translated
by Ralph Manheim, 1978)

   *is a representative, highly accomplished novel by an Austrian
   writer whose flat, behavioristic descriptions of human life conceal
   a tender sensibility.*

The Man without Qualities by Robert Musil
(translated by Eithne Wilkins and Ernst Kaiser,
1955–1960)

   *is a plotless, three-volume study of the decay of traditional
   bourgeois Vienna. Not quite finished at the author's death, it is
   considered the foremost experimentalist novel in the German
   language.*

Maison de Rendez-vous by Alain Robbe-Grillet
(translated by Richard Howard, 1987)

   is a seminal work by a leader of the French nouveau roman
   *("new novel"), a movement of the 1950s and 1960s that
   attempted to go beyond conventional plot and character. Often
   parodying detective novels, Robbe-Grillet devoted his most loving
   attention to toneless renderings of the surfaces of objects.*

Portrait of a Man Unknown by Nathalie Sarraute
(translated by Marie Jolas, 1958, with a preface by
Jean-Paul Sartre)

   is the first novel by a more humanistic leader of the nouveau
   roman. *Sarraute's* The Age of Suspicion: Essays on the
   Novel *(translated by Marie Jolas, 1963) spells out her theory of
   "tropisms," psychological responses that are the human equivalent of plants' automatic attraction to light, earth, and water.
   Often using unnamed characters in her fiction, Sarraute tries
   to bring to light the "subconversations" that occur in the psyche
   on a level at which emotions cannot yet be labeled.*

Part Two

PROCESS

Chapter 13

How Writers Think

When you get down to it, it's really just daydreaming.

When writers are doing their most intense, creative work, they look like they're doing nothing.

That's why it's so hard to show the creative process in a movie. The screen version of a writer is a distraught eccentric throwing crumpled pages onto the floor, muttering, pounding on the typewriter, and screaming at anyone who comes near. I've done all those things, but only in rare, self-destructive moods. Done habitually, that sort of behavior is probably an obstacle rather than an aid to writing. Blow your stack at your loved one for interrupting, and you'll end up losing a day's work in guilt. (That's one of those genuine, inside tips of the trade I learned along the way somehow.)

The real version of a writer at work is me lying on the floor looking at the ceiling. Day in and day out. Hoping—and trusting—that in the emptiness of the ceiling, the window, the wall, life will suddenly take form like the first primitive organisms in the empty prehistoric sea. And the amazing thing is, it usually does. Vague, not quite visual shapes, not quite heard lines of dialogue, random motions that will select themselves into a story line pop into my mind.

At some point, I'll get up and write some of it down, but for now, patience is the key. Let the life on the empty ceiling reveal itself and play its game. In the movie *Searching for Bobby Fisher,* the chess teacher tells the young prodigy not to make the move when he first thinks of it, but to wait till he *really* sees it in his head. "Wait till you see it!" A good motto.

That's why bystanders are confused and upset by writers' behavior. They think we're wasting time. They think we're lazy. They think we're not really working, when in fact the reverse is true: we're using our time in the most constructive way possible, working with our brains as hard as human beings can (which is why we do it in restful postures: we don't have any energy to spare).

What's going on, in these quiescent, private, early stages of invention, is that I have activated my fullest attention, and yet there's nothing I'm paying attention *to*. Therefore, I have to make it up. I have to make up some object for my attention. And the object of my attention, very hazy at first, looks like people-shaped clouds; and the more attention I pay them, the more solid and definite and real they become.

If, at the beginning of such a session, you asked me, "What are you thinking about?" I might have to say, "I don't know." But at the end, I could tell you, "I'm thinking about my new story." The story arises so that I won't be stuck without an answer; or, to put it another way, the story arises because when a human being's attention is activated, it finds an object, even if it has to create one.

The psychological state I'm in during these thinking sessions could be described as a self-induced trance, but that would give you the wrong idea. It is not dulled, zombified, passive, unaware, or controlled from outside. It is receptive, aware, and highly concentrated, and I control it at will. It is a search operation: a brain looking to uncover its own hidden contents. Its emotional coloring is sometimes pleasant, sometimes frustrating, sometimes neutral. That doesn't matter very much. The search is what matters.

It's a form of meditation in which the only doctrine is, "I've got to think of my next story." Its rituals are ones I developed over a period of years, and they belong only to me. Every writer develops his or her own.

There is an element of tenderness in it. Every writer loves his or her own characters and is grateful for their arrival. They may have qualities that I would dislike in people made of flesh and blood, but the negative qualities of characters can't hurt anyone. Thus they can be forgiven without cost. (Forgiveness in real life can be much more difficult.) Creating fictional characters can train you to view human beings nonjudgmentally. After all, the flesh-and-blood people you meet can be raw material for characters—*especially* if they have negative traits. If you're a writer, nasty people become magnets, worthy of detached, sympathetic study.

It may sound as if what I'm doing is lying around waiting for inspiration—and that's exactly true. It's common nowadays to belittle inspiration, but I highly recommend that you get yourself inspired if you want to write anything worthwhile. If that sounds absurd, it's intentional, for I'm now coming to the real secret, and real secrets usually sound absurd at first.

You can train yourself to get inspired. You can get inspired as a habit.

That's where the work ethic comes in, for writers. Not, "Another day, another page. I'll punch the clock at 9:00 a.m. and write my thousand words, then my conscience will let me knock off to go swimming." If writing a work of fiction is drudgery, then reading it is likely to be as well. Try swimming first and writing afterwards; you might write better if you throw off your slave mentality.

The writer has to keep the spark of life in the story, and that is much harder to do if the writer doesn't feel alive while working. The work ethic for writers is a matter of disciplined inspiration: inspiration at one's own command.

If I lie down for fifteen minutes, I'm pretty sure to come up with an idea for a story or a character. That doesn't mean the story or character is going to be any *good*. Quality is another matter entirely. What it means is that the creative switch is on: something is happening. If it doesn't lead me anywhere this time, it may the next time. If I lie down for fifteen minutes a dozen times, and eleven times the result is boring, predictable, and trite, and one time the result is an interesting, unexpected, original story, the process has worked superbly.

You can't duplicate this process in a classroom; you can't rope it into a semester's calendar. The process I'm describing takes years to learn, years in which, very often, there are no visible results and no feedback from outside. Young people are not often the best candidates for this process: they want quick results. Writing, like parenthood, is an experience many people get into without knowing what's in store for them—and fortunately so, because if they knew, they might not do it. And like parenthood, it's an experience that can eat up your youth.

FORMAL PREWRITING

In order to make the process more visible, to give it a tangible result and make it seem to work in classrooms, teachers and other creative writing gurus usually recommend various techniques of "prewriting." The term *prewriting* is inaccurate: there's nothing "pre" about it. It happens as much during the third draft as before the first. Controlled daydreaming—thinking—dreaming the scene—*is* writing, in the same sense that dreaming the moves *is* chess. (Another secret, without which nobody would be able to write anything: writers aren't daydreaming creatively only when they're staring at the ceiling; they're doing it all the time. No wonder it's so hard to get a civil word out of them. Small talk is a distraction, an irritant.) Without it, you're just putting words on paper.

If putting words on paper helps you dream the scene, fine. You can keep a journal. You can freewrite. You can draw your characters' physical appearance and make story charts, outlines, and lists of traits. Your scrap paper will not be graded. That stuff is just to help you. If it helps, do it, and if it doesn't, don't feel remiss in getting directly to the story. It's definitely worthwhile to try out some formal prewriting techniques during your apprenticeship to find out which ones, if any, suit you. In writing my first unpublished novel, I made a numbered list of chapters and their major events; that's the only outlining I've ever done. I kept a journal intensively during my early thirties; now I only make entries on widely scattered occasions—they usually turn out to be ideas for silly titles and character names—or when I'm traveling.

To say that students in America today have been overjournalled is putting it mildly. If you are now, or have been, an American student, I don't have to tell you what a journal is and how to keep it.

Freewriting should be just what the name says: writing freely, letting the pen move quickly over the page for a comfortable period of time so that you don't censor your flow of ideas. Afterward, you look back and see if any of the ideas are usable. This is essentially the same process as lying down and staring at the ceiling, except it leaves a record you can refer to later. Leaves a partial record, that is, because you can't write as quickly as you can think; freewriting always, no matter how hard you try, involves summarizing and self-editing. You're trading away some spontaneity, some richness of thought, in exchange for a permanent, written record. If the process works well, you can regenerate the whole from the part, the living idea from the summary: you read the note, "Louie and Stella meet through a wrong number," and the initial fantasy resurfaces, enriched by touches and afterthoughts—revisions—that weren't there the first time. If the process doesn't work well, you look at "Louie and Stella meet through a wrong number" and think, "Hm, what did I mean by that?" Maybe that's a sign that the fantasy didn't have as much potential as you first believed. Or maybe it's a sign that it withered during storage.

If freewriting is just an additional segment in an assignment, just another "should," just another opportunity for unnecessary assessment, it's not free; it's a redundant interim procedure, and you may be putting your best, freshest ideas into a form that no one will see, and when you recast them into fiction, you'll have left their life behind.

Whether freewriting and journal-keeping help you or not may depend on how good your memory is. If you're prone to forgetting your good ideas unless you write them down immediately, I heartily suggest that you use these techniques. I'd go so far as to admit that if you resist formal prewriting techniques, that's all the more reason you should try them at least once: we often resist what we most need.

But if you can remember an inspired idea simply by having it, dwelling on it for a few minutes, and recalling it now and then, you've got an advantage.

These things are the hard part of writing. The easy part is the words. Creativity is a state of being:

- alert
- absorbent
- explorative
- flexible
- hypersensitive
- independent
- foresightful
- opportunistic
- synthesizing
- self-replenishing
- intense

GETTING TO THE KEYBOARD

The transition from daydreaming to word-writing involves the delicate art of knowing when to get up off the couch and start tapping at the keyboard. Cut off the flow of fantasy too soon and the shapes on the ceiling may evaporate, leaving you nothing to tap the keyboard about. Linger too long and you may succumb to torpor, your fantasies drifting into back-channels: you begin by thinking about your characters, but then you wander into thoughts of what magazine you ought to send the story to when it's finished, and how badly you're being treated by the publishing world, and whether you should sign up for a course next term, and what your teacher is really like. . . .

This sense of when to move from stage to stage, like the ability to dream the scene, is acquired from years of silent, patient repetition. Sometimes you'll write useless, vapid pages because you hadn't dreamed them out sufficiently in advance. Sometimes you'll waste time daydreaming—fooling yourself into thinking you're working—when you should have gotten right to the computer. If you grope through all the possibilities often enough, you'll get a feel for when the process is working efficiently and when it isn't. You'll tend to repeat the behaviors that promote positive results and give up the ones that don't. You will feel confident in your ability to get good results and avoid bad ones. When bad results do occur, you'll get through them with minimal distress because you know that while they're inevitable, they're not dominant. And you'll know that the process fits you. This is known as "developing good work habits" or "acquiring self-discipline." (See Chapter 16.)

If anyone had told me, when I started out, that I would become an extremely self-disciplined, hard-working person, I would have said, "You've got the wrong boy." But I have become so. That's another thing writing did for me.

Do It

1. Do exactly what I've described in this chapter: choose a comfortable resting place such as a couch, a bed, a floor, a chair, a forest. Sit or lie down and stay there for a while—anywhere from ten minutes to an hour or more. Don't expect anything to happen. Don't try to make anything happen. Don't even think, "I want to think up a story." When you get bored, get up and do something else. Repeat as often as you wish. Eventually a story may appear.

2. Keep a notebook of your dreams and/or daydreams. Make at least two entries before deciding whether this practice suits you or not.

3. Keep a notebook of interesting things people say, interesting quotes you read, and events and people you encounter. Make at least two entries before deciding whether this practice suits you or not.

4. Try freewriting in order to see if it suits you. Start out when you have the vague beginnings of an idea for a subject or character, but not a specific plan for how the story will progress. Write the name of the character (choose one at random if you don't have one in mind) or a phrase that summarizes the subject, such as "Shipwreck" or "Life of a racing jockey." Then just start writing whatever comes to mind, even if it's off the subject. Spend at least five minutes; write at least half a page. Then read your freewriting and see if any ideas or phrases in it engage you. Use those, in turn, as starting points for a second round of freewriting. Hold as many rounds of freewriting as you feel is beneficial. Stop at a point where you can say, "Now I know basically what I'm going to write

about." If you like this practice, do it whenever you are trying to formulate or refine story ideas.

5. In a classroom or writing group, Exercise 4 can become a group activity: the teacher, or a group member, proposes a topic and everyone freewrites on that topic individually, exchanging papers or reading them aloud. This can lead to a fruitful cross-pollination of ideas.

Writer's Bookshelf

Becoming a Writer by Dorothea Brande (1934; reprinted with a foreword by John Gardner, 1981)
    pioneered the idea that the writer can train himself or herself to enter a concentration state.

Notebook for Crime and Punishment by Fyodor Mikhaylovich Dostoyevsky (translated and edited by Edward Wasiolek, 1967).
    As if the pressures of writing to pay his debts weren't enough, Dostoyevsky kept voluminous notes while planning his novels. His agonizing creative process involved major plot and character changes from draft to draft. Also available are Wasiolek's editions of the notebooks for The Possessed *(also known as* The Devils, *1968) and* The Brothers Karamazov *(1971).*

On Not Being Able to Paint by Joanna Field (1950; 2nd edition, 1958).
    The British psychiatrist Marion Milner was an amateur painter who, under the pen name Joanna Field, analyzed her creativity and its inhibitions in order to find out what she most deeply wished to express and how to free herself to express it. The result was an intimate and sometimes profound study of the creative process, from which any artist at any level of accomplishment can benefit. Field had previously written two equally valuable books of personal exploration: A Life of One's Own *(1934) and* An Experiment in Leisure *(1937).*

The Notebooks of F. Scott Fitzgerald, 1932–1940 (edited by Matthew J. Bruccoli, 1978),

in which the entries were categorized and numbered by Fitzgerald himself; they're rich in story ideas, descriptive passages, and aphorisms ("Show me a hero and I'll write you a tragedy").

Passages from the American Note-Books by Nathaniel Hawthorne (1910 and other editions).

Hawthorne was one of the most introspective and technically conscious of classic fiction writers. His notebooks make us privy to the conception of his works and to numerous story premises that never got past the jotting stage. A recent supplement, Hawthorne's Lost Notebook: 1835–1841 *(1978), contains a manuscript facsimile.*

Letters by John Keats (various editions, e.g., *Selected Letters of John Keats,* edited by Robert Pack, Signet Books, 1974).

Keats' letters served as a proving ground for his philosophy, his metaphors, and often the first drafts of his poems. Energetically written and ceaselessly inspiring, these casual scribblings say the best things ever said about what makes people artists.

Journal of the Fictive Life by Howard Nemerov (1965).

The distinguished American poet wrote a novel and, perhaps more importantly, kept a journal of his thoughts and emotions during the writing process.

Chapter 14

Necessary Roughness: The First Draft

This sentence is part of the first draft of *Writer's Mind*. If you can read that sentence, it made the cut into the final draft.

The initial wording of the second sentence was, "I don't know whether it will survive into print." I changed it because—well, I don't really know why I changed it. You think we have an airtight technical reason for everything? Mostly we go by feel. I guess I changed it because the new version was more active, and because it seemed arrogant to assume my words will get into print. (And I know from experience that the assumption is often incorrect.)

You'd be surprised how much in the readable, loose-limbed paragraphs above was reworked. The first paragraph was three sentences long; the sentence, "If you can read that sentence, it made the final cut," was a late addition. The last two sentences were rephrased repeatedly—should I say "wrong" or "incorrect," for instance? Sometimes I changed a phrase—"airtight technical reason"—only to change it back again. The opening sentence and "Mostly we go by feel" were the only sentences left un-touched. To be recklessly candid, *this* entire paragraph was moved up from a position further down the page.

Once in my life, I would like to get a passage right the first time. Just once. It never happens. I don't know whether it's because my prose isn't tight enough in a first draft or because I have a compulsion to fiddle. But the point is, when I write a first draft, I know I'm writing something I'm going to throw out later. It's not going to be good enough. I'm going to be disgusted by parts of it. I'm going to wonder how I ever got bogged down in such a dull, futile project. (That usually happens half to two-thirds of the way through the first draft. Let's see—Chapter 14 out of 21—where would that be?)

The key points to remember about writing first drafts are:

- they don't have to be any good, and
- you keep writing them anyway.

The greatest danger in a first draft is being too self-critical, too inhibited. A first draft is a place not to be inhibited. It is, in fact, a place where, if you are inhibited, you can *learn* not to be.

There are many brilliant, gifted people who want to write and have something to say, but can't get past page 1. I've known some personally and used them as negative examples—I wasn't going to turn out like them. They can't accept the idea of putting something less than perfect down on paper. In their scrupulous self-doubt, they can't write the second sentence before they have polished the first sentence to its ultimate. And what is its ultimate? If you're smart enough, you can keep finding alternatives, and reasons to be dissatisfied with the alternatives, into infinity. The ultimate is never reached. And so they barely get started, and the world is poorer for not seeing the products of their struggles. Which, maybe, is what they secretly intended all along: to deprive the world, and themselves.

My purpose in this chapter is to persuade you not to be like that.

Just start writing and keep going—that's the best method for producing first drafts. Resist doubts. Leave mistakes alone. Let it be as clumsy as it is.

The first draft is where everything is provisional, in flux, up for grabs. Since nothing need remain in its first form, you can take any risk. The risks that turn out successfully, you will keep; the ones that don't, you'll throw out. (This is one reason why first drafts are usually longer than final drafts: there are so many risks that don't work out.) If you write something awful, there's no reason to be alarmed: no one will ever know.

CONSTRUCTIVE EXAGGERATION

Many of the risks you take will be in the form of exaggerations, and that's a good thing. If real life were narrated exactly as it is, hour after hour, there wouldn't be many exciting stories in it. Exaggeration is to fiction what shoving is to basketball: the accepted bit of cheating that lets you win. Exaggeration is to fiction what accuracy is to fact: it's the current of conviction. The magic formula for turning the small conflicts of every day into the big dramas of fiction is one word: exaggerate. (I'm exaggerating, of course.) If two teenagers exchange angry words in real life, it becomes a knife fight in a story; if two business partners have a contract dispute and give each other the silent treatment, the written version has them hiring hit men, going bankrupt, and dying miserably in jail. The emotions remain the same, but the actions become larger, more visible, more gripping. If this kind of constructive exaggeration tends to elude you during the planning stages (as it does me), the drafting stage is a good place to catch up on it. In the sway of invention, you can whip up scenes without worrying about whether they're the right scenes. Give yourself an occasional reminder to go for big gestures and tumultuous events. If they seem phony, take them out afterward.

The let-it-rip approach to drafting has two major advantages. First, it allows you to finish what you started. Being unable to finish is one of the saddest and most easily preventable of writers' ills. If you can't finish what you've started, no one will ever read it. This is an ailment of writers who fear they aren't good enough; it turns inadequacy into a romanticized "block." The cure is not to become attached to the first draft. You aren't attached to the first draft because you have confidence in your ability to improve it.

The second advantage is that by leaving your self-critical faculty behind during the first draft, you will inevitably write some things you didn't plan on writing, and a certain percentage of them will be worth keeping. Your characters will say unexpectedly witty things. Your descriptions will sound fresh, and figures of speech will appear on your screen almost before they have occurred to you. If you keep self-criticism at bay, you will become a more inventive, more thought-filled writer, not a sloppier and more thoughtless one, even if the initial product is sloppy.

Worrying about perfection in your first draft is like worrying about the tidiness of your kitchen counter when you're cooking: it bears no relation to the taste of the finished dish.

Does this mean you should never cross out a word in a first draft? Of course not. Individual temperament and work habits come into play: everyone has his or her own drafting method. It's a rare writer who finishes a first draft straight through, never backtracking to cross out a line. A certain amount of on-the-spot revising is natural. I do a lot of it, testing out different versions of sentences as I type them. I always assume, however, that there are many imperfections, small and big, which I will either not notice in the first draft or consciously leave untouched for a later go-round.

There's no need to define pure drafting as opposed to pure revision; it wouldn't match the reality of the process. We're talking about tendencies, overlapping phases. The phases are more or less equivalent to mental states. There's a time when I say to myself, "Now I'm just writing the first draft; it doesn't matter if I write garbage," and a time when I say, "Okay,

I'm starting to rewrite—gotta get more serious." But these phases are not clearly demarcated. In the middle of what is "officially" the revision of the middle of a novel, I may come up with an idea for a new scene; when I write it, it's the first draft of that scene. And who's to say how many times I turned a sentence over in my mind, perhaps unconsciously, before I first typed it out? In that sense, even a first draft is a revision.

There's not much point in counting drafts. It's hard to tell where one begins and the next ends. Nor is there a sure way to know when you've reached the end of the process—the so-called finished product (see Chapter 15).

There are, it's true, some writers who hate to revise on paper. They won't write a sentence down until they've got it the way they want it. Their first drafts are very clean—it seems as if they've hardly changed a word. Actually, though, they've done a lot of rewriting in their heads; the first written draft may be the fourth or fifth mental draft. It's like playing chess without a board. Some great writers, such as Charlotte Brontë, have worked this way, but I believe it's much less common among ordinary good writers. A poetic gift is required just to use this approach at all, it seems to me, much less to create something beautiful with it.

I don't favor this approach, not only because I'm not personally suited to it, but because it eliminates the creative communication among scenes that results when you draft swiftly, revising lightly on the wing and returning for heavier changes later. That sort of back and forth movement from beginning to middle to end keeps you aware of what's happening at all points of your story. I'm thinking about Louie and Stella's first encounter, their developing romance, their breakups, and the final reunion simultaneously; I keep a vision of the shape of the whole work in my mind. Therefore it's more likely that I'll have last-minute ideas that will fit into the pattern of the work and enrich it. The story is not just the product of a bygone inspiration that I have doggedly fleshed out; its inspiration is continuing.

This method also helps keep the details consistent at different points in the work. By moving back and forth freely, I instinctively make sure that Stella, who was twenty-six in April at the beginning of the story, is twenty-seven the following July, forty pages later. If an inconsistency does get into the first draft, I will discover it in the second. If, on the other hand, I were creeping along, polishing each sentence as it arose and not doubling back, I might goof and make Stella twenty-seven the following February, before her birthday, and I might not notice unless I were working from detailed outlines or notes. Surface polish is not necessarily actual perfection.

By not thinking too much about the details, you paradoxically manage them more efficiently. You don't have to worry about minutiae until you revise. Then those details become very important.

VARYING YOUR METHOD

Whether your drafting is slipshod or scrupulous, the order in which you compose a work is a matter of inclination. The obvious method is to start at the beginning and work page by page to the end, but it can be self-defeating to turn that into a rule. If you're stuck in Chapter 2 of your first draft, you might as well skip to Chapter 3 and return to the difficult scene after you've written the rest of the book. Among other things, you'll have a much better feel, at that point, for the thematic and psychological connections you want Chapter 2 to make with the rest of the material. Perhaps you'll have written something on the next-to-last page that unexpectedly illuminates the problem passage.

By all means experiment with different drafting sequences; try a new one just for the sake of widening your experience. Writers who keep extensive notes or outlines are best equipped to draft out of sequence; they can simply look at their index cards and find out what they're supposed to be writing in any given scene. Writers who don't outline are more likely to draft in sequential order as a way of not getting lost. Even the strictest, however, should be able to depart from lockstep when doing so will solve a problem that threatens the work. For instance, in writing this book, I drafted Chapter 6 first, then wrote the other chapters in order from 1 to 21, except for 9, which came last, and the introduction, which was a break after Part I.

Nor do you have to know the ending of a story when you begin drafting it. A fairly common method is to work toward a vaguely sensed but not finally decided goal, trusting that by the time you get there you'll see it more clearly. A corollary method is to write the first draft three-quarters of the way through, until you've settled on an ending, then return to the beginning and revise in accordance with the planned but still-unwritten ending, which you finally write as the frosting on the cake.

Rough drafting is a kind of willed imperfection. By accepting the fact that your first draft will be flawed, you develop a higher-order competence: competence to control the process. There's a Japanese word for it: *isagiyosa,* having the courage to relax one's hold.

Do It

1. Recall a story idea you once had and did not develop into a story. Start drafting that story now, this moment, without any further preparation.

2. Recall an interesting event that you recently experienced or observed. Write a rough draft in which you exaggerate the event for dramatic effect.

3. If you are working in a class or writers' group, have someone propose an opening sentence. Then have each member write at least one page of narrative starting with that sentence. If you wish, set a time limit, such as thirty minutes per page. If you are working alone, simply choose a first line and do the exercise. Change the narrative point of view and/or the characters' genders if you wish.
   Here is a bouquet of first lines, some fresher than others:

- You won't believe what I'm going to tell you.
- The family got together every seventeen years, when the cicadas came out.
- There was a time in my life when I used the radio as an oracle.
- I could hear every word through the wall.
- If you want to save yourself, save someone else.
- There was one question he never wanted to hear.
- There are two kinds of people in this world.
- Everything had changed.
- It was supposed to be simple.
- It was over.

Writer's Bookshelf

The Last Tycoon by F. Scott Fitzgerald (1941; corrected edition, 1990)

is that rare spectacle: a published, very rough draft by a great writer. It might have turned out to be Fitzgerald's masterpiece if he had lived. As it stands, it shows Fitzgerald groping toward his plot and characters; some of the chapters exist only in the sketchiest form. Thinking about how he might have expanded and polished it is a valuable exercise.

The Garden of Eden by Ernest Hemingway (1986)

is a posthumously published, incredibly messy, revealing novel from Hemingway's great period of the 1920s. The published version was reduced from more than 1,000 pages to 247. The distance from The Garden of Eden *to* A Farewell to Arms *is the distance from rough draft to fully realized art.*

Dark as the Grave Wherein My Friend Is Laid by Malcolm Lowry (1968)

is the posthumously published rough draft of a companion novel to Under the Volcano, *by a writer who almost never finished anything. It includes an informative preface by Douglas Day.*

Lucien Louwen by Stendhal (1834–35).

As is often the case with unfinished novels, there are critics who consider this the author's best work. Drafted several years before his death, it was not published in Stendhal's lifetime. Even Stendhal's finished works were written hastily, however: The Charterhouse of Parma *took just fifty-two days.*

Chapter 15

Revising—Or Should I Say Rewriting?

Technically the difference is this: revising means making changes in a draft, while rewriting means starting a new version from scratch. In common parlance the two words are interchangeable. I could idle away a half hour trying to decide whether to say "revising" or "rewriting"—or "reworking," "redrafting," or "recasting"—in a given sentence, but the correct term for *that* would be "wheel-spinning."

Revision should improve a text. That may sound so obvious as to be not worth stating, but it's a hidden problem for many writers: they sweat and strain, crossing out and filling in, and what they end up with is not noticeably better than what they started with. Perhaps going through the rewriting process makes them feel professional. When every page on your manuscript is half crossed out and there are illegible sentences traipsing through the margins, you feel like you've been working. The problem is a familiar one for creative writing teachers: they assign their students a rewrite, and the work comes back much altered but not much improved.

Rewriting is the most important phase of the writing process, which is what makes it so dangerous. Some writers fall prey to the dangers and spend eternity rewriting, never finishing. Others, scared of the dangers, try to skip this phase without looking.

Everything needs a second draft. Nothing is ever exactly right the first time. If, upon reading your first draft, you are distressed and want to hide and realize that it can't be shown to anyone and you must change it right away, this is not a sign that you've done anything wrong or that you lack ability; it's a sign that you have something in common with every creator. Knowing what to save is a skill no one is too big to work on.

There are levels of revision; in ascending order of breadth, they are:

- diction
- scene
- structure
- concept

DICTION

The level of diction—word choice—is probably what most amateurs think of when they think of revision. Finding *le mot juste!* The setting sun diffused its effulgent rays through coral clouds—or shall I say *nacreous*?

Albert Camus diagnosed this literary illness in *The Plague,* in which one of the characters is a novelist who is perpetually trying to perfect his first sentence.

If you are hitting yourself on the forehead with your thesaurus, trying to shake loose the exact right word, there is every possibility that the word you finally choose will be precious and posey rather than right. Good prose is readable. It sounds natural. Even if it's the product of seventeen drafts, it sounds as if you were speaking it or penning it at leisure. Good prose is clean, not overburdened with ornate touches.

You know the words already. You may not be able to summon them up immediately, in their best order, and that's why recasting sentences and searching thesauruses is useful.

Trim your sentences; make them swift; make every word an arrow. Go for the plain word over its fancy synonym, the concrete and sensory over the abstract, the one-syllable over the two-syllable (except where rhythm favors the two-syllable), the exact over the approximate.

It's a mistake to think, though, that rotating every phrase this way and that, running a complete synonym search for every noun and adjective, is the secret of good prose. The phrases you fix upon will still be stamped with your stamp. They will be on your level of accomplishment, not above it or below it. The new version will be different from the old, but in order to make sure that it's better, you must read it with an open mind. Re-revising, painful as it is, can become necessary to recapture good things you prematurely tossed away: in the end, after all that polishing, you might go back and see that your first impulse was the freshest and truest.

Professional writers often reach a point where they realize that no matter what they write, no matter how they tinker, it's always inescapably, exasperatingly *them.* That's one of the things that makes revision so hard. After a lot of trying, you may still not know which version is best. It may seem like a toss-up. You may despair. Don't despair. (I said there were no don'ts in this book, but I think that one's excusable.) A better writer than you said:

> Why write I still all one, ever the same,
> And keep invention in a noted weed,
> That every word doth almost tell my name,
> Showing their birth, and where they did proceed?
> —Shakespeare, Sonnet 76

The thesaurus will not lead you out of yourself. And that's a good thing. The only alternative to yourself is falseness.

Revising on the level of diction is, most of the time, for most writers, a matter of taking things out rather than putting things in. First drafts tend to be loose; they usually need tightening. They tend to be pleonastic—containing extra words or phrases that add to the length of a statement without adding to its meaning. (That sentence was pleonastic.)

Sentence structure in first drafts requires particular going-over. In a first draft, we tend to fall into a syntactical rut, using the same patterns repeatedly. One writer writes first drafts almost exclusively in simple declarative sentences; his roommate keeps him up at night with the rapid-fire clicking of complicated, clause-laden, spiralling sentences. Both need to look over their drafts and increase sentence variety.

If your simple sentences become monotonous, try combining some into compound or complex sentences. If your long, elaborate sentences become hard to read, try splitting them.

Sentence variety should not become a mania. Every sentence need not have a different structure from its neighbors. How it sounds is the main thing. A work in which every sentence had a markedly different structure from its neighbors would probably sound unfluent. Many writers like to follow a string of long sentences with one or two very short ones for effect, but that too gets tiresome if overdone.

Another rut that's easy to fall into is the habitual use of certain words or phrases. Every writer has his or her tics, automatic verbal twitches that would be better off suppressed. An editor once pointed out that I used the word "now" too often. It was good advice: I crossed out a lot of "nows." (But it left me with a lot of "nows" inside me, trapped and yearning to break free. Now I think I'll let a couple out.) Now, your tic might be some other word, or a form of punctuation such as the semicolon, or a sentence pattern such as the rhetorical question. The things you repeat may vary from passage to passage: at one point you use the word "however" four times on a page, and later you modify four verbs in a row adverbially. Finding your tics is easy; it requires mere attention. Read your draft. Note whatever verbal devices you use repeatedly. It's possible that they are conscious repetitions that enhance the sound of your prose, but it's more likely that they're tics. If the latter, simply get rid of them.

There comes a time in everyone's life when he or she must use a checklist, and for me that time has come. Here is a checklist for revising on the level of diction:

1. Delete unnecessary words and phrases.

2. Find accurate, preferably concrete words for the things you're describing.

3. Inject adequate variety into sentence structures.

4. Locate and remove verbal tics.

If you've done those four things, then you've done the essential minimum of revision on the word-and-sentence level. Adding inventive, expressive, striking turns of phrase is desirable but goes beyond the essential minimum: it comes from inspiration assisted by research.

I'll add a fifth checklist item that leads to the next level, the level of scene:

5. Control your tone.

Tone arises from word choice, but as a practical matter it builds up from many such choices over the course of a passage, a scene, an entire work. Tone is best assessed when you come back to a work after a hiatus, when your first infatuation has cooled. After a day or more away from a piece of writing, there's some part of you that can approach it as a reader encountering a new text, not as its author who is in love with it. Let this part of you be the part that responds to tone. Is the piece sarcastic when you intended it to be lightly humorous? Hard-breathingly melodramatic when you intended cool suspense? You will notice these things and be shocked and embarrassed.

Fortunately, changes in the overall tone of a scene can often be accomplished through the changing of a few words. They're the superfluous words: the little, verbal dig of the elbow you were giving the reader, the curl of the lip, the extra adjective, the cloying attempt at intimacy. At other times, tonal change can be achieved by filling in omissions, inappropriate terseness, and affectlessness: *"Louie had what trendy postcards call 'a bad hair day'"* becomes *"Louie had a bad day."* Or vice versa.

Within a passage whose overall tone works, you may find the occasional sentence that slips unintentionally out of tone. (Intentional variation in tone is a different matter, of course.) The procedure for this is the same as for a longer passage: reread it and find the places where you want to wince.

SCENE

On the level of scenes, revision usually involves adjusting the pace. A scene, like a sentence, has a rhythm. It has a shape: it starts at a point, builds through a process, and at its end has accomplished a goal. Extra actions, extra moments of dialogue or explanation or digression, are like unnecessary words, interrupting the rhythm and distorting the shape.

Let's say the scene is one in which Stella, uncertain of Louie's seriousness, tries to reignite her failed relationship with her former beau, Griswold. She makes a coffee date with him, and, halfway through his orange cappucino, Griswold reveals that he has booked tickets to Rabat for the following Tuesday for himself and his secretary/companion, Dorothea, but is willing to dump Dorothea for Stella if she wants to go. Of course, I don't have to write a full-fledged scene at all. The shortest way of reporting the action would be simply to tell the reader, in one sentence, "Stella met a former boyfriend, Griswold, for coffee, and though she was tempted by his offer of a foreign tour—touched by his lingering affection—in the end she couldn't say yes to his possessive need." But let's assume I've decided that a scene would illuminate the characters justifiably. How long should the scene take?

As long as is required to implant the reality of the scene in the reader's mind. If a feeling of reality can be achieved by implying some things rather than stating them, it should be.

I'll get Stella to the coffeehouse, perhaps with a brief transition from a previous scene, but more likely not. In real life, there might be many minutes of small talk, but in fiction you can reduce that to two lines of dialogue or eliminate it entirely. There's just enough description of the surroundings to make us feel we're sitting at the next table, eavesdropping. A touch of atmosphere: four old gangsters playing dominoes at the back table, the waitress' boyfriend hanging around examining pastries. Almost immediately, the ex-lovers are talking about important things. There is enough indirection and mundane detail in their conversation to make it seem like real talk and to hint at the style of their relationship, but the indirection is not digressive; it's aimed at bringing the characters to the point. Stella's idle touching of the flower in the centerpiece induces Griswold to make a premature move for her hand, which in turn leads her to blurt out her current ambivalent status with Louie. Remarkably soon, the conversation is more intimate than it would be in real life. Griswold, with a dismissive comment about Dorothea, lets loose with his Rabat offer. And the scene can end there. Stella doesn't even have to make her decision—that can be implicit in the next scene, where she's laughing with Louie about the terrible mistake she almost made. After Griswold's offer, a single line of dialogue, a gesture, or a thought can be a suspenseful or enigmatic link to the next scene, enabling Stella to make a memorable or charming exit:

"Come to Rabat with me."

"Rabat?" She laughed at how the two syllables, common bits of sound belonging to hundreds of words she used, seemed, because *he* had used them, to have no meaning at all; he had barked and waited for her to bark back; but she had no idea what he was asking.

Among the things I'll cut from the first draft of the scene are:

- the guarded, menacingly inconclusive remarks of a hit man on the phone:

  "Five? You don't get me for no five. Do the job right, costs more than five. You said five, I didn't say five. No second man—I work alone. So bring 'em in from Miami, so why are you talkin' to me? No, look, *you* listen. . . ."

- The probing glimpse into the sordid past of the waitress and her boyfriend:

  "It had only been six months since that day—the day they never talked about. The day that had cost Frankie his job at the direct-mail company and created a breach between Rosie and her family that might never be repaired. Frankie and Rosie knew what love was like. They could have told Stella and Griswold a lot. . . ."

- The realistic but digressive chatter about things that the reader has no investment in and that don't contribute to our understanding of character and event:

  "Gris, you cut your hair!" she said.

  "You like?" He rubbed his hand over his scalp. Oh, the trouble she'd had trying to resist that preening boyishness!

  "I always liked your hair. I think it was probably better when it was long, but I like this, too. You planning to do anything special with it?"

"Well, I've been thinking of growing it out on one side and keeping it buzzed short on the other. . . ."

- The cutely random intrusion:

Suddenly the waitress hugged Griswold with startling ferocity. "Oh, I have all your albums! I saw you in concert last summer! Here you are ordering orange cappucino from me, I'm like totally stunned!"

People were always mistaking him for a famous singer-guitarist whose music, as it happened, he despised.

"I'm not him—it's okay—it happens a lot—"

"Okay," she laughed conspiratorially, and for the next half-hour she lurked behind the espresso machine, ogling Griswold and Stella and doing her best to hear what they were saying.

- The redundant explanations that stop the action cold:

"What do you think, Gris?"

Griswold looked at her. Had he missed his chance for genuine love? Yet here it was, offering itself to him again: an opportunity he had not anticipated. If only he could believe in second chances! For he was a bitter man, with a bitterness that stretched far back in time. . . .

And it stretches on for a page and three-quarters, until by the time Griswold answers Stella's question, we've forgotten what it was.

- And, perhaps most dangerous, the tendentious windings and turnings of conversation that seem as if they might have some bearing on the action at hand, but leave the scene stronger when omitted:

"Griswold," Stella said abruptly, "you know, I always loved you."

"Love!" he laughed.

"And you always laughed at me when I said it."

"That's not true. I didn't laugh at you. I respected you enough to think that you would understand my laughter for what it was: an expression of regard and, incidentally, an expression of my soul. I'm amused—bemused, really—by this world in which we live. That's my demeanor. Maybe it masks some kind of fear. Afraid to show my true feelings. Whatever."

"You showed plenty of feeling to me, but it wasn't always such positive feeling."

"Yes, I could be cold. I could be angry. But you can't have the negative without the positive. That was always your problem, Stella. You want only one side of the coin of life. Remember that night in Oconomowoc—"

"Waiter! Check, please!"

"No, listen to me, this is important—"

Whew—I'm glad *that* didn't last too long. The clue to the material's superfluousness is the insistence, "This is important!" Whenever you tell yourself, "This is important! I've got to put this in whether it fits or not!" it's a sign that the material is iffy and you ought to reconsider. Your inner urgency comes from the strain of trying to push down the thought, "This isn't as brilliant as I hoped; better leave it out."

Which isn't to say that there's never a proper role for passages like Griswold's soul-baring or the personal history of the waitress and her boyfriend. I can imagine stories in which they would be central. There's no role for them *in this work,* that's all. After writing those passages in a first draft, I might want to save them in an outtakes file, for possible cannibalization in a future project, rather than throwing them out entirely. But in the story about Stella's decision whether to go with Griswold or to give Louie another chance, Griswold and Stella's dead romance doesn't need to be fully exhumed. We only need to learn enough to give an intuitive understanding of why Stella decides against him. There might be a sentence or two of physical description of Griswold at his entrance, with a sentence or two of background information (the introduction of the fighter on stepping into the ring). After that, everything Griswold does and says should be focused—as the reader is focused—on his present interaction with Stella, with its goal of the travel offer. We've defined that as the perimeter of this scene. Anything we learn about him—and it can be a lot—occurs within that boundary, not in his life outside.

It would be equally a mistake to pass over Griswold so quickly that we got no impression of who he is and no idea why Stella declines his offer.

I want Griswold to make a memorable cameo appearance as a foil for Louie, a contrasting character: where Louie is blunt, candid, down to earth, and tends to hide his loyalty behind self-mockery, Griswold is urbane, loquacious, and tries to hide his narcissism behind a facade of therapy-talk. Therefore, too much conciseness would be self-defeating. I want to show enough of the scene to make the reader believe in it.

The reader's belief in a scene is to some extent a function of time. The characters are using up a certain amount of their lives in the coffeehouse, and the reader must feel that he or she, too, is in the scene long enough to experience its events. The reader's emotional response to a scene rises and falls along a natural trajectory; if the trajectory is cut off prematurely, the response doesn't develop, and if it's sustained too long, the reader gets bored. If Stella and Griswold are in and out of the coffeehouse too fast, the reader is left wondering, "What was that all about? Why was it there at all?" Some reading time—some number of lines or pages—is necessary. Of course, readers' time and characters' time are on two different tracks: it may take two minutes to read a scene that occupies two hours of the characters' lives. But two minutes may feel like enough where three would feel like too many and one like too few.

Let the scene play, but recognize when it's played itself out. Let the emotional confrontations build without pausing for the interruptions and wandering into the side-issues that would prolong it in real life.

Whenever you've finished a scene, it's a good idea to reconsider the last paragraph or so. The curtain line, the last clever fillip, is often not worth it.

Heed what Stendhal said in *The Red and the Black:* "Though it is my intention to tell you about life in the provinces for some two-hundred pages, I will not be so barbarous as to inflict on you the long-windedness and 'witty turns' of a provincial dialogue."

And remember that everyone is a provincial.

STRUCTURE

Revisions in structure affect the plan of an entire work or a significant portion. They may involve deleting unnecessary subplots or elaborating underdeveloped ones. They may involve removing unproductive characters, combining two or more feeble characters into a single strong presence, or inventing a new character to fill a gap where something seems missing. Rearranging scenes—like putting Stella's conversation with Griswold *before* Louie's similar conversation with his old girlfriend rather than after it—and cutting entire scenes (Griswold's coffee hour is certainly a prime candidate) are probably the forms of structural revision writers do most on a day-to-day basis.

As with the other kinds of revision, a structural change may mean putting something in or taking something out. Taking things out is probably more common, for most writers in their first drafts err on the side of overinclusion, but that doesn't mean that putting things in, when they're called for, is any less important.

First drafts tend to suffer from overpopulation. Secondary characters multiply like rabbits. At the beginning of a project, you're probably at your highest level of excitement, full of ideas, each one calling forth a character to exemplify it. Later, when you're straggling toward the end and have to fudge the answer to "What next?" you tell yourself: "When in doubt, throw in a new character." A very dubious dictum. Better in more cases to give deeper traits and new developments to the characters you've already got.

How to tell when you've got unnecessary characters? For one thing, compare characters with each other. A classic structural flaw is to have two characters performing essentially the same function at different points in a work. Let's say I gave Stella two old boyfriends in the first draft—Griswold and Chumley. Griswold was the one who lived in her city and occupied her present thoughts; Chumley appeared only in flashback, in scenes set in college. Is Chumley really necessary? He's different from Griswold on the surface, of course—it would be unprofessional of me not to think of some distinct traits for him—but underneath he's the same sort of guy, playing the same role in Stella's life. It's hard to tell the two apart. Like two slightly different shades of green, Griswold and Chumley clash because they're too similar.

Harsh population-control measures have to be used that would never be acceptable in real life. Mercilessly we snap our fingers and an unsuspecting, innocent first-draft character simply ceases to exist—he or she vanishes from the finished work.

I get rid of Chumley—but not exactly. What I do is make him part of Griswold. There are aspects of Chumley that are genuinely interesting— for instance, the way his snobbishness about clothes contrasts with his democratic attitude toward people. I graft these traits onto Griswold, and instead of having two little ex-boyfriends who blur in the reader's mind, Stella now has one: the inimitable, larger-than-life Griswold. He's Stella's old college boyfriend who broke up with her just before graduation, but moved to the same city to get a job and then, after a couple of years, began seeing her on an on-and-off basis. Griswold is a composite character consisting of Griswold and Chumley, but no one knows that except me. I've done a significant structural upgrade, strengthening the work, and all it took was changing a name and a few lines of exposition.

It's as if Chumley and Griswold were two folders on a desktop. If there are some documents in Chumley I want to save, I select them and move them into Griswold; the rest of the Chumley folder, I throw in the trash.

It may be that a character doesn't clash with any other character but just doesn't have enough of a reason for existing. Ask yourself, on the character's behalf, the second of Stanislavsky's four questions: "Why am I here?" Is it really necessary for Louie to visit his therapist in midplot? The therapist doesn't have any role except as a passive audience for Louie's feelings, a sounding board. If Louie has any insights worth revealing, he can reveal them in conversations with Stella or some other necessary character. Likewise for any valuable insights the therapist states about Louie.

As with Chumley, it wasn't a *mistake* to write the therapist into the first draft. If I hadn't given those two minor characters their chance to act and speak, I wouldn't have thought of their insights and character traits at all. But once I've thought of those traits and insights, I can detach them from their origins like bits of clay and pat them onto other figures.

In looking for superfluous characters, do a thorough search of any whom you introduce near the end of a work. Sometimes they duplicate characters you introduced near the beginning but forgot to develop fully. Well, you *have* fully developed them, but under two names instead of one.

Think of your work as if it were a play. If your characters were actors, would they crowd the stage? Maybe you've cast two roles where there should only be one. As a fiction writer, you don't have to pay actors, but there are reasons of literary economy for trimming your cast.

On the other hand, maybe your stage is too bare. If Louie and Stella were the only characters in the story, it would seem thin. Even the most complex characters—which, as you may have realized, Louie and Stella are not—can become tedious company if they're a reader's exclusive companions for two-hundred pages. And it's hard to achieve richness in main characters if they don't interact with secondary characters who open up the scene and give them opportunities to show multiple aspects. I behave differently with my children than with my friends, differently with one friend than with another; they might be surprised at what they learned if they could see the whole range of my interactions. Every relationship between one character and a second character should show sides of their personalities that are different from the sides shown in their other relationships. Therefore, friends, relatives, and colleagues hang around the fringes of love stories; sidekicks go along on adventures; clowns pop up in tragedy; and villains and bystanders proliferate in all kinds of action, commenting chorally on fate, choice, and chance.

We can make similar points about superfluous plot lines and impoverished plot lines, but those are easier to discern than superfluous or impoverished characters. Causation is the criterion. And it's a material thing: if an event fits causally, you can state its effects. A leads to B, which in turn is causally connected to the rest of the plot. If I show Stella going out dancing with Griswold and resisting his advances, does it have a material effect on the plot? No: Stella goes home and does exactly what she would have done anyway with regard to Louie. Therefore, the dancing-with-Griswold scene is unfit. I worked a week on it; it's eight pages long; but I throw it out without a qualm. With a sense of relief, in fact, because I know I've improved the story.

The opposite problem occurs if there's a gap in the action: something is missing, but you don't quite know what. I might have to go back to the thinking stage, give myself a day or two away from the keyboard to stare at the ceiling until I know what Louie and Stella do and say in their next-to-last scene, where they have talked about parting but are still clinging to one another from fear of loneliness. Without something to fill that gap, they don't know themselves well enough and don't seem mature enough to justify their ultimate decision to reunite. It's a matter of pace, too: without something in that gap, the resolution happens too abruptly. So I send them to a furniture auction. Who shows up at the other end of the room but Griswold! Louie and Griswold engage in a vicious bidding war for a rolltop desk; Griswold is richer than Louie and forces him out with a heart-stopping last-minute raise of a thousand dollars, but Stella, who has seen Griswold's power plays before, is disgusted by his crassness and charmed by Louie's graciousness in defeat.

CONCEPT

What we're approaching here is the level of the work as a whole. What is its shape and pattern? What, essentially, are you trying to build? Whether or not you outline at the start, conceptual revision is an ongoing possibility, painful but sometimes necessary. The entire work asks itself Stanislavsky's questions—"Who am I? Why am I here? Where did I come from? Where am I going?"—and if it can't answer them satisfactorily, the work must be reconceived. Should Louie and Stella stay together at the end, the way I first thought, or should they break up? (Conceptual revision is especially common, and perhaps easiest, in endings.) What about the idea of Stella's wrong number—should I invent a more original way of having them "meet cute"? Should the love story of Louie and Stella take place in modern America or in medieval England? For that matter, should I write about Louie and Stella at all, or should I set them aside and turn to that science fiction novel I've been planning for years? These are revision questions at increasingly basic levels of concept.

Unlike the revision of details, where innumerable small decisions affect minuscule portions of the text, conceptual revisions involve a very few, very big decisions, each of which affects large chunks. The decision can occur in a finger snap, but once it takes effect, it creates big changes.

These decisions demand a lot of thought. You might find yourself pondering for a day, a week, or several months over whether to keep a first-draft concept or revise it. This is not wasted time. You may feel as if you're getting nowhere; be assured that your unconscious processes are going forward, slowly approaching a solution that, when it reaches consciousness, may feel like a bolt from the blue.

Making a radical change on insufficient grounds can be fatal to a writing project; not making it when it's called for, equally so; and trying to tell the difference, excruciating. Giving yourself time is the only way to ensure that you avoid an ill-considered decision. Sleep on any conceptual decision at least overnight. Beware of the impulsive decisions that you're tempted to make when you're in "down" moods, at times of artistic despair or external stress. If the decision is correct, it'll still seem correct after your mood picks up. If you're tempted to make an impulsive decision at a time of despair and the impulse seems wrong after your mood improves, trust your improved mood as more realistic.

ON DISCARDING PROJECTS

Every writer, from the greatest to the smallest, goes through painful emotions during the writing process. Learning to read those emotions is a skill in itself. There are many times when you have to write through the pessimism, the lagging confidence, the anxiety about success, and the doubts about your ability, just like an athlete playing with physical pain. There may be times when your mental pain is so great that you'd be wise to take some time off to heal, as an athlete might need to be put on the disabled list, because insistently continuing to work would harm your performance. The majority of the time, in my experience, mental pain is not a true indicator of a textual problem. A significant minority of the time, however, mental pain is a valid signal that something's wrong with your concept.

Writing would be a lot easier if it weren't so emotional—if it were just a "process," as it's sometimes called in textbooks. It's not just a process, it's a rite of passage you volunteer for; it's the ordeal of growing into your limits; it's a love affair with your own imagination, with all the approaches and avoidances, illusions and disenchantments of real love. I've described the four levels of revision in analytical terms for teaching purposes, but at every stage of the real work, emotion is the fuel. That's why work habits, the subject of the next chapter, are so important: destructive habits can make your writing the hostage of your mental life, delaying and weakening your output, while constructive habits can convert your emotions into work-energy.

The most important fact to understand about the anguish that accompanies writing is the same fact we all learn (most of us belatedly) about the anguish of puberty and adolescence, the anguish of setting out into the adult world and making a living, the anguish of dealing with life's failures: everybody goes through it. If you think, "I'll never make it, I'll never get anywhere, my writing is terrible," remember that everyone has thought the same thing—both the ones who got somewhere and the ones who didn't. The fact that you have the anguished thought means absolutely nothing as a predictor of success or failure. If anything, it means you're normal.

Sometimes your doubts are so great that you want to throw a project out. This too is normal. I would like to meet the writer who's never left a project unfinished. On second thought, I wouldn't like to meet such a writer; it would be too demoralizing. I've written unpublished novels—plural—since becoming a published novelist, not to mention before becoming one. Sometimes you're stuck and you just can't get moving. Sometimes you can't solve your dilemma at your present stage of development, but you'll be able to in a decade or so. Sometimes you're in the middle of one thing and you suddenly get a better idea and wish you could turn right to it. (Judith Rossner did that when she was working on *Attachments* and suddenly got the idea for her breakthrough novel, *Looking for Mr. Goodbar*. Later, rich and famous, she returned to finish *Attachments* and got a lot more money and attention for it than she would have otherwise.)

Knowing whether to keep going and finish a project or scrap it is the biggest conceptual decision. A few suggestions:

- If the decision seems a toss-up, keep writing till the decision becomes clearer. Perhaps you will finish the project without ever finally deciding to!

- Err on the side of staying on course; changing course requires a higher degree of certainty. Better to finish a bad story than to let a good one die, because bad ones, even among published works, greatly outnumber good ones. The good ones are treasures, blessings, to be cherished when they appear. And finishing projects is good discipline no matter what their quality. You can always decide to keep a story in a drawer rather than try to publish it; and you can let friends read it and give you more objective advice.

- Always keep a backup copy. If you make the romantic gesture of tearing up a manuscript, throwing it out, burning it, you've destroyed something you may later wish you'd kept, at least to reexamine for purposes of assessing your growth. Once you've decided to quit a project, it's not going to hurt you to keep a readable copy somewhere out of sight.

• If you're writing something as an assignment or to a deadline or under a contract, finish it no matter how much you hate it. Not turning in what you're obligated to turn in can be a serious detriment to your career. Believe me, I speak from experience. Much better to become known for delivering poor work than for not delivering at all; editors and teachers know that anyone can have a slump. They want to see that you are capable of fulfilling your responsibilities and turning out a product. If it's bad—and if they notice that it's bad, which is far from a sure bet—confess your sins and ask for help in making it better.

ON FINISHING PROJECTS

The four levels of revision are not independent during the real writing process, though there are certainly times when you could say to yourself, "Now I'm doing a diction change" as opposed to "Now I'm making a conceptual change." There may be days when you're occupied in diagramming plot trees and days when you're tinkering with sentences and scenes. Each broader level of revision, however, involves all the levels narrower than itself. If you decide to change a major concept, you'll want to make its structure of events economical and each scene within the structure effective and each sentence and word in each scene the best sentence and word; if not, if you just say, "I'm going to change that ending," and hurriedly rattle out a happy ending in place of a sad one, you've only substituted one first draft for another.

All four levels of revision have a planning component and an execution component, and in every case, in everything you write, you may have to go back to the thinking stage at any point, whether it's early or late in the process. This too is normal, and there's no need to be discouraged if, three pages before the end, you pull up suddenly and have to spend a week reconsidering what comes next or what has come already. Some of my working time consists of pure thinking, some of pure writing, and some of a mixture, every single day. (When you lapse into a thinking mode, it's a good opportunity to press "Save" on your computer.)

At any level of revision, you will at times be taking things out and at times putting things in. Many writers find that they alternate between the two in a rhythmic series. In the reworking, a draft contracts and expands like an accordion. I tend to add things in odd-numbered drafts and take them out in even-numbered ones: a fairly natural rhythm since the first draft is by definition a putting-in draft. Two or more putting-in drafts or taking-out drafts in a row, however, is not unusual. And of course, even if we broadly label a draft as "putting-in" or "taking-out," there will be individual words, lines, or passages within a draft that go against its general trend.

The accordion rhythm can sometimes seem like it could go on forever—and it probably could if writers didn't force themselves, sometimes arbitrarily, to stop. How can you tell when a work is finished? How do you know when to stop revising?

Well, "know" is a misnomer and "finished" is relative. We might consider a book that's been published to good reviews "finished," but the author, rereading it a couple of years later by the fireside the book enabled her to afford, might be appalled by its callowness and wish she could either do it all over again or bury every copy in the sand. You never know, and nothing is ever truly finished. You just have to accept your best, if you're sure it's really your best. And your best, you hope, is better than it used to be; the hardest you can work is harder than you've worked before.

Writers often say that a book is finished when they hear a satisfying mental "click," as if the story or novel is a box that, when carved to perfection, can be latched with a nice, final sound. I believe that when you hear this click, it means a *draft* is finished; it doesn't necessarily mean the work is finished. Send that tightly latched, perfect-seeming work to an editor and, after the editor accepts it and tells you she loves it, she'll point out a dozen ways you can still improve it. Follow those editorial suggestions—the ones you agree with—and you'll find, when you receive the galley proofs to correct, that there are hundreds of sentences you desperately want to tighten, rephrase, elaborate upon, or otherwise rescue from shameful amateurism. Cover the galleys with handwritten changes, and you'll find, when the book is in print and it's too late, that there are countless horrible mistakes you wish you'd caught in time—that the whole thing, in fact, is a spill you wish you'd wiped up.

For the nth time: this too is normal. Just heave your sigh and keep working on your next project.

Having said all this, I can think of a few ways you can tell when a project is finished:

- When the expansions and contractions of the accordion rhythm keep getting smaller and smaller and ultimately hardly visible— you've put all your ideas into effect and have no more.

- When, on rereading, your alterations don't seem to have improved the quality of the work—or have even lowered its quality—you've reached the point of diminishing returns.

- When you repeatedly make changes only to undo them—you've reached the point of paper-shuffling.

- When you can't tell the difference anymore—you've reached the point of exhaustion.

Feeling euphoric or despondent is not a reliable sign. Reliable signs are more likely to come when you're feeling calm and self-accepting.

If, when you write, you are consistently bored by your own work, in first drafts and revisions, near the beginning and near the end, it may be a sign that your work is genuinely boring and you should be doing something else. After all, it's hard to imagine readers sustaining interest in a story that doesn't interest its own author. Occasional boredom, or boredom at a particular stage, especially the revision stage, does not mean the same thing; it's another of those inevitables of the process. The longer the piece, the more likely you are to get bored at some point while writing it. Even consistent, chronic boredom may be a sign of inhibition—of being afraid to feel your own excitement over your writing—rather than of true lack of interest.

Others' opinions may or may not be reliable, and their reliability may not be directly proportional to your degree of intimacy with the advisor or to the advisor's professionalism. General readers often give better advice than professionals. Listen carefully to advice, wait at least overnight, and treat it as one factor in making your own decision.

And when it seems as if you've been revising forever, think back to your first inspiration, your vision of the work, your spontaneous first impulses. Did your rewriting help fulfill them? If so, it was productive rewriting; if not, it may have been counterproductive. Sometimes you may have to rewrite just to get back to where you began. For this reason, it's a good idea to preserve your first draft in pristine form and make a separate copy of it to revise on. This ensures that when you feel lost and dull and stymied and wish you could recapture the freshness of the initial idea, you can actually find it.

The great paradox of revision is that we polish our work tirelessly to make it spontaneous and quick. No matter how much you've scribbled over a passage, it should read as if you just thought of it that morning—and happened to think of it in the most lucid form possible. That's why it's valuable to rewrite from scratch at least some of the time, rather than revising on top of a dozen imperfect versions. Then, even the hundredth attempt is in a sense a first attempt—but with the advantage that you know about all the previous attempts. This method takes time and is impractical for long works, but it can resuscitate a passage you feared was dead.

The important question about a work of art is not, "Is it flawless?" or "Is it innovative?" or "Does it contribute to the intellectual dialogue of the moment?" The important question about a work of art is, "Is it alive or dead?" In Stendhal and Hardy and Dostoyevsky—those clumsy stylists!—in Manzoni and Gaskell and Frank O'Connor—those failures at exhibitionism!—we find a life so fine we wish we were in it. There are writers long buried who are living writers; and there are dead writers whose bodies are still moving around.

Ideal revision would make every version seem fresher than the one before. But revising can go on forever if you don't put a stop to it somewhere, and I could say the same about this chapter. So it stops here.

Do It

1. Revise a rough draft you wrote for one of the exercises in Chapter 14.

2. Exchange rough drafts of a piece of writing with another writer. It may be an exercise you did for Chapter 14 or for any other chapter or a work of fiction you drafted independently. Each of you is to review the other's draft, giving as much care to it as you would to your own work. Then, return the revised draft to the original writer to read. Discuss the merits and flaws of the revisions. Refrain from violence.

3. Choose a published short story that was written at least a generation ago. Revise it in your own style. Start fresh with a new draft rather than making changes on a copy of the old story. Make as many substantive, conceptual changes as you wish, as well as stylistic ones.

4. Retrieve a short story you wrote at least two years ago. Rewrite it in your current style. Start fresh with a new draft rather than making changes on the old copy. Make as many substantive, conceptual changes you wish, as well as stylistic ones. Make sure you improve the story.

5. Choose a story at random from the current issue of any popular magazine. Rewrite it according to the principles in Exercises 3 and 4. Give the two versions of the story to a friend or classmate to read; discuss the effects of your changes.

6. Show one of your recent works of fiction to someone you trust. Ask him or her to point out weaknesses and flaws and to suggest ways you might improve the work. Think about your reader's comments for at least 24 hours. Then rewrite the story, adopting the comments you agree with and ignoring the ones you don't.

7. Read a short story written by a friend or classmate, then write the author a memo giving your ideas on how to improve it through

revision. Then do the same thing for one of your own stories: read it and write yourself a memo.

Writer's Bookshelf

An American Tragedy by Theodore Dreiser (1925)
is perhaps the most sloppily written of all great novels. Try rewriting random passages for practice.

Stephen Hero by James Joyce (1955; corrected edition, 1991)
was the first draft of A Portrait of the Artist as a Young Man *(1916). Longer and much more conventional than the final product, it shows how far Joyce progressed during revision. A scholarly companion volume is Don Gifford's* Joyce Annotated *(1982; a revised edition of* Notes for Joyce, *1967), which contains Joyce's notes for* A Portrait of the Artist *and* Dubliners *(1914). A facsimile manuscript fragment of* Stephen Hero *was published in 1978.*

John Thomas and Lady Jane by D. H. Lawrence (1972)
is the second of three existing versions of Lady Chatterley's Lover *(1928), the once-banned novel that now looks sexually rather humdrum. Lawrence was mistaken to revise further, for* John Thomas *is a finer work than* Lady Chatterley: *richer characterization, lovelier descriptive writing, and less strident polemic. The first version has also been published, as* The First Lady Chatterley *(1944).*

Chapter 16

Work Habits, or, Do I Have To?

Once I lived in an apartment complex with a coffin-sized garden area in front. The plot was overgrown, dominated by one big, ugly bush, a weed the size of a young tree. I decided I was going to plant flowers there. First I tore up all the lesser weeds by the roots; that took a few hours. Then I took a handsaw and got to work on the counterfeit tree. Cutting it off at the stump and dragging away trunk and branches was the obvious, easy part. Digging into the soil, I found, in dismay, that each of the main roots was as thick as my arm. Each one had to sawed away separately, the soil around it dug up, and the entire root—twisting and narrowing for perhaps a yard until it hid under the pavement—pulled up by hand. Then I would have to go over the whole patch of soil, to a depth of two or three feet, making sure I hadn't left any roots behind that would grow again and starve out the flowers. It was a hot summer; I drank a lot of water, but no amount seemed to be enough; my skin was wet and my eyes stung from salty sweat. Then I realized something that made me stand up straight and laugh. I had done this kind of work before. I did it all the time. It was the work I loved best.

"This is just like writing a novel," I said.

For short stories, I have an equivalent analogy. Writing short stories is like planting flowers, one by one, all your life—digging the soil, planting the seeds, watering, pruning, keeping the bugs away—and never knowing whether or not any of them have bloomed. If you're lucky, perhaps, you'll see one or two or three of them bloom in your lifetime, amid a field of thorny branches.

Writing would be hard enough if it were just a matter of getting the words on paper and trying to find someone to read them. The real killer is trying to figure out whether the words are good enough. It's difficult to exaggerate the uncertainty, bewilderment, and isolation that are the normal, daily working conditions of the writer. If I said it's like volunteering for solitary confinement without being told the length of your sentence, that would not be an exaggeration but a realistic analogy.

Writing is made tough by the following facts:

- You have to generate your own work.

If you're an architect, a client comes up to you and says, "I want you to build a house," and has long discussions with you about what kind of house he or she wants. If you're a movie director, an agent or producer comes to you with a script, a book, a "treatment." If you're a fiction writer, you must come up with your own idea from nothing and see it through with little or no feedback from beginning to end.

- There's really not much demand for your work anyway.

This is true for all but a very few bestselling writers at the top of the commercial pyramid. Contrary to what the public imagines, no one is calling the typical published fiction writer on the phone and asking, "When can we see your new novel?" (I speak from experience.) Hundreds of novels that nobody notices are published each year. Many of them are by writers who previously scored hits. Plus, each year there are more people who want to write and fewer people who want to read. Editors know these things. They've seen writers come and go and they're not breathlessly waiting for anyone's new work. You are writing because you want to. Period.

- There's no objective yardstick for success.

If you're a politician, you know you've succeeded when you win an election. If you're a baseball player, you know you're good when you hit .300. If you're a writer, when do you know you're good? When you get published? Most published books fall quickly into oblivion, and if you're unpublished you can say, "They just don't recognize talent." When you write a bestseller? Most bestsellers are poorly written; they sell on the basis of concept, subject matter, sensationalism, and the writer's track record. When you win an award? Literary awards are given primarily on the basis of literary politics and only secondarily on the basis of excellence. When you write a classic? It doesn't become a classic until you're dead.

You can't know you're good, you can only feel good about your work; but your subjective feeling is not a reliable indicator of the work's value to others. T. S. Eliot said—as quoted in Jon Winokur's *Writers on Writing*— "No honest poet can ever feel quite sure of the permanent value of what he has written: he may have wasted his time and messed up his life for nothing." *T. S. Eliot* said that. And the same thing applies to fiction writers.

- You have no colleagues.

You may have fellow students or fellow teachers or fellow complainers; you may like one another personally and enjoy each other's company; but they are all, also, your rivals. None of them is working on the same project as you; all of them are in the same confused, isolated position as you; and they are all competing with you for a place in an eternally shrinking market. Most importantly, each of you has his or her own personal aesthetics, habits, and strategies, his or her own improvised method for trying to shape something beautiful in a fog. If you ask them for advice, all they can do is tell you their own individual methods, which, for you, may or may not be helpful. And that's assuming they have your best interests at heart. It may be asking too much to expect them to throw you their own lifeline.

To combat these difficult working conditions, you need the following:

- blind faith
- discipline
- devotion

Blind faith to get you started in this high-odds gamble and to help you shrug off the doubts and difficulties. Discipline to keep you advancing toward your goal with steady persistence. Devotion because having the ambition and working toward it are not enough; because if the work becomes mechanical, it is worthless; because one page of truth is worth more than a thousand you've filled up just to prove to yourself you could do it. If discipline is the ability to keep working whether you feel like it or not, devotion is the ability to feel like it.

The title of this chapter posed a question, and the answer to the question is No. You don't have to do it. You don't have to be a writer. If you aren't, the world won't know the difference.

You only ought to do it if you *have* to do it. Wanting to is not sufficient motivation; thinking it might be a nice way to live is not sufficient motivation. Writers do it because, for psychological reasons that would require a book in themselves to explain, writing makes them feel complete and worthwhile, and not writing makes them feel incomplete, inadequate, irritated with themselves and the world. If you can't say that about yourself, be glad. If you can't *not* say that about yourself, you are in danger of being a writer, and this book is intended as a cry of fellowship, a small lantern in the dark, a spiritual aspirin.

If you can leave it alone, do so, but if you have to do it, do it all the way. There's no harm in not being a writer. By deciding, "Well, I don't really want it that bad after all," you may save yourself years of fruitless struggle. However, if you are a writer, there's harm in not trying hard enough, or sticking to it long enough, to achieve something.

No one who has not been through it really knows how long it can take. The amount of naiveté with which writers begin their careers is colossal and probably adaptive. Talented people are admitted to excellent creative writing programs and sincerely believe that, after they get their degrees, they'll become successful, famous writers pretty soon. They are amazed to learn that you can be a star in grad school, get a job teaching at a good university, and not be able to sell your novel; or that you can sell your first novel, get good reviews, and not be able to sell the second. What if I told them that, yes, most of them are capable of becoming published writers, but most of them will have to work hard for years—often for a decade or more—before achieving it? That even if they succeed in publishing a story or a handful of stories in their twenties, and even if they get a teaching job, this is by no means equivalent to a stable career—no guarantee of future publications or of a job with tenure, as opposed to a life of academic nomadism?

We can always name a few people who have achieved early, stellar success, and we all have fantasies of being like them, but it's very important to realize that such success is the result of nonliterary as well as literary factors, and most of us, talented or not, have as much chance of achieving it as of being elected to high office.

In a situation like this, where you must do it all yourself and you can never be sure it's worth it, you had better buckle up. Your salvation is that you know you know how to do it. You can sit down at that console every morning, and by afternoon you'll have two or three pages, or whatever your personal daily product is. When you're young, you're prepared to do it for a long time; and when you're older, you look back and see that you've done if for a long time, and that feels good.

The reward for succeeding as a writer is not swimming pools, lovers, or interviews. The reward is that you get to keep writing. If that's enough for you, you can call yourself a writer. (If it used to be enough for you and it no longer is, you can call yourself a commercial writer.)

HOW WORK HABITS AFFECT QUALITY

Every writer has a different set of work habits. I can't tell you what yours should be. I can tell you what mine are, and I can point you toward developing your own.

I have a strong intuition that a writer's work habits affect the shape of his or her writings. If Flaubert and Simenon had traded work habits—the latter perfecting every sentence, the former zipping through a novel in ten days—they surely would have produced very different works from *Madame Bovary* and *The Little Saint*. Whether their works would have been better or worse than what they actually left us, I don't know. Sheer difference is what I'm talking about.

If you write three hours a day every day for forty years, your life's output will be quite different than if you write ten hours a day for one year, then cool off and write nothing for a decade, and then heat up and write ten hours a day for another year; or if you write nothing at all till you reach retirement age, then concentrate all you know into one big book. There's no guarantee that the first method will bring the best results, but it's where the probability is the highest. All else being equal, regular, long-term work habits are recommended. If the wise retiree had been writing for an hour or two a day all along, then her one big post-retirement book would probably turn out better, even if she'd thrown every previous page she'd written into the trash.

This brings us to the answer to the eternal question, "Why do I have to write so much bad stuff in order to write a little bit of good stuff?" The bad stuff is your equivalent of a musician's practices. Writers tend to think that they ought to produce something of lasting value every day; if they approached their work the way musicians or athletes do, knowing that most of the hours are practice, they might attain greater peace of mind. If our hypothetical sixty-five-year-old writer began writing her masterpiece with no previous preparation, all she could bring to it would be her wisdom; if she had already written forty years' worth of practice fiction, of which, let's say, one story was publishable, she would have wisdom plus craft.

Regular work habits help you in two major ways. First, they help you learn to finish what you start. But if that were all that regular work habits did for you, it would only mean that you would learn to write long, finished pieces of mediocre writing rather than short, unfinished ones. The real value of work habits is that they help you become inspired. They ease your entry into the concentration state I described in Chapter 13.

Basketball players talk about being "in a zone," a state of spontaneous rightness in which every shot seems to drop effortlessly through the hoop. Psychologists refer to it as "peak experience" or "optimal experience" or "flow." Sometimes I've thought of it as "writer's high," equivalent to runner's high, but it's a highly productive intellectual experience rather than empty euphoria. It happens to everyone, in every field, at certain unpredictable, transient moments. It happens to writers and other artists during scattered hours of heightened creativity.

The aim of regular work habits is not to maximize the amount of time you spend sitting at your desk. It is to maximize the amount of time you spend in the optimal state.

You can teach yourself to maximize it. It already happens naturally, from time to time, and you can extend those moments by extending the activities that you are doing when those moments occur.

Moments of inspiration may occur to you while you are sitting in front of your computer screen, while you are lying down looking at the ceiling, while you are drinking a cup of coffee fifteen minutes before turning the computer on, while you are exercising after your work session, and so forth. Your typical, everyday preparations, your cooling-down period, and the work activities they bracket are all conducive to arousing the concentration state. By making a ritual of them, you permit the concentration state to emerge day after day. At first, like a novice in any ritual, you will feel clumsy and doubt that your activities are doing any good. After performing the same actions trustingly, year after year, you will reach a point where your simple work habits place you in the concentration state most of the time. You will never reach the point where they put you in the concentration state all the time.

Most writers prefer working conditions that increase their privacy and quietness. That is an aid to contemplation. Few writers feel comfortable working when other people are in the room—although it's certainly desirable to be *able* to write with other people in the room, as Dickens could. A writer who can work in a noisy, populated room is either a superficial writer or a writer who's concentrating so deeply that he or she scarcely notices the presence of others, even when keeping up his or her end of the conversation. (The uniqueness of Dickens was that he was both.)

My own work habits are very average. While writing this book, I've been getting up at about eight o'clock in the morning and having a light breakfast and a big mug of strong, black coffee. I turn on the computer at about nine—any day I turn the switch on before nine is an exceptionally promising day. The effort of having gotten up, breakfasted, and turned on the computer usually wears me out, so I immediately fall back into bed for about fifteen minutes of first-rate ceiling-staring, assisted by the remnants of the coffee. At some point during this preparation, my gears shift; I know I'm going to be working pretty soon. If I feel a mild dread, that's a good sign, because I happen to suffer from fear of success: I dread the good writing that's going to come out of me, exposing my insides to the world and perhaps changing my life. Guilt, too, is starting to act on me—as well as, let's fact it, a simple love of writing—and I'm telling myself, "Quit stalling, it's time to work."

I'm so accustomed to the routine after all these years that the simple act of turning on my computer sends me into the fiction-state. I'm plugged in; I'm in cyberspace; the beautiful lake twenty feet outside my window belongs to another universe. I write fast in this state, but periodically my stamina gives out and I have to stare around, grooving on my screensaver, sometimes returning to the conveniently located bed to recharge my batteries and think of new profundities to type. The cycle of fast typing and stupefied staring continues for about two hours, by which time I generally have about three pages written. Then I stop. I know from experience that if I press myself to keep going, I'll be able to turn out a couple more pages, but they won't be as sharp, as fresh, as the first three; I'll be babbling, and I'll have to rewrite most or all of it the next day. In other words—dig this excuse!—writing a little bit *less* on a given day is often more efficient.

What I've just described is one work session, a personal, modular unit of time. Two sessions per day is ideal, but because of outside responsibilities, it's a rare day when I can fit in two sessions of fiction. The second session is usually in the evening, from about eight to about ten. I generally take afternoons off for errands, business correspondence, and exercise. Occasionally I'll have a work session in the afternoon and skip either the morning's or evening's session. I usually work at least one day each weekend, using the same rhythm I've described above.

You may have noticed something strange about these work habits: they seem revoltingly lazy and admirably diligent at the same time. (Or is it admirably lazy and revoltingly diligent?) I'm taking breaks, I'm lying in bed, I'm skipping sessions, I'm only working two hours at a time—and yet I'm sticking to a self-imposed schedule that allows me to write a book in a year or two or a story in two to four weeks. If I continue to be as lazy as this for another forty years, I'll have a long shelf of books with my name on them.

I have developed these work habits over a couple of decades while working full-time jobs or taking full-time care of my two children. I have written novels in the evenings, during my spare time from a hack job at which I wrote—this is a literal fact—a million words a year. I have written novels while my children napped.

The flexibility of my work habits, the allowance for my human frailties and my nonliterary responsibilities, is of the highest importance. It keeps me from feeling like a zombie and therefore helps me achieve the concentration state. And because my work is broken into two-hour sessions (sometimes they're one hour, sometimes three), I can write whenever there happens to be time available. If necessary, I can compress the warm-up phase—the cup of coffee, the staring at the ceiling—into five minutes and still, often enough, attain concentration.

I stick most closely to this schedule when writing first drafts. When revising, I can put in longer hours. If I've reached a point in the revision process where I'm polishing sentences rather than dreaming up new ideas, I put in six to eight hours a day, buffing ten to twenty pages.

I keep a rough idea in mind of where I want to be by a certain date, and if I'm ahead of my self-imposed deadline—which I usually am—I can take a day off whenever I want. After a day off, I'm feeling mildly guilty and return to work the next day with extra energy.

The days off, and the interludes between sessions, are not just for fun or for a sense of personal freedom. They are necessary because it takes time to think of ideas. On any given day, I've found, I have enough fresh ideas to fill up one, two, three pages. "Ideas" may be ideas for scenes, for plot threads, for aspects of characterization, for new stories, or whatever. On some days, I have no new ideas. I accept that fact. By submitting to a relatively disciplined, self-evolved work regimen *and* allowing reasonable departures from it, I maximize my concentration.

I put in shorter hours than most workers—even than most artists—but my activity during those hours is more intense and comes from a deeper part of my mind. Painters spend hours gessoing and stretching canvases; directors spend hours setting up lighting and camera angles; executives talk on the phone, space out at meetings, harass their secretaries, and look busy. Writers don't do any of that. It's all pure work, even the quiescent parts, and none of it is mechanical.

I can never be certain that these work habits have brought my achievement up to its maximum potential. Perhaps I would have achieved more if I worked eight hours a day like clockwork. Perhaps I would have achieved more if I indulged in all-night writing binges, separated by long stretches of bohemian experience-seeking. I don't know. All I know is that my work habits are compatible with my temperament and have allowed me to keep being a writer all my adult life. If I were omniscient, I would know how my work habits have limited my achievement, just as Simenon's limited his and Kerouac's limited his and even Flaubert's and Shakespeare's limited theirs. (My man Will could have done a lot more revising. Those last two acts of *Hamlet,* for instance! What a mess!)

That which permits you to do the work is also that which limits you.

I do recommend, in the strongest terms, remaining entirely sober while you're working. Malcolm Lowry, a legendary alcoholic, produced his only great work, *Under the Volcano*—a brilliant *description* of alcoholism—during periods of sobriety, before relapsing and drowning in his own vomit.

This brings up the question, "Should I devote my time to writing or to building up life experience to write about?" Some people write so much that their lives become vestigial; some live so much they lose the faculties they'd write with. Clearly Malcolm Lowry could have used a bit less experience of a certain kind.

There's no special kind of life that makes people writers and no need to seek out extreme or strenuous experiences if you are not an extreme or strenuous soul. You will find material no matter what. You can't avoid it. Don't worry if you have lived a "normal" life. That's worth writing about, too. There's no such thing as a normal life; every life, when closely examined, is extraordinary and interesting. Of course, if you hit the road, spend a year hitchhiking through South America, work on a oil rig, go through medical school, and return with the skill to write about it, that's a plus. The primary effect of such experiences, however, will be to make you a better hitchhiker, oil-rig worker, or physician, not a better writer.

Your work habits will vary in some individual way from what I've described, to a small or large degree. What matters is that you observe your own work experiences and develop a rhythm that reinforces your concentration state.

And after you've done so, what then? Good work habits alone will not make you a good writer; they can only make you a better writer than you otherwise would have been. I would be dishonest if I didn't point out that there have been a great many aspiring writers who worked industriously, dauntlessly, indefatigably, without success. Was it a waste of time, as Eliot implied? If you deprive yourself of a family life and social life for a year and end up with a pile of mediocre fiction no one wants to read, is that a waste? What if you do it for twenty years? What if you do it for twenty years and the result is a handful of mediocre published works that don't make you rich or famous? What if the result is published works that *do* make you rich and famous but aren't of high literary quality—and you don't enjoy fame and fortune as much as you might have enjoyed a family life? What if the result is high-quality fiction that doesn't get published? Or gets published but isn't noticed? Or brings you brief acclaim and is soon forgotten? Or brings you the status of a classic and the feeling that you've never lived? Eliot's self-doubts apply to every writer at every level of accomplishment.

I have solved this problem to my own private satisfaction by telling myself what I tell you at the beginning of each chapter's exercises.

Do It

1. Keep a log of your writing sessions for a week. When you look over your log afterward, what insights do you gain that might help you improve your work habits?

2. Discuss work habits with a group of fellow writers. It's quite possible you'll each glean some tips you can adapt to your own work.

3. Videotape yourself while writing, if you can stand it and you have the facilities. Watch the tape while trying to remember what was going on in your head, and on the page, at the time. What activities correspond to your periods of greatest inspiration or productivity? What activities seem not to have led to constructive results? Try to adjust your work pattern accordingly.

4. This is one I've never heard of anyone doing, have never done myself, and am suggesting only as an experiment. Make a pact with a fellow writer to observe one another's work sessions for a day or two and give one another feedback. Your findings may surprise you or may confirm what you already know about yourself. In either case, it will teach you something.

5. Force yourself to make a major change in your work habits for a limited period of time, say a week. If you have been writing in short stretches, try long ones, and vice versa. It might be particularly useful for writers who feel they can only work in solitude and silence to force themselves to work amid noise and company.

6. If you have been using an excuse—perhaps you call it a "reason"— to avoid writing, if you've been saying, "I wish I could write, but I don't have the time or energy because of (fill in name of obligation)," write anyway in your spare time, no matter how limited. If you have only an hour, write for an hour. If you have only half an hour, write for half an hour. If you only have the time when you're commuting or eating lunch, compose something in your head while you're commuting or eating lunch. By using what time you have, you will become an expert at expanding your opportunities.

Writer's Bookshelf

The Craft of Crime: Conversations with Crime Writers, edited by John C. Carr (1983),
is an informative set of interviews with writers who tend to be very much aware of the nuts and bolts of their trade.

Winged Words: American Indian Writers Speak, edited by Laura Coltelli (1990),
> contains interviews on work habits and a wide range of other topics with eleven authors, including Louise Erdrich, Michael Dorris, Paula Gunn Allen, James Welch, and M. Scott Momaday.

Writers at Work: The Paris Review Interviews, edited by George Plimpton (nine volumes and counting; 1958–),
> is the great ancestor of all compilations on this subject: an inexhaustible source of insight on the writer's calling. Interviews are first published in the literary quarterly The Paris Review, then periodically collected into book form. The tables of contents are rosters of internationally famous authors; being asked to participate is a high honor, and many of the interviewers, too, are eminent writers or critics.

Conversations with American Writers by Charles Ruas (1985)
> contains fourteen interviews; subjects include Eudora Welty, Toni Morrison, Joseph Heller, and Truman Capote.

The Confidence Woman: 26 Women Writers at Work, edited by Eve Shelnutt (1991),
> includes poets and essayists as well as fiction writers. It is valuable precisely because the writers tend not to be as well-known as the subjects of similar compilations.

The Writer on her Work: Contemporary Women Writers Reflect on their Art and Situation, edited by Janet Sternberg (1980),
> contains candid, inspiring articles by sixteen prominent writers, including Anne Tyler, Joan Didion, Maxine Hong Kingston, Erica Jong, Margaret Walker, Alice Walker, and Gail Godwin.

Black Women Writers at Work, edited by Claudia Tate (1983),

conveys advice, anecdotes, and inspiration from fourteen writers, such as Toni Cade Bambara, Nikki Giovanni, Ntozake Shange, and Gwendolyn Brooks.

Chapter 17

Audience

My ideal audience is a hundred thousand me's. Actually, a hundred would do. But, tragically, there's only one, and his visa for this world is temporary. So I have to find an audience among *other people,* a group that has baffled and tormented me all my life.

My hope, then, is to find other people who are like me. I don't mean I'm looking for other male, lower-middle class, Jewish Bronxites who emigrated to Midwestern college towns. Quite the opposite: the greatest delight would be to find someone with a very different exterior who was like me. A Frankfurt veterinary student who was like me; a Tokyo mechanic who was like me; a Soweto schoolteacher who was like me. My art would then serve its purpose of creating connections across boundaries, showing social categories to be illusory.

Most of the time, I don't think about audience at all. For years I had no readers; later I attracted a small number; someday I hope to attract more. But if the number and identity of my readers had a noticeable effect on what I wrote, I would be less of a writer than I hope to be.

One's audience is one's best self. That is really what people mean when they say, "I write for myself." I don't write for myself as someone who worries about the bills and has problems relating to authority figures; I write for myself as someone who loves beauty and seeks truth and hopes for freedom and justice. By writing for that self, I make it more possible, I hope, for that self to come into being.

On a more down-to-earth level, one's audience is most likely to be a teacher, an editor, fellow students, or a mate. Some of the best writers I know do not solicit opinions from such people, do not welcome their suggestions, and do not talk about work in progress. If outsiders' opinions agree with what your inner creative force is saying, you've neither gained nor lost anything; if their opinions differ from it, you're in a quandary. Of course, you may feel you're in a quandary *without* outside feedback; that's when it may be useful to get people's reactions. However, this creates the subsidiary quandary of whether or not to believe what they're telling you. It is good to learn to get out of your own quandaries. Workshops and support groups notwithstanding, we are not engaged in a communal activity. We are doing something we would do no matter who was there and whether they rewarded us or not.

If you feel things are going well, resist the temptation to fish for compliments; they can only distract you. After someone has praised an aspect of your writing—"I just love your descriptions of the setting"— you're likely to overdo and overthink that aspect, damaging its spontaneity. Once, I was staying at a country inn where the host was playing cocktail-lounge piano. At the reprise, he changed keys nicely. "Oh, I like that key change!" one of the guests foolishly said. Sure enough, the pianist changed keys every verse for the next two hours, driving us all crazy.

It happens from time to time that, after reading your finished work, your instructor will give you a B instead of an A; your editor will ask you to change the ending; your fellow students will remain silent instead of gushing enviously; your mate will change the subject to your holiday plans. This, alas, is when most of us are most keenly aware of our audience.

Writing for your instructor or editor is sometimes an unavoidable corruption; writing for your fellow students is simply a weakness; writing for your mate is insidious, almost impossible to stop doing, and doesn't even benefit your relationship. It is a supreme danger.

Some writers, lacking real audiences, write for imaginary ones. You write for the editor you hope will accept your book; for the critic whose review you prematurely write inside your head; for the standing-room audience at the reading you may never conduct. The fantasy can help you believe in yourself. Make sure, though, that your fantasy audience is a faithful externalization of your own values, not an internalization of alien values that you imagine will make your work acceptable.

Writing for the market, for what you think will either shock or comfort (the two are ultimately the same) the faceless masses into buying, not only cheapens your work but underestimates the audience. In addition, it is almost impossible for an inexperienced outsider to calculate market demands accurately. Reading in a popular newsweekly that a certain style is fashionable among the twenty-year-olds of the Pacific Northwest, you write a novel aimed exactly at that target—only to find, five years later, when the book is finished and you've been rejected by forty publishers, that the target has moved and the style is no longer fashionable. Attempts to meet a predetermined market need are almost always dated by the time they're finished, because entertainment trends move along a much faster time track than the writing and publishing of books (even of short stories, in many cases). The only exception occurs when the attempt is initiated by an insider, such as an editor who knows what his or her publishing house is going to want to promote in eighteen months.

Even if you do manage to anticipate a marketing trend with uncanny precision, the effort of doing so will probably rob your work of its vital force, its expression of an independent, unique spirit. And that's what people will want to read your work for—not for your uncanny ability to anticipate a trend.

Sometimes writers do meet actual flesh and blood members of their audience or receive letters from them. This is always nice; it's surprising and reassuring. They usually don't match our images of what our ideal audience would be like, though. Should I change my writing because I get fan mail from suburban women on the threshold of middle age rather than from doctoral students in Comp Lit? Neither reader has more intrinsic value than the other—some indeed belong to both categories—and I write what I want.

Growing away from one's audience is a problem many artists face. Rock musicians find that by the time they achieve stardom, they no longer identify with the adolescents who buy their albums. Some respond by quitting; some by pandering to a mass audience they don't respect; others by doing what they have always done; and others by changing and trusting that they'll find a new audience. Exactly what the makeup of that new audience is, they don't have to think about, though their handlers may wish they did. Strong artists are comfortable with the fact that their audience changes over time. The audience for Victorian fiction has narrowed since the Victorian age; the audience for Salinger, Steinbeck, Stevenson, and Kipling has grown younger. None of this invalidates their work.

ON SELLING OUT

In planning this book, I wondered whether I ought to discuss the question of audience or ignore it. After all, everyone knows that a true artist writes only for himself or herself; but if a true artist sneaks in a fantasy about being mobbed by adoring readers, it may be a helpful crutch. The reason I decided to write about audience is, paradoxically, that so *much* has been written about it in other books on writing. We live in a world where every presentation of the self has been reduced to salesmanship, and almost all communications, from political discourse to news to everyday conversation, are dumbed down. (It's impossible to write *up* to an audience—impossible to be smarter than you are.) I'm distressed by English education that views the targeting of an audience as one of the fundamental writing skills. I fear the rise of a generation who are expert at giving people what they want, not at saying what they believe; who will settle for the audience at hand, enthusiastically adopting its limitations, rather than seeking, improving, creating the audience they deserve, a process that may require doing without one for a while.

Writers used to write for themselves without giving the audience a thought. The result was a thriving, adventurous literature and an audience that was delighted by the innovations of its writers. Now, writers are advised to keep the audience in mind, and the result is a stagnant, imitative literature and an audience chronically unsatisfied by the bright, empty packages they buy—when they *do* buy—at the bookstore.

In ancient times—the 1950s—there was a phenomenon called "selling out." Let me explain this archaic term. A writer who had sold out was one who had sacrificed his or her artistic vision and personal integrity for the sake of worldly success. People used to *worry* about that—can you imagine! Those who did want success felt guilty. Others were authentically appalled at the thought of writing a bestseller, giving lots of interviews, doing a multicity tour, and taking a soft job at a university. They didn't *try* to make it happen as we do today. This was before writers reaped the benefits of the high-tech devolution and the mass-media devolution—before they learned that worldly success is not the most important thing, it's the only thing.

From our vantage point, we can only pity them.

Do It

1. Imagine that you have an audience. Describe it, or one representative of it, in a paragraph or so; or, if you're tired of writing by this point, draw a picture of it. How does visualizing this audience help or hinder your writing?

2. What kind of writing do you imagine that your imagined audience (in Exercise 1) would like most? Try to write that kind of fiction. How does it feel?

3. Try to write a short piece of fiction for an imagined audience that is different from your usual imagined audience. How does it affect your work?

4. Seek out an audience by presenting your writing to people who haven't read it before—perhaps by reading it aloud or giving photocopies to friends or relatives. Listen to their reactions, examine your counterreactions, and think about the extent to which you want their influence to determine your writing.

5. Form a mutual audience with a group of friends, colleagues, or classmates. Agree that you will always be available to read and respond to one another's work. Try to be your own ideal audience toward one another.

6. Do you write the kind of fiction you most like to read? If not, try to.

Writer's Bookshelf

The Writer's Chapbook, edited by George Plimpton (1989),

is a one-volume collection of pithy passages from the Writers at Work *series. The chapter "On the Audience" contains the views of Saul Bellow, W. H. Auden, John Cheever, William Faulkner, Margaret Drabble, Gabriel Garcia Marquez, Edna O'Brien, John Steinbeck, John Updike, and others.*

Part Three

PRACTICALITIES

Chapter 18

Writers' Ed.

The question is, "Should I take the academic route to a writing career—major in creative writing, go to grad school for a Master of Fine Arts degree?"

The answer is, "Unfortunately, yes."

There are drawbacks to the academic route—the foremost of which is the fact that it probably won't make you a greater writer—but there are big advantages from the standpoint of establishing a career. The best graduate programs in creative writing are, for a few people, highways to publication and recognition.

I did not take that route. I took the scenic route. I majored, idly, in anthropology and never went to grad school. I held jobs and lucked into publication. Sometimes I wonder what things would have been like if I'd taken an M.F.A. I doubt if I would have become either a better or a worse writer than I am today. As I've said, you tend to reach your own level of accomplishment. I think I would probably have become a more fashionable writer and a more orthodox writer. I think I would probably have learned how to incorporate the standard modernistic devices (see Chapter 12) into my work, instead of seeking the simplest technique for narrating any given story. I think that under the influence of peer pressure and instructor pressure, I would have written fiction that was less personal, more concerned with characters who don't resemble me, people I might become acquainted with by interviewing them or doing research. Perhaps my style would have been less "inward," with more descriptions of the outer appearance of things, the details of setting, and less exploration of characters' thoughts; more dialogue about external events, less confessional dialogue about psychodramatic issues.

The differences I'm describing are differences that might have made my fiction resemble more closely the fiction that's printed in the *Atlantic* and the *New Yorker*. People who go the workshop route tend to end up writing that way. It's the officially approved, acceptable way of writing realistic fiction, which has been dominant since the mid-1970s. It tends to be emotionally cool and to value narrative distance. Although enthusiasts of this kind of fiction often give lip service to the ideal of deeply exploring characters' emotions, in practice they flinch from it. The reader of this kind of fiction may feel that the author is observing the characters from outside, through a high-powered telescope, with patronizing irony. There are several writers of this kind of fiction whose work I admire, but somehow I can't seem to get the hang of it myself. I must have eaten too much chopped liver as a boy.

THE NETWORK

The pressure to write a certain way is quiet and cumulative; no one ever says outright that they want you to (although they may sneer at your sentimentality, or simply withhold comment, if you write in a more impassioned, less distanced way), but after a couple of years, you may find yourself doing it reflexively. If you go to writers' workshops, be aware of this pressure. It's up to you to decide whether to resist it and write another way or whether the workshop style is actually best for you.

There have been strong writers who went through grad school and retained, even intensified, their individuality. They probably would have done so in any environment. Meanwhile, they gained the social and political benefits of education, which are considerable.

In writers' workshops you will make friends. You will meet people who don't think it's weird that you want to write and love to read; people you can talk with about your frustrations and goals; people whose personalities may even resemble yours, proving that you *aren't* the only one. There's a family resemblance among writers; you're members of the same secret club, citizens of the same country.

Most writers I've met are highly intelligent and quick-tongued, with colorful backgrounds and an endless repertoire of moods; they are tolerant of eccentricity but somewhat set in their own ways, with sporadic social lives that alternate between periods of glum seclusion and ones of giddy guestship. They're dauntingly witty raconteurs and professional-quality gossips; it might be naive to depend on them when push comes to shove, but they make excellent dinner companions and most presentable escorts.

Some of them will become successful writers before you, and therefore they are contacts. Writers are notoriously envious of one another's success, but there's really no reason to be; if your classmate gets published, it increases rather than decreases the chances that you will. You now know someone who knows an editor and an agent. Your foot is inching toward the door.

The same thing can be said of your professors. At the grad-school level, they will be published writers or very close to becoming so. Their recommendations, their sponsorship, can enhance a student's career to a breathtaking degree. Editors and agents occasionally talk to them, asking who's new, who's on the horizon. They are the minor-league scouts of the publishing industry, not very powerful in themselves but possessing the capability to alter a career. These professors may nevertheless be struggling in their own writing and looking, like you, to widen their contacts; if they see you as a future success, they'll be just as eager to cultivate you as you them.

In short, you will be in the network.

There's a bus—figuratively speaking—that leaves Iowa City at the end of every semester, express for Manhattan, with stops at Knopf, Viking, Harper, and points around town. Get on board if you can. The people on that bus (and those departing from other campuses) are the only exceptions to the rule that it gets tougher all the time to break into publication. It got easier for them throughout the seventies and eighties, though it has flagged a bit since.

That's the most glowing scenario, the case of the unknown writer who stars in grad school, is ushered enthusiastically into the offices of a publisher, "discovered" by reviewers, and made an instant celebrity. It's important to understand that only a very small percentage of students are that lucky. Even the ones who are are only that lucky for a short time. Everyone in the network *knows* people like that, but very few *are* people like that.

The world of workshops can be a cruelly hierarchical place. Some faculty tyrant used to assign military ranks to writers based on prestige: if you self-published, you were a private; published in obscure quarterlies, a lieutenant; in well-known quarterlies, a colonel; and if you published in the *New Yorker,* you were a general. This kind of vicious nonsense ("Corporal Kafka, reporting for duty!"), uttered by failed masters and repeated in giggles by anxious apprentices, can make grad school a much more stressful experience than it need be. There's a lot of snobbery, status-mongering, and velvet-gloved competitiveness at these places. Remind yourself that it's all part of your education.

At least after you and your classmates have gotten degrees and scattered to teaching jobs, you'll have friends you can visit all over the country.

WHEN TO ENTER GRAD SCHOOL

If you decide to get an M.F.A., planning when to do it is crucial. This isn't medical school, where the earlier you enter, the better. Going straight through from college to grad school is the exception in this field, not the norm, and being in a hurry is not the best way to become a writer. Writers are ready at different times. The best time to enter is when you are on the threshold of literary maturity: when you've already written a good deal of fiction, making noticeable progress, and have begun to consolidate a style of your own. The ideal is to time it so that when you leave school, you have a manuscript—a novel or a sheaf of short stories—that's ready for publication. It's a mistake to expect graduate school to form your style for you; it's smarter to arrive with your style already mostly formed. This is a matter of careerspersonship. Also, if you already have a style when you get there, there's less chance that you'll be tainted by the orthodox workshop style.

You may be twenty-five when you enter grad school, or thirty-five or older. You may even be twenty-two, but that's least likely. Writers who enter graduate programs so young are in many cases not making the best of their opportunity. Talent and ambition mislead them into going through the process prematurely. At the end, they have more growth left to do than they expected. They emerge armed with their address book full of contacts, their briefcase of recommendation letters, and a manuscript; shivering with confidence, they call their professors' agents, one of whom accepts them for marketing—and the manuscript doesn't sell. They have been psychologically thrown for a loss and no longer have their group to pick them up. Of course, they may pick themselves up and achieve success later, but my point is that their timing has not allowed them to exploit their education to greatest advantage.

What's more, they don't have as much material to write about as they would have if they'd taken a break after college. If you work at a job for a year or two before going to grad school, you'll have that much more understanding of the world and that much more to write about. If you've held jobs, had one or more serious romantic involvements, perhaps started a family, you are in a vastly superior position as far as material is concerned. You may worry that you've missed years of writing time or learning time, but it's a groundless worry. There's a kind of equalization in literary careers; writers who start late tend to catch up. One of the very nice things about the grad school environment, helping counteract the competitiveness, is that everybody is accepted as a member of the group regardless of history, personality, or age. As Jesse Lee Kercheval has sagely observed, you begin counting your age again, from zero, when you enter an M.F.A. program. The people in your class year are the same literary age as you, whether their chronological age is twenty or forty.

Grad school is a great place to develop a literary persona and acquire a final layer of polish, but if you're seeking to learn the rudiments of the craft, take some extra undergraduate courses or spend some time in a community-based writing group. This will place you on a more even footing with your future grad school classmates, not to mention giving you a better chance of being admitted to the program in the first place. It also allows you to test the waters before making a full commitment. And it gives you an external motivation to write, if you need one.

Writing courses are perhaps most worthwhile for a kind of person I described in Chapter 16: people who say, "I'd like to be a writer," but have never gotten around to it. Enrolling forces you to test the reality of your hopes. There are disadvantages in the semester framework, however: your phases of productivity might not correspond to the instructor's schedule. And in a single semester, writing anything longer than a novella is practically out of the question.

As for learning how to write, there's no way to know beforehand which school will be best for you or whether school will be better than real-world experience. It's like picking a doctor, and then, at the office, hoping you'll get cured and not catch another patient's infection.

Do It

1. Research the creative writing programs available at the undergraduate or graduate level. Send away for grad school or college catalogs and application forms; talk to your teachers and anyone else you know in the writing field. Find out where and when the writers you admire have gone to school. Learn which distinguished writers are at which universities. Then continue the process: write letters to those writers, asking for advice, and apply to the schools if you think you're ready. Let the momentum of your search carry you along so that, if you're undecided, you'll keep progressing, perhaps encountering unforeseen opportunities.

2. If you're a relative newcomer to writing, or have limited time and mobility, enroll in a course at the local level and/or join a local writers' group as a proving ground for your ambitions and a training ground for your skills. Junior colleges, technical colleges, and extension schools often have excellent writing courses, taught by graduates of top M.F.A. programs (given the scarcity of tenure-track jobs at four-year colleges).

3. If you're looking for a writers' group and can't find one you like, form one. Ads for writers' groups are often found in free neighbor-hood newspapers and on bulletin boards in grocery stores, laundro-mats, community centers, and so forth.

Writer's Bookshelf

***Writing Past Dark: Envy, Fear, Distraction, and Other Dilemmas in the Writer's Life* by Bonnie Friedman (1993)**
> *is a well-written, honest memoir of the author's experiences as a grad student, creative writing teacher, and aspiring fiction writer. Friedman urges us to transcend the subtitle's emotions; despite them, she obviously gained a great deal from formal education.*

***The Iowa Writer's Workshop: Origins, Emergence, and Growth* by Stephen Wilbers (1980)**
> *is the semiofficial history of that institution, published at the beginning of a boom decade.*

Chapter 19

Careers

People who have gone to grad school tend to think that the only career available to a writer is teaching creative writing. It isn't true. Before there were such things as creative writing courses, writers made their livings somehow. Today, they still make their livings in those old ways and in some newer ways as well. Many of these jobs involve writing or editing. Others don't but have become traditional for writers in the same way that waiting on tables is traditional for actors. I'll examine a number of means of survival for creative writers, starting with the ones that most closely involve writing and working my way outward. The list won't be all-inclusive, because writers often invent their own career niches, and because a writer can make a living any way anyone else can.

MAKING YOUR LIVING WRITING FICTION

This is such a long shot that no one ought to count on it beforehand. The main prerequisite is luck. If your work is both skillful and fashionable, you may become one of the few who make a public impact early in their careers and parlay it into earnings. Some great artists have done it, as have some talented, honest writers whose work did not survive their eras, as have a good many sincere commercial writers. Serious artists who succeed in the blockbuster universe often do so at its fringes and need to supplement their royalties with grants and fellowships. Bear in mind that even after success comes, writers' careers are still subject to the vagaries of market demand and the unpredictability of inspiration. Your first novel may be trendy, but the trend may change before you publish your second. Or, having succeeded, you may lose your inner drive and start repeating yourself rather than climbing to new peaks.

If you score an early hit, hire a good money manager. It's better to set up a comfortable but modest lifestyle and invest your earnings than to blow it all on a mansion and a sports car. That way, you can keep writing what you want to, rather than turning out uninspired hits to pay a whopping mortgage. Innumerable promising writers have failed to fulfill that promise after a big, early success; one reason is that they become accustomed to a standard of living that requires all their books to be bestsellers. Their later books don't come with labels saying "Hack Job—Beware," but astute readers and critics can sense that the writers have lost something. What they've lost is their innocence; they're writing to pay the bills.

In starting out, it's best to assume you will not be able to make your living writing the kind of fiction you want to. That assumption is 99 percent likely to prove correct. If it proves incorrect, it will still prepare you to deal constructively with the problems of success.

WRITING SOME OTHER KIND OF FICTION

This can be an honorable career path or a sleazy one, depending on the kind of fiction and on your attitude toward it. If your serious fiction isn't selling, you may find you can sell genre fiction: suspense thrillers, science fiction, gothic romance, or horror, for example. You may be proud enough of your genre work to publish it under your own name, as Graham Greene did, or you may do it under a pseudonym, like Gore Vidal, who in the 1950s became the mystery writer Edgar Box. If you make a sale in a genre, there's a good chance of establishing a steady track record and making a living from advances and royalties.

For best results (as they say), do the work honestly. Pick a genre for which you have genuine affection and respect, one you've enjoyed reading. It's okay to view your genre work as less serious than your "real" writing, but it's dangerous to feel contempt for it. Better to view the genre work as a hobby, even if it brings in more money than your primary work. This is a delicate mindset to achieve. Preserve a clear distinction between your serious and your commercial writing, but approach both as a diligent artisan. It would be self-deceptive to think, "I'm going to transform the spy thriller genre through my superior gifts, creating high art in a popular form." The chances of doing that are no greater than the chances of writing an esoteric bestseller. But it's equally self-deceptive to think, "Alas, I must wade through the muck of shlock fiction in order to finance my art." It's hard to write while you're holding your nose. Many is the ambitious but second-rate literary writer who found he or she was a first-rate genre writer instead—a worthwhile trade-off.

The rung below honest genre fiction is fiction done for hire at a breakneck pace: cheap paperback romances that you turn out at a rate of one every two to four weeks, using a pen name such as "Loretta Von Swett" when your real name is more like Gerald Torres-Horowitz. Many romance writers are sincere fans of the genre; others are hacks with bad attitudes. This kind of work is okay for a short time if you need cash, especially if you're young and don't have a family to support and find the grubby side of the literary life glamorous. It can get you used to filling up pages quickly—for better or worse. It can also burn you out.

The major problem with writing genre fiction for money is finding time to write your other fiction.

WRITING NONFICTION

Nonfiction traditionally sells better than fiction. It's an easier market for unknown writers to enter. Writing nonfiction is also easier than writing fiction, since you don't have to make up your story line and characters. All you have to do is find an attractive, timely subject and apply the skills of your craft to it. Many writers who've had difficulty getting their fiction published, or who've gotten it published without big financial returns, have established their names in nonfiction. Piers Paul Read, a highly respected but obscure British novelist, achieved fame and increased his later fiction sales with a bestselling nonfiction book about a plane crash, *Alive*. The American novelist Evan S. Connell has not had sales to match the quality of his fiction, but his nonfiction study of General Custer, *Son of the Morning Star,* became a major bestseller. Conversely, several writers have published bestselling novels as follow-ups to nonfiction bestsellers with no previous fiction credits. Nonfiction in our era is becoming more personal in tone, its techniques merging with those of fiction. Even a computer manual, *The Macintosh Bible,* expresses the distinctive personalities of its authors, who interrupt one another in the course of the work.

At a time when the audience for serious literature is declining, the ability to cross over into nonfiction has been a lifesaving compensation for some fiction writers and poets. It's certainly saving *my* life at this very moment.

WORKING IN PUBLISHING

A time-honored route. Some textbooks belittle it; I found it an excellent way to establish a writing career. My first job out of college was as a manuscript reader for a literary agency; I got it by taking a test that consisted of reading and evaluating a short story. It was not the most high-toned of publishing venues, but it gave me the contacts who sold my first two novels, and it taught me a lot about writing and marketing. To work for a publisher or agent is to learn what kinds of fiction get marketed and why. That can be a disillusioning experience. If you're undeterred—if you can keep faith in your personal vision after learning that publishing is a mercenary business—it can strengthen you. Toni Morrison and E. L. Doctorow are two distinguished contemporary novelists who built successful first careers as editors.

The major problem is that it's a low-paying, overworked field. Another problem is that it's a many-branched business in which most of the jobs are not in the glamorous, literary branch. If you're hired as an editorial assistant at a prestigious publisher or literary magazine, it gives you personal contacts who can boost your career as a fiction writer; if you're hired as a production assistant (helping oversee the physical manufacturing of books rather than their acquisition and editing) or a copy editor or layout editor or publicist, it's a worthy credential but gives you fewer such contacts.

The unglamorous work is what gets books and magazines into print. These are respectable jobs, and many college graduates enjoy doing them; they can involve writing (for instance, writing jacket copy for books or press releases) but offer few opportunities for meeting influential people.

Still further from the "core" are jobs on trade journals and other specialized publications. If you work for a magazine of the pet food industry, a magazine for motorcycle enthusiasts, a labor union newsletter, a journal of engineering abstracts, or whatever, you can build a solid middle-class career that uses your writing and editing skills—period. You won't be any closer to becoming a famous writer than if you were a cabbie or a cop, but you'll be surviving by using words.

Help-wanted ads and employment agencies are good places to look for the unglamorous, bread-and-butter publishing jobs. The more prestigious entry-level jobs are infrequently advertised and often filled by word of mouth. Many are filled by people with degrees from the finest colleges—sometimes master's degrees—and recommendations from figures in the literary world. If you're looking for a glamor job in publishing, be prepared to initiate the job search with slick-looking letters and résumés, and be prepared for a lot of semipolite rejections. It helps a great deal to have edited a college literary magazine and to have taken summer courses in publishing. (Radcliffe College and New York University give the most prestigious publishing courses; there are several other fine ones.)

To find out where the book and magazine publishers are and who to contact, consult *Literary Market Place*—its friends call it *LMP*. This fat handbook, updated annually, is the standard reference source for the publishing industry. It contains the address and phone number of just about every American publisher, literary agency, and publishers' service (such as book design, typesetting, advertising), along with the names and titles of editors. It is available in good public libraries and some book-stores. Other valuable reference sources are the annual editions of *Writer's Market, Novel and Short Story Writer's Market,* and the *International Directory of Little Magazines and Small Presses.* The magazine *Publishers Weekly* is the trade journal for the publishing industry; its articles are worth reading to acquaint you with the trends, leaders, and general spirit of the industry, and it has some classified ads, though not usually for entry-level jobs. Another magazine, *Poets & Writers,* published in newspaper format by Associated Writing Programs, provides vicarious immersion in the world of serious writing: articles on small presses, ads for small-press books, notices of fellowships and contests, and interviews with writers; it might give you some ideas about where to apply for jobs.

EDITORIAL SERVICES

Shocking as it may sound, many books are not entirely written by the people whose names are on the covers and not entirely seen into print by the publishers whose logos are on the spines. Increasingly, the development and packaging of books is being farmed out to intermediaries, small companies known as "book packagers" or "development houses." The book packager, typically working out of a small office or even an apartment, hires writers, editors, and designers to meet publishers' specifications and deadlines; this reduces publishers' overhead, since freelancers, unlike in-house editors, aren't paid benefits and don't take up office space. If you hook up with a thriving development house—and if the developer itself remains in business—you can often enjoy an ongoing relationship through a series of short-to-medium-term projects for a variety of clients on a variety of topics: you may find yourself writing entries for a biographical dictionary one month and articles for an encyclopedia of woodworking the next. There are brisk periods and slack periods in the book development business, and you may be lucky enough to send your résumé to a developer who happens to need an extra freelancer to fill a slot on a project. Developers are reluctant to take on novices, because a developer's business depends on its reputation for delivering competently completed assignments on schedule. If you can wangle a personal recommendation from another writer or editor and can claim expertise on the subject of a developer's current project, it helps a great deal. Sending a writing sample is a good idea. It's best to send a published piece in its printed form; next best, a published piece in manuscript form; next best, an unpublished but well-written piece. Its topic and format should be as close as possible to those of the projects you hope to work on.

Similar conditions apply to ghostwriting. Celebrity autobiographies, novels with celebrity bylines, and a wide variety of general nonfiction are ghostwritten. There is a hierarchy of ghostwriting prestige: it's best to be listed as coauthor ("By Susan Celebrity and Richard Writer"), next-best to be listed as a "with" author ("By Susan Celebrity with Richard Writer"), next as an "as told to" author ("By Susan Celebrity as Told to Richard Writer"), next to be left off the byline but included in the acknowledgments ("special thanks to Richard Writer for his invaluable editorial assistance," or other code words), least-best to be unlisted. Ghostwriters whose names are on the cover usually share the royalties. Other ghostwriters—and they make up the bulk of the profession—get paid on a work-for-hire basis, either by the hour, by the page, or for a flat fee. The ghostwriter is an independent contractor and negotiates each project separately with the publisher; and the publisher, as always, has the advantage of knowing the terms of other writers' contracts.

As an entry-level ghostwriter, you are likely to belong to the unlisted, work-for-hire category, unless you arrive on the scene with high-level credentials in the field you're ghostwriting about. For instance, a well-known rock music journalist hired to ghostwrite the autobiography of a rock star may be able to work out a deal for coauthor credit and royalties.

How to become a ghostwriter? The easiest way is to move laterally from another field. Sportswriters end up ghosting sports stars' autobiographies; movie critics end up ghosting film stars' memoirs; and so on. If you're straight out of college and don't have a name in some field of expertise but are relying solely on your writing skills, it's harder. There are ghostwriters' agencies that farm out projects to freelancers; some are listed in the "Editorial Services" section of *LMP;* send a résumé and writing sample. They take care of the contractual negotiations, but they take a cut. A flukier way of becoming a ghostwriter is to work in publishing and to happen to be around when an editor expresses a need for a writer. If you're a published writer looking for extra cash, tell your editor and agent that you're available for ghostwriting assignments—and keep reminding them.

There's a wide range of other literary services for which people get paid, and most of those people are aspiring writers. People get paid to edit and revise academic manuscripts and theses (especially those written by nonnative speakers of English), to do research for writers, to read and critique manuscripts, to teach creative writing for correspondence schools. Some of these activities are on the border of respectability; some are on the wrong side of the border. For instance, it is considered sleazy to charge writers a fee to read and assess their work. Nevertheless, some people do it—my first employers did it. Again, the "Editorial Services" section of *LMP* is a good place to look for employers of this kind. You can take out an individual listing for yourself, too, though if you don't have a track record, you're more likely to find work through an agency.

The yellow pages are a potential source of employment ideas, in their "Editorial Services," "Publishers," and "Writers" sections. Though the American publishing industry has traditionally been centered in New York and Boston, computerization has spurred decentralization. New literary presses keep sprouting up all over. In the nonliterary sector, any city of appreciable size is likely to have publishers who serve local businesses, universities, and government, as well as magazines aimed at the regional audience. They all use writers and editors, sometimes on-staff, sometimes freelance. Nonprofit associations, such as the American Bar Association and the American Medical Association, have been dependable sources of work for many freelance editors.

JOURNALISM

This classic career for aspiring fiction writers has become less popular in the past generation and deserves to become popular again. American novelists from Mark Twain to Joan Didion have started out as reporters. It gave them knowledge of the world, gave them subjects to write about, and taught them to write concisely and vividly. The rise of academic creative writing has meant that most aspiring fiction writers now go to grad school rather than looking for jobs on newspapers, magazines, or wire services. In turn, the fact that fewer creative writers enter journalism means that there are fewer usable connections between the world of reporting and the world of fiction publishing. Nevertheless, it's still a good way to earn a living by writing.

It's not necessary to be a journalism major or have a master's in journalism to become a reporter. Many news editors—and not just the older ones—look down at journalism school. They know that the best training for a reporter is to work on a college or small-town newspaper. Nor is it necessary to begin as a reporter; you might begin as an office flunky for a newspaper or a researcher for a magazine or television station.

ADVERTISING AND PUBLIC RELATIONS

Another classic career for aspiring writers, similarly less popular than it was in the past and for similar reasons. Advertising copywriters write commercials for television and radio, ads for newspapers and magazines, and posters and billboards for roadsides and buses. Public relations writers write press releases, speeches, brochures, newsletters, direct mail letters, and other assorted publicity materials for clients. In both fields, there are big, general, national agencies as well as smaller, local, or specialized agencies. Some agencies specialize in a particular medium, such as radio ads; others specialize in content areas, such as ads for movies. The primary reference book in this field is the *Standard Directory of Advertising Agencies,* published three times a year, with monthly supplements, by National Register Publishing Company. The yellow pages listings for "Advertising Agencies" and "Public Relations" are helpful local sources.

People who want to become copywriters or p.r. writers often start out as entry-level office workers or researchers. A very nice thing about advertising agencies is that the biggest ones conduct in-house courses to train their employees in copywriting.

TECHNICAL AND BUSINESS WRITING

Technical writing may range from an instruction manual for a software program to a book of specifications for sewage treatment. There is a steady demand for people who know something about a technical or scientific field and can write clear English. As more new technologies arise, there's every reason to expect that the demand will increase. Writers who can explain computers to laypersons can usually make a living at it. Technical manuals are produced by businesses, government agencies, and the military. Some are produced by in-house employees; some are farmed out to agencies specializing in technical writing within the given field. The yellow pages' "Writers" section may contain the names of technical-writing agencies in your city. A master's degree or undergraduate major in a scientific or technical field is a plus.

Business writing is a very diverse field. Let's say you're the International Breakfast Cereal company. Somebody writes the drivel on the sides and back of the cereal box, which millions of glaze-eyed breakfasters read every morning; somebody writes the speech the chairperson of the board gives at the annual convention of the Breakfast Cereal Makers of America; somebody writes the brochure that explains IBC's health-care plan to its employees; somebody writes the company house organ, "International Breakfast Cereal Facts 'n Faces Monthly"; somebody writes the five-hundred-page *Brief History of International Breakfast Cereal,* a copy of which sits on the shelves of all three thousand IBC vice presidents; somebody writes the annual and quarterly reports that IBC sends to its stockholders. Not only does somebody write each of these, but somebody edits and proofreads them. Some of these writers and editors are in-house: IBC employees working in the public relations department. Others are freelancers working for public relations or editorial service agencies. In-house jobs can be found through employment agencies or through the personnel departments or (preferably) p.r. departments of the corporations themselves. If you're not sure whom to send a résumé to at a huge corporation, you can simply call up and ask a receptionist.

EDUCATIONAL WRITING

Educational publishing is perhaps the biggest single branch of nonliterary publishing, and it's what I know most about—I've made my living at it since I was in my mid-thirties. The warhorses of the field are the big, multivolume basal programs—*Adventures in Postmodern Multicultural Literature Grade 10, Adventures in Pomo Multicult Lit Grade 11,* and so on. These series take years to plan and produce, and the successful ones are revised in edition after edition as pedagogical standards in this wacky land of ours keep changing. Most are national; some are local, such as textbooks on the history of a state. For each volume there is a pupil's edition and a teacher's edition, in which the answers to questions are given in the margins, along with annotations suggesting activities. There may be a separate teacher's manual as well, rehashing the annotations in a separate form. There is also an assortment of ancillary materials: worksheets to keep pupils busy; transparencies for teachers to copy and distribute; packets of activities generated by the lessons; and guidelines on how teachers can assess students' work. Aside from basal programs, there are also textbooks in more limited areas: a multivolume grammar text, for instance, or a one-shot creative writing manual, for that matter. Textbooks on the school level tend to be written and re-written by teams of freelance writers and editors, recruited either directly by the publisher or by a development house; those on the college level tend to be written by the one or two professors whose names are on the cover, perhaps with assistance from editors or graduate students.

The ideal writer of school-level educational materials has teaching experience at the level the text is intended for. Retired or burned-out schoolteachers sometimes enter this field; practicing teachers sometimes do it as a second job. However, it's common for publishers to hire teachers to write textbooks and then to find that the teachers' work needs professional revision. That's how I got into this line of work: I knew an editor who had a relatively easy project—a teacher's manual—that needed revision. By rewriting other educational writers' work, I learned the methods and lingo of the field. Having completed one assignment, I had a writing sample I could send "cold" to publishers. To find the names of editors, I looked in *LMP* for the listings of textbook publishers and of development houses that listed "el–hi" (elementary to high school textbooks) as their specialty. I wrote to the executive editors in my fields of interest (language arts and social studies).

JOBS THAT DON'T INVOLVE WRITING

Police work, medicine, law, the military, the foreign service, espionage, and the clergy are professions that expose their practitioners to life and death situations. Even one year in such a profession can give you a career's worth of literary material. Numerous great and good writers have continued to practice these professions while writing fiction in their spare time. It is eminently sensible to plan on this from the start. The drawback, of course, is that these professions are true vocations in their own right, consuming not only time but emotional energy; being a writer in addition burdens you with a second vocation. A surprising number of writers find that they are able to handle it; energized by their full-time jobs, they turn gratefully to writing as an outlet for observations and feelings built up at work, which they wouldn't otherwise have time to discharge. Some of these professions involve writing: legal briefs, sermons, debriefings, and what have you.

I would add homemaking to the list, though it has not been an income-producing job in our society. A homemaker is in the thick of the best kind of literary subject matter: private life, the family, marriage. The job usually leaves little spare time for writing, of course, and thus is comparable to any of the others on this list. Homemakers who write and who have preschool-age children have to steal time for their writing in the few hours when the kids are napping or at nursery school. It gets easier when the kids are old enough to be at school all day. The advantage is that you don't have to travel to the job. That saves a little time. The emotional disadvantages of homemaking—isolation and low socioeconomic prestige—are major incentives to do creative work. At least they were in my case. I was a homemaker for six years, with full-time care of two preschool children and full responsibilities for the usual tasks such as shopping, cooking, and laundry; in that time I wrote two published novels. Was I frustrated by the conflicting demands on my time? Yes. Did I complain? Sometimes, though in retrospect I feel I had nothing to complain about. Am I glad I did both things at once? Very. Could I have written more if I had held a full-time paying job? The answer is not obvious. As I've said, writing rarely requires eight hours a day. Make a two-column list of the great works of fiction; in one column list those written by people of leisure, and in the other, those written in the spare time of people under economic pressure. I'm not sure which list would deserve the laurel.

There are other jobs that don't place you in the thick of crisis in quite the same way as police work but still put you in touch with a broad spectrum of humanity: cab-driving, schoolteaching, psychotherapy, and social work are examples. The difference here is that the jobs themselves are not as interesting to write about. Doctors' and lawyers' "war stories" are more likely to make exciting fiction than cabbies' stories of their eccentric fares or teachers' stories about students and administrators.

The truth is, writers can support themselves, and have done so, doing any job imaginable: farming, fishing, manual labor, secretarial work, business, and so on ad infinitum. Some have found their material in these professions; some have merely used their jobs to pay the rent.

Jobs that offer good pensions after relatively short service are perhaps the best way to finance a writing career that starts in middle age. If you enter the military at eighteen, you can retire at thirty-eight with a pension and write full-time for the rest of your life. Something similar happens to homemakers after their kids leave the nest.

TEACHING

So far in this chapter I've discussed alternatives to the teaching of creative writing. But what about that profession? I think it's a good choice if it suits your temperament. The big advantages are that you're in a network of contacts and that your work is directly related to writing. You think and talk about writing all the time. Some creative writing professors feel that their jobs require them to think and talk about writing *too* much, and that once they're finished reading and discussing their students' stories, giving introductions for colleagues' readings, participating in writers' confer-ences, and attending committee meetings, they have no creative energy left for their own work. They concentrate on their writing during vaca-tions, and sometimes they wish they had jobs where they didn't have to use their minds and pens and voices so much. Whether you're the kind of writer who prefers to make a living in the creative writing milieu or far from it is a question experience can answer for you.

As I write this, the job situation for creative writing teachers on the college level is a tough one. Tenure-track jobs, which lead to permanent, stable careers, are increasingly scarce, and many fine writers find that they have to scratch together a living from a visiting professorship here one year, somewhere else the next year, or by teaching courses at more than one college in the same geographical area during the same semester. Teaching creative writing at the high school or prep school level generally offers more stability, but imposes a heavier teaching load and places you at the margins of the network.

Every job in every walk of life has its drawbacks. I've tried to arm you with knowledge of the drawbacks of writers' jobs, but they aren't more severe than the drawbacks of anyone else's job. Try any of the options I've mentioned or invent one I haven't. Writing is the basis of our society. Everywhere you look, you'll find words that have been written by people who were paid to do it. Finding such opportunities requires a bit of imagination and effort—but not nearly as much as writing itself.

Do It

1. Read interviews with writers, such as in the *Paris Review Writers at Work* series or in the many literary quarterlies that publish such interviews. Learn how they built their careers.

2. Look around you for written words: in commerce, in education, in the media. Who wrote them? How did they get their jobs? Brainstorm a list of conceivable writing and editing jobs and ways to get them.

Writer's Bookshelf

What Color Is Your Parachute? by Richard Nelson Bolles (1970; updated annually)

> has become the standard source of advice and inspiration on how to create the career you want to fit the life you want. Bolles' The Three Boxes of Life and How to Get Out of Them *(1981)*

goes even further in the direction of advocating self-fulfillment as a career goal; he calls his approach "what to do until systemic change arrives."

Opportunities in Book Publishing Careers by Robert A. Carter (1987)

is a trim, down-to-earth overview that points the reader toward further sources.

Career Choices for the 90's for Students of English by Career Associates (1990)

offers a concise, practical survey of opportunities in a variety of fields, including publishing.

Careers for Bookworms and Other Literary Types by Marjorie Eberts and Margaret Gisler (1990)

is short, chatty, and fun: a good starting point for a search.

Book Publishing Career Directory, edited by Ron Fry (1987),

is a solid, practical reference book.

Directory of Internships, edited by Katherine Jobst (1988),

is a Writer's Digest *book that focuses on internships in the publishing field: a major pathway for entry-level positions.*

Liberal Arts Jobs: What They Are and How to Get Them by Burton Jay Nadler (1989)

is a slim, large-format entry in the Peterson's Guides series; its capsule descriptions might be springboards for brainstorming.

150 Best Companies for Liberal Arts Graduates by Cheryl Woodruff and Greg Ptacek (1992)

is informative on the personality as well as the statistics of 150 corporate workplaces; each company's profile includes a "report from the trenches" by an employee.

Chapter 20

Going Public

Most writers are shy, self-doubting people who desperately want to be recognized and loved. Writers spend their entire lives shrinking toward the spotlight. The conflict between the desire for privacy and the desire for publicity can lead to personal imbalances and career difficulties. Some writers resolve the issue by becoming recluses—but that only works for those who are already famous. If you run from the spotlight before it blinds you, it might never find you at all!

Thus, even the shyest, most hand-wringingly modest writers seek publication. In fact, it's hard not to think that the definition of "writer" is "someone who has had something published" and that the unpublished are simply aspiring writers or would-be writers. Try as we might to be self-motivated and pure of heart, we all need confirmation from outside at some point, even if we know that the standards of the world are not our own.

In this chapter, I'll talk about getting published. There are good books on the subject, such as Judith Applebaum's *How To Get Happily Published,* which has become something of a standard reference book, so I'll just briefly review the nuts and bolts of how and where to submit manuscripts and how to worm your way into publishability. Then I'll wax expansive on what the publishing world is all about—what gets published and why, and what to do about it.

HOW TO SUBMIT A MANUSCRIPT

Submitting fiction manuscripts is done by old-fashioned mail, usually first-class mail. If you have the money and are impatient, you can use express mail or an overnight shipper, but there's really no reason to. To save money, you can use fourth-class book rate, but if you're sending a manuscript a long distance, book rate can take a couple of weeks each way. Short stories are sent in manila envelopes, with a manila self-addressed, stamped envelope (SASE) inside. Book manuscripts are placed in nice clean boxes, such as boxes of typewriter paper, and sent in padded shipping envelopes, with a padded shipping envelope as the SASE. Buying a postage meter will enable you to figure out how many stamps to put on the SASE. Or, you can take your package to the post office unsealed and ask the clerk to put postage on both the inner and outer envelopes, then seal and mail it.

It's very important to send a clean, neat copy. Use a letter-quality printer or laser printer or an electric typewriter. Keep your ribbons fresh, and keep hand corrections to an absolute minimum. Use good paper, preferably with a 25 percent cotton fiber content. Medium-weight paper is fine; heavy paper adds to your postage costs. Avoid staples and folders; keep the pages of book manuscripts loose in their box, and use a paper clip for a short story. Use a title page for a book; it's not necessary for a short story. The title page contains the title and "by (your name)" at the center, with your address and phone number below, usually to the side. If you use a pen name, put the pen name in the byline and your real name with your address and phone number. On a short story manuscript without a title page, your real name, address, and phone number go at the top left, the page numbers at the top right. Then skip one-third to half a page, center your title and byline, and skip another couple of spaces before the text. Each page of the manuscript should be numbered at the top right, and at the top left it should have your name in case the editor slips and falls while carrying a pile of manuscripts. The title can go there, too, if you wish. (Of course, when applying for grants, you'll be required to send manuscripts *without* your name and so will need to print new copies.)

It's perfectly okay to submit the same story or novel to two or more places at once. Everyone does it. Most editors, at this point, are willing to read such submissions, and if they aren't, you don't have to tell them that it's a multiple submission. Nowadays, photocopies are often cleaner and more readable than originals anyway; the whole concept of an "original" manuscript is obsolete. The chance of having a work accepted by two editors at once is very, very small; it will probably never happen to you, and if you're clever enough to write something that was accepted in two places at once, you're clever enough to make up a plausible alibi.

There are still a few editors nasty enough to refuse to read manuscripts that they know (or think) are being submitted elsewhere simultaneously. There is no excuse for that sort of behavior. Traditionally, the consideration time for a story was one or two months; lately, three or four is average and five or six not at all uncommon. The number of competing writers has grown so large, and the number of magazines so small, that no newcomer can expect to sell a story quickly on the basis of quality alone. Submitting a story to a magazine is equivalent, in a very real, pragmatic way, to applying for a job. Do these editors expect job applicants to apply to only one prospective employer at a time and to refrain from applying anywhere else for months until they've heard the results of that application? You can grow old submitting a story to one publisher at a time. The process does not permit a career to develop. Anyone smart enough to edit a magazine or journal is capable of understanding that simple fact. People who are capable of understanding such facts and yet persist in refusing to read simultaneous submissions are either abysmally out of touch (and some prestigious editors, in fact, live on trust funds and have never applied for a job they were not assured of beforehand and would never dream of publishing the work of someone to whom they hadn't been properly introduced) or pettily, arrogantly cruel. Editors have a responsibility to nurture good writing. To act cruelly toward people you are supposed to nurture is to be abusive, sadistic, bullying.

QUERYING

It's not necessary to query beforehand if you're sending a short story to a magazine. Just send the story without warning. It's advisable to query beforehand if you're sending a novel or novel portion to a book publisher. Send queries to lots of places at once. A query is simply a brief letter— no longer than one page—describing your project and, if applicable, stating any special qualifications on your part. It should be written in clear, concise, straightforward, ungimmicky, but lively prose; it should not try to be cute or clever, yet should spark the editor's interest—it should not be boring. The interest comes mainly from the project itself, but secondarily the query letter demonstrates that you can write. Convey the subject of the book and the most enticing aspects of its story line or major characters or themes, in one paragraph, without giving away the entire plot or making the editor feel bogged down in details. Your hope is to arouse the editor's interest so that he or she actually wants to read the book—to entice the editor. If you know something about the subject—for instance, if your novel is about firefighters and you are a firefighter—mention that. If you have some publishing credits, state them; if you won a college writing award or edited a literary magazine, state that; if you have or are working toward a M.F.A. or have taught creative writing or have won a grant, include that. If you come to the editor through personal recommendation or indirect acquaintance, by all means mention that. Such credentials don't truly impress editors, but do help separate you from the mass of aspiring writers who lack them.

Your query will usually be a request to submit the whole, finished manuscript rather than a rough draft, portion, or outline. Unestablished writers usually sell first novels *after* writing them. Exceptions are (a) formidably well-connected grad-school hotshots and (b) commercial writers of high-concept blockbusters, in which the subject and the angle, rather than the quality of the writing, sell the project.

Send a SASE with your query letter, as with all submissions. If an editor writes back asking you to submit the manuscript, it is then a solicited rather than an unsolicited manuscript and will usually get at least a longer glance and a more courteous rejection.

It is not, repeat not, advisable to send a manuscript or query letter to a publishing house or magazine without addressing it to a specific editor by name. It's a sign that you don't know the ropes. (Editors, unfortunately, tend to be snobs. They're underpaid, as I've said, and take their gratifications where they can find them.) Unsolicited manuscripts pile up somewhere in a corner unread—that's called the slush pile—until finally they're processed with a minimal glance, when some editor decides to clean up the office, and returned with a form rejection slip. It's a waste of time and postage. I only know of one novel in the past generation that was accepted off the slush pile: *Ordinary People,* by Judith Guest. The event was so unusual that the discovery became a large factor in the book's advertising campaign. Guest had previously submitted several novels in that manner, which had been routinely rejected.

TRACKING DOWN EDITORS

Bizarrely enough, simply including a human being's name at the top of your letter and envelope increases the respect with which that human being will greet your package. How to find the names of editors? One way is simply to look in *LMP* or the *Writer's Market* books, where hundreds, perhaps thousands, of editors are listed. The listing is only about 75 percent reliable, because editors move around a lot; the person who was at Viking last year may be at Atheneum this year. A little extra effort will track them down, though. You can call the publishing house and ask the receptionist for the name of the editor who has replaced the editor who has moved and for the new location of the editor who has moved.

To find the names of magazine editors, buy (or browse!) a copy of the magazine and look at the masthead, the list of staff members that is usually near the table of contents. The usual reference books also contain names of magazine editors, as do the annual *Best American Short Stories* anthologies, in a list at the back. Send your story to the fiction editor, if one is listed; otherwise, to the top editor. A few literary quarterlies edit anonymously or have editorial boards; that's a case where it's okay to address the submission to "The Editors" or "Fiction Editor."

The fine print at the bottom of a magazine's masthead page sometimes gives instructions for submitting manuscripts, such as the times of year when the editors consider fiction. Many literary magazines only read scripts during certain months; send a story at the wrong time—often the summer—and you'll get it back unread. The *International Directory of Little Magazines and Small Presses* is a good source for this information.

Writing to names without knowing anything of the individuals behind them is a scattershot affair. Ideally, you want to submit your material to an editor whose tastes are inclined toward your kind of writing. You can do a little intuitive research by reading the acknowledgments and dedications of books you like; editors are often mentioned there. Look for articles by, and interviews with, editors in periodicals such as *Publishers Weekly, Poets & Writers, Writers Digest, The Writer, Writer's Journal,* and *The Writing Self.* Again, calling the publisher's receptionist can sometimes give you a clue; you can simply ask, "Could you tell me the name of an editor I could send a realistic first novel (or whatever) to?"

This is where agents come in. They know editors personally, know who's buying fiction at the moment and who isn't, know what kinds of books the editors have bought in the past and what literary longings they've expressed. They also know what prices are currently being paid and can usually compensate you for their commission by getting at least 10 to 15 percent more money than you could on your own.

Agents have their limitations. Some deal with new writers in a half-hearted way, testing the waters briefly and soon losing interest. Some deal with the same few editors over and over again; if your work happens to be right for one of those editors, you're in luck, and if not, you're out. The number of editors an agent will send your manuscript to is always less than the number of editors in existence, and each agent, like each editor, has his or her personal tastes; an agent is always an extra gate you have to pass through on your way to publication. (That's why publishers like to deal with agents: they know the agents have screened out the unprofessional submissions. For the same reason, being represented by a reputable agent enhances your prestige a bit; it's a kind of recommendation.) Many writers have sold a manuscript on their own after their agent lost heart and returned it. Working without an agent, you can also

send a manuscript to more than one editor at the same publisher—
something agents generally won't do.

So an agent is not a necessity but a major aid and convenience. Finding
one involves the same process of search and submission, rejection and
luck, as finding a publisher and can take almost as long. Look in the
reference books, the writers' magazines, the acknowledgments and
dedications; ask around among writers and creative writing teachers. Get
personal recommendations from agents' clients if you can. Send queries
first, both for novels and short stories. The words you will hear most
often, as always in publishing, are "no" and "sorry." If you *ever* hear "yes,"
you're doing all right.

THREE CONSTRAINTS ON PUBLISHERS

Which brings us to the question, "What gets accepted and why?" To
understand the answers, imagine yourself not as a writer but as someone
on the other end, an editor.

That much-maligned figure, the editor, is usually an intelligent,
sensitive person with a deep love of reading. If editors could publish
everything they wanted to, whenever they wanted to, a lot more good
fiction would appear in America. But editors work under three major
constraints:

- time

- space

- money

The time constraint is a result of the immense number of submissions
editors receive. A publishing house or magazine typically receives several
thousand manuscripts a year; smaller houses probably receive more, per
editor, than bigger houses. Editors don't have time to give each script a
careful reading. Not only that, they usually are not paid to read manuscripts and must do it during their off-hours. Publishers no longer retain
employees as manuscript readers *per se*. The more promising the manuscript, the more time it takes to read—time at lunch, at home, on the train,
on vacation. To prevent severe emotional distress, editors learn to
winnow the possible wheat from the probable chaff with a glance. For
sheer survival, they have to rely on first impressions. This is terribly unfair
to writers, because many fine works of fiction build slowly or have
untrendy subject matter and unflashy styles or are hard to categorize.
Fiction of that kind starts off with a strike against it. There is nothing to
be done about this unfairness, short of publishers' hiring a reasonable

number of editors for the workload—something they are not historically inclined to do.

Because of the time constraint, the shrewd contemporary writer develops a flamboyant, attention-getting style. This is a sad development, because what first appears flamboyant and attention-getting is, as a rule, soonest to appear stale, pretentious, and dated and least likely to contain lasting wisdom or beauty. The story or novel that beings with a quiet, simple description of a man walking down a road—for instance, *Tess of the D'Urbervilles*—is going to be overlooked by today's editors. Let's face it, sometimes writers do have to adjust and adapt to the realities of the marketplace if they want to get anywhere.

Thus has arisen the ignoble but true maxim, "Hook the reader with the first sentence." Or first paragraph or first page. It's an unpleasant fact of life that editors tend not to continue reading if the first page doesn't grab them. In response, for the past generation, we have evolved a national literature dominated by stories and novels whose first lines sound like, "Cousin Boo ran in with the knife still dripping, so's he wouldn't miss Final Jeopardy." Note the slick mimicry, the kinky soft-core shiver, and the condescension toward popular culture. We can put a self-referential spin on it: "A story about a man running in to watch Final Jeopardy while carrying a knife dripping with entrails shouldn't begin this way." Or compress it into the affectingly minimal, "Entrails." The typical catchy first line of our era sounds wry, hip, ironic, five-minutes-from-now; it aims to startle, giving the appearance of originality whether or not anything new is really being said. Most such works of fiction tail off rapidly after the beginning—but who ever finds out?

Textbooks often proclaim the need for a catchy first line as if it were a literary criterion. It isn't. It's a commercial criterion that has shaped contemporary tastes—and for that reason, it's something to take seriously.

The space constraint on editors follows from the fact that a publishing house or magazine can only publish a few works of fiction per season. The set of books a publisher publishes in a given season is called its "list." Within the house, each editor has his or her own personal list, which forms a fraction of the overall list.

Let's say that Picky Press has twenty books on its fall list, eight of which are fiction, and that it has four acquisitions editors (editors who read manuscripts, offer contracts, and deal personally with authors). Each editor, then, can accept two books of fiction per year. It's unlikely that both will be by unestablished writers; at least one will be by an author the editor has worked with before or an established author switching over from another house. This leaves one newcomer's slot per editor per season. Competing for this slot are well over a thousand writers, dozens of whom arrive with impressive credentials or recommendations backed up by manuscripts of genuine merit, the fruits of years of loving labor. The editor regrets having to return all but one of them, yet must do so; there is simply no choice.

But it's not just a matter of picking the submission the editor likes best, although that's a big part of it. To an excessive degree nowadays, editors only offer publication to first novels when they fall in love with the books—or, more precisely, become infatuated with them during the crucial period of consideration. As anyone knows who has ever fallen in love at first sight, this is not a reliable guide to long-term potential. It favors the superficially attractive over the deeply meaningful, the sensational over the worthy. But love is not enough; the project must also fit the list. It must be compatible with the other books on the list, without competing directly with them. Suppose you've written the great novel of Tibetan history. The editor loves it, wishes you success, but admits that her publishing house is just about to issue another novel of Tibetan history, which they acquired a year ago. Tough luck! They can't publish both! This kind of thing happens more than you might think. Writers pick up ideas for subject matter from the culture around them—and they all watch the same programs, read the same books and newspapers, swim in the same intellectual currents.

Magazines are even more restrictive. The amount of space available for fiction in American magazines has been shrinking steadily since the invention of television. If you are the fiction editor of *Young Self* magazine, you are working under an editorial policy that allows you six pages of fiction per month—period. You can't exceed that, any more than an astronaut can change the orbit of Mars. When you receive a story you love that happens to be eight pages long, you either return it or accept it on condition that the author cuts it by one-fourth.

Further, every magazine has its own editorial slant, its distinctive style. No profit-oriented magazine publishes a story solely because it's good fiction. It publishes a story *because it's a good example of the kind of story the magazine publishes.* There are women's magazines, men's magazines, and literary glossies such as the *New Yorker* and *Atlantic*. Each category publishes a different kind of fiction, and there are variations within categories as well. A *Cosmopolitan* story is different from a *Redbook* story and so on. If you're the fiction editor of *Young Self,* you may personally prefer *New Yorker* stories as your recreational reading but your job is to find *Young Self* stories.

There's a certain amount of flexibility here, because editors are human and personal taste is a big factor. You may seek out *Young Self* stories that bear more resemblance to *New Yorker* stories than the ones your predecessor found. You'll ask agents to send you that kind of story; word will get around. If your editor-in-chief deems that your new stories are boosting circulation, you've succeeded; if he or she thinks they've hurt, you may be told, "Our readers don't appreciate that kind of stuff," or given only four pages instead of six—or fired.

For the most part, however, a magazine's slant is a strategic response to its audience demographics rather than a simple expression of taste. Every magazine is specialized; it survives by occupying a particular niche in the market. It publishes material aimed at appealing to a very specific, scientifically profiled sector of the readership: for instance, professional women between 21 and 35 making $25,000 to $60,000 a year. The magazine prints stories and articles aimed at that audience in order to convince companies whose products aim at the same audience to buy advertising space.

This brings us to our third constraint, money. Editors as individuals may love literature, but publishing corporations are not in the business of literature. They are in the business of making money. They publish what they think will sell enough copies to bring in a profit. Calculating profit involves calculating costs: a story by a famous writer costs more to publish than a story by an unknown but attracts more readers; a two-hundred-page novel costs less to publish than a four-hundred-page novel. It's also a matter of calculating audience: the four-hundred-page novel, by virtue of its subject matter or genre or, for that matter, because a lot of people like to read long novels, may attract an audience large enough to make it a better investment than the two-hundred-pager.

The decision to accept or reject a work of fiction is largely a budgetary decision. And editors are supremely, uncomfortably aware of this; they are under intense pressure to acquire books that turn a profit. Even worse, most editors don't have the power to offer a publishing contract single-handedly; they must get approval from their editorial boards for each manuscript they buy. Increasingly in recent years, as publishing companies have been bought by large conglomerates for whom books are only a sideline, the decisions of editorial boards are influenced by the shallow enthusiasms, faux-worldly doubts, hidden prejudices, and merely human myopia of the marketing department; in more and more cases, members of that department sit on the board and vote on what to publish. It was hard enough in the old days (the 1980s) for a work of literature—by definition unique, hard to categorize, highly personal in style—to get past the qualms of a majority of a board. It's even harder when marketing has the last word.

These three constraints mean that writers are often rejected for reasons other than literary quality. That can be a disheartening reality to confront for the first time, but in another way it's heartening too. When you receive a manuscript back in the mail, there's no reason to assume that it was rejected because it wasn't good enough. There's every reason to keep sending it to other places, hoping that the next editor will have a slot on his or her list for the novel of Tibetan history or the women's-magazine-cum-*New-Yorker* story. Rejection letters from editors rarely go on at sufficient length for the writer to get a true idea of why the work was turned down. If you get any kind of personal note at all, even the one word "sorry" scribbled on a printed form, that's a genuine reason to be optimistic. Someone has taken time out of his or her day to scribble that as a gesture of goodwill.

REASONS TO HOPE

This would be a very bleak picture if there were only one publishing house in the world, only one slot on one list. Remember, though, that there are a lot of publishers' lists. By last count, there were at least two hundred editors acquiring novels in America. The same group of manuscripts tends to migrate from editor to editor over the course of a season or more.

The thing to do is to keep at it until your manuscript finds its home. It's not at all unusual for a book or story to be rejected by twenty or more editors before being accepted; in fact, it's par for the course. A half dozen rejections is not much; we tough guys shrug it off.

There are hundreds of small literary magazines, and being less dependent on advertising than commercial magazines, they are relatively free to search for literary quality, bound only by the personal tastes of their editors. (They aren't totally free, because they're funded by universities or foundations or rich individuals who subtly impose their literary and political views on the editors and because of the creeping market-consciousness of our society even at levels where it's uncalled-for.) Tastes vary widely, of course; one journal will publish dense works of ornate quasi-Jamesian prose, while another will scoff at anything that uses conventional punctuation. The best way to learn about these editorial slants is to read the actual magazines; the second-best way is to look at the listings in the reference books already mentioned.

There are new publishing houses and magazines all the time, filling the vacuum left by ones that have folded or changed their editorial policies. Small, new publishers tend to be more receptive to new writers than prestigious, established publishers, largely for economic reasons. It can be a stroke of good fortune to join such a publisher on the ground floor, if it endures and prospers.

In this publishing climate, patience and perseverance are absolutely necessary—and often surprisingly effective. One reason for believing them effective is the prospect that, in the next few years, electronic books will make it easier for new writers to get into print. Computers have already made self-publication easier and less expensive, returning to it the respectability it enjoyed in the nineteenth century. Soon it should be possible to self-publish by uploading a text from disk to computer network: a fast, low-cost process that should also save huge numbers of trees. This mode of publication has always been available, of course, simply through the circulation of manuscripts by hand—*samizdat,* as they called it in Eastern Europe—and through reading aloud. I've long wondered why American writers don't initiate our own form of *samizdat* in order to protest and subvert the restrictions on artistic freedom that are posed by corporations, restrictions that are not officially acknowledged but are very real. No doubt we crave prestige and comfort too much. Electronic books will at last give writers an easy way to get their work into the hands of large numbers of strangers, all over the world, without betting their fortunes on the results, and—most importantly!—to look cool doing it. Publishing houses will doubtless continue to exist, because they're expert at designing and packaging and because readers want reassurance, a stamp of approval saying, "Somebody in authority thinks this book is worth printing." Big changes are coming soon, though, and they may very well help writers.

Do It

1. Go to the library and find the publishing reference books cited in this chapter. Acquaint yourself with them. Notice what kinds of information they give and what kinds they don't; ascertain their strengths and weaknesses, their categories, their slants. Choose one publishing house or magazine and compare its listings in the various reference books.

2. Research the editorial slant of a magazine. Read at least one recent issue, preferably more. Answer the following questions: How much fiction do they print per issue? Per year? Who is it by? What genre is it? What is its subject matter and literary style? What socioeconomic level and what culture or subculture do its characters tend to come from? What are the subjects and styles of the nonfiction articles? What products are advertised in the magazine? What kinds of models—by gender, age, race, and intangible stylistic factors—are used in the ads? What political views, if any, are expressed in the editorial contents? Compose a one-paragraph description of whom you think the targeted reader of the magazine

is. Then write a one-paragraph description of what you think the "slant" of the magazine's fiction is. Then assess how this type of fiction helps the magazine appeal to its targeted readership.

If you do this exercise in a class or writers' group, you can build up a file documenting the editorial slants of many magazines.

3. Found a literary magazine of your own. Its purpose at first may be to print your and your friends' fiction or to be a new forum for the writers in your college, school, or dorm; if you make a go of it, you may actually start attracting and soliciting submissions from outside.

Writer's Bookshelf

How to Get Happily Published by Judith Applebaum (3rd edition, 1988)

is the authoritative text on the subject—especially good on self-publishing.

The Writing Business: A Poets & Writers Handbook, by the editors of *Coda: Poets & Writers Newsletter* (1985),

gives useful advice on locating resources, selling a manuscript, and what to do after selling it.

The Writer's Legal Guide by Tad Crawford (1977)

is indispensable for those who have achieved publication, if only to make sure that your agent and lawyer know what they're doing. The author is a lawyer who specializes in representing writers and artists. Also totally valuable is Crawford's Business and Legal Forms for Authors and Self-Publishers *(1990).*

Editors on Editing: An Inside View of What Editors Really Do, edited by Gerald Gross (1985),

does for editors what the Paris Review *interviews do for writers—and thus is eye-opening for writers as well.*

***The Writer's Essential Desk Reference,* edited by Glenda Tennant Neff (1991),**

>   *gives well-organized, practical information on the art of living as a writer: taxes, legal matters, selling your work, finding employment, and researching fiction.*

***Words in Our Pockets: The Feminist Writers Guild Handbook,* edited by Celeste West (1985),**

>   *contains articles by various writers on publishing, self-publishing, finding support systems, writing for genres, and other topics; it's aimed at women writers, but men too can learn from reading it.*

Chapter 21

Living

I have good news and bad news.

The good news is that writing is a life of freedom and potentially limitless personal growth.

The bad news is that writing is a life of rejection and frustration.

In the spirit of the true writer, you probably want to hear about the bad news first. Actually, I told you the worst of it in the previous chapter. If you've pressed on to read this chapter, you have the beginnings of a writer's resilience.

If you try to become a published writer, the chances are very high that you will experience rejection—not just one or two rejections, but continual, chronic rejection. This is true whether or not you ultimately triumph and are accepted. It remains true after you're published. It's a mistake to expect that once you sell your first story or novel, the days of rejection are over. Rejections continue for professional writers, even well-known ones, because of the external constraints I discussed in Chapter 20. The "no" will come from a higher source—it may be the *New Yorker* turning you down with a warm personal note rather than the *Oshkosh Review* with a form slip—but it still feels like "no."

The key to dealing with it is to change how "no" affects you.

Frustration is the writer's companion on successful, lucrative projects as well as unsuccessful ones. After you get something accepted, you will have the enviable opportunity of learning all about the frustrations of success. To start with, your editor may ask you to revise your manuscript, which you thought was finished but which he or she calls a draft. The ending is a downer, the editor tells you, and the title will have to go, and the whole thing should be fifty pages shorter. You may feel intimidated and powerless: the editor is the gatekeeper to a land you've been dreaming of for years, and just when you thought you'd stepped through, he or she poses another test. This kind of meddling is particularly rife among high-paying, slick magazines. Should you follow the editor's suggestions or hold firm to protect your artistic vision?

I recommend fighting for your principles but not martyring yourself for them. If you think your ending is the proper one, say so; have long phone conversations with the editor about it; barrage your editor with memos justifying your ending with well-reasoned arguments. The chances are that a book editor will let you have your way; magazine editors, more beholden to space limitations and rigid editorial policies, are more stubborn.

Most editors, in any case, don't really believe they're infallible. A few enjoy battling with writers and, like dentists who always find cavities, seek out problems that may not be there. Short of that kind of pathology, any editor will have the usual personal insecurities; he or she may have suggested the revision partly in order to gauge, from your reaction, the suggestion's validity. The editor understands that it's your work and that no one knows it as well, or cares about it as much, as you.

A moment may come, however, when an editor says, "I can't publish it unless you make this change." Take that editor at his or her word and think carefully. The chances are that, if this editor turns the book down with a "Good luck placing it elsewhere," you will return to the endless round of submissions, with no greater likelihood of finding "elsewhere." If you huffily withdraw the manuscript, you may be throwing away your big break. Learning to compromise is part of any adult's training, not just a writer's. Dickens changed the ending of *Great Expectations* for a publisher; Hardy changed the ending of *The Return of the Native*. In both cases, the publishers were wrong; in both cases, the writers resented the pressure; but in both cases, the work has survived. Every writer I know has had to compromise with publishers.

There's a motto that has helped me when I've been calm enough to remember it. I forget who said it first. It's this: if you throw a pile of garbage on a small fire, the fire is smothered and goes out, but if you throw the same pile of garbage on a big fire, the fire uses it for fuel and burns brighter than ever.

Try to become a big fire, because you're going to be dealing with a lot of garbage.

After you've come to terms with your editor, more problems. You may find that your publicist doesn't return your calls—if you even know who your publicist is. (I recommend learning the identity of, and cultivating as your best buddy, this important person.) You may find that the marketing department isn't as enthusiastic about your book as the editor was, and that their indifference has infected the editor. For that matter, your editor may leave for a better job at another publishing house or may leave the publishing industry entirely. What do you do then? It's often best to follow your editor to House B; if you stay at House A, you'll be assigned to an editor who didn't discover your book and feels no personal connection to you. Indeed, your book will not be on that editor's personal acquisitions list; he or she will not get credit for its sales if the book succeeds. The editor will give the bulk of his or her attention to projects that improve his or her personal track record; your book is likely to be put through the motions, perhaps given to an assistant as a training project. As I've said before in this humble tome, "Believe me, I speak from experience."

Or your entire publishing house may be bought out by another publisher (B.M.I.S.F.E.—see previous sentence). You become simply a contract the new corporation has to obey, not a commitment it wants to fulfill. Your new owner may, for reasons of economy, send a memo to all its editors demanding that they cut one book from that season's lists— and that one book may be yours. Or your book may survive the cut but be delayed by several months or more, with the result that it's no longer as timely as it used to be and sales don't meet expectations (B.M.I.S.F.E.). (By the way, when sales don't meet expectations, no matter why, it's always held against the writer.) Or things may go smoothly, but your book must compete with another on the same subject, by a more famous writer, issued a month before yours by a publisher with better distribution. (B.M.I.S.F.E.) You may visit your neighborhood bookstore and find that your book is not on the shelves and, when you ask the clerk about it, be greeted with a humiliating, blank look and informed that the book isn't listed on the computer from which the store places its orders. (B.M.I.S.F.E.) You may be on the computer and the shelves but panned by the reviewers—or not reviewed at all. (B.M.I.S.F.E.) You may get great reviews and it still may not make a difference to your sales or your public exposure. (B.M.I.S.F.E.) You may get great reviews and good sales by virtue of the fact that the publicity misrepresents the book, embarrassing you. (B.M.I.S.F.E.) You may be exhausted by the promotional tour and find that you don't have much time left to write. You may want to write something very different for your next project, then learn that your editor is only willing to accept your work when you repeat yourself. You may dutifully repeat yourself and may be told that "the magic is missing." Or you may get a free ride and achieve every possible worldly success and realize, in midcareer, that you weren't Jane Austen after all; you were just—well, a success.

HOW TO DEAL WITH REJECTION

Becoming a professional writer is a process of learning to absorb punishment and come back for more. Joyce Carol Oates, in her book *On Boxing,* says that she knows only one profession, aside from boxing, whose participants willingly undergo continual punishment to the head: writing. I would add that boxers, unlike writers, expect it beforehand.

The reason you can absorb these blows to the head is that there are so many rewards, both during the fight and afterward. Learning how to keep your fire burning is a wonderful experience. Purifying the garbage can make you self-confident and mentally tough. I have some advice on how to do it: how to process the negative experiences so that rather than warping you, they straighten you out.

First, when something frustrating happens to you as a writer, recognize it. Meet the emotional impact head-on. Admit that you have been rejected; admit that it makes you sad and angry. Talk to yourself about it; write about it in your journal. Cry if you want to cry—but try to do it in private. Scream if you want to scream—as long as you aren't screaming at an innocent bystander. Hit something if you want to hit something—as long as it's inanimate.

This will help you avoid making a terrible mistake, the mistake of taking your frustrations out on those close to you. (B.M.I.S.F.E.) Perhaps the most damaging effect of the frustrations of a writing career is the effect they can have on a writer's interpersonal relations. Remember that the people around you aren't the cause of the frustrations—nor are you the cause. The people around you probably care about you and love you and are probably willing to help you through the frustrations if you treat them right. Ranting and raving and cursing the publishing world can wear on the nerves of the most loving observers; they may come to feel that it's the dominant aspect of your personality. Drinking or taking drugs to suppress the frustration has even worse results. (Fortunately, I don't speak from experience here.)

Just tell yourself and your loved ones, "I got a rejection—I feel awful." Mope about it for a while; meditate if that's your style; go out and exercise; talk to your therapist.

Regulate your relations with the people around you to your own and their advantage. You have no duty either to tell them all your plans or to hide everything. You can do either one when you sense it would smooth out your relationships. If you tell a friend, "I want to be a writer," and the friend is encouraging and interested, keep talking to that person about it. If the friend asks to read some of your work, do so if you feel the experience will strengthen the friendship or benefit you as a writer; if not, feel free to say, "Sorry, I don't feel ready" or "I'm shy about showing my unpublished work—maybe some other time." If, on the other hand, your hoped-for confidant says, "Who, you? A writer? What would you write about?" (B.M.I.S.F.E.), drop the subject. You can still be that person's friend to play tennis with, have coffee with, or whatever, but there's a subject you're going to keep from him or her. You've discovered a limitation in your friend, not in yourself.

For similar reasons, reading one's reviews can be a trial. I don't read my reviews in full and never have; and I don't even glance at articles about me. I get the gist of what they've said from others' comments, and I do peek at the really nice passages that appear in reviews from time to time. My theory is that the negative comments will depress me and the positive ones will give me a swelled head and that neither type of comment can be counted on as the objective truth. I have recommended this approach to writer friends when they've expressed frustration with reviews; to my knowledge, no one has ever adopted it.

Obtuse reactions from well-meaning people, in person or in print, can be irritating. Perhaps when you're young you tell your parents about your ambitions, and they give you the old line about how writers starve and how it isn't a respectable career. Well, for one thing, as I've indicated in Chapter 19, writers don't starve. (B.M.I.S.F.E.) Those antiliterary prejudices are totally obsolete. We live in the age of information, and information is written. Writing is a thoroughly upstanding career; I've found that when I tell people I'm a writer, they're invariably respectful, even admiring. And, thank goodness, gone are the days when Americans considered male writers sissies (and going are the days when they thought there was such a thing as sissyhood at all); that ridiculous prejudice drove some great men to alcoholism and suicide. If you are male and anyone still confronts you with that prejudice, be assured that they are totally, totally out of step and that in your writing life you will find innumerable people who scoff at such bigotry and support your ambitions.

If you are female, you may face an equivalent bigotry (for both stem from a fear of tenderness): the idea that women's writing is "minor." In that case, you have the privilege of belonging to a generation of women who are putting the lie to stereotypes and, in the process, changing our ideas about what constitutes "major."

The quickest cure for the frustrations of writing is to write something. Open the document file for your current project and renew your effort. The quickest cure for a rejection slip is to send the manuscript someplace else soon—the same day or the next day if possible. Once it's in the mail again, a new cycle of hope has begun.

IT'S A WONDERFUL LIFE

If the rewards of writing consisted only of learning to deal with bad news, it would be better to avoid bad news in the first place. But the rewards go far beyond that. Writing is the best life I know—that's why I became a writer in the first place. I am a free human individual. I live where I want. I do what I want. I keep regular hours to the extent I want and vary them whenever I want. I work at exactly what I want to work at, and it's creative work that enriches my soul. I don't have a boss; I have colleagues and clients whose requests I can turn down (as long as I'm willing to accept the consequences in terms of lost assignments). I keep short, flexible hours—for, while it's true that writers write all the time, you can write all the time on vacation or at a party.

I love my work, even when I'm not fully satisfied with the products of my labor. I'm always trying to do better, and I have enough confidence to believe I will. I enjoy dreaming the scenes, thinking of the words—I'm so addicted, I even enjoy typing them out.

What I love best is the feeling that I'm making progress. No one is better situated for lifelong learning—or more dependent on it—than a writer. Writers are naturally meliorists; their entire careers are a step-by-step striving for improvement, driven by the faith that they can get there. They may not get all the way, but they'll get somewhere worth arriving at; to some small degree, they hope to be instruments of the larger improvement.

When I finish a project, I kiss it goodbye—so to speak—and go on to the next as if is were the first thing I had ever written. I'm starting fresh, meeting new difficulties, and discovering new ways of mastering them. Of course I'm aware that this is an illusion, that I've written a great deal in the past and am starting from a higher point than I started last time, but it's a useful illusion. The truth underlying the illusion is that a writer must do something new, and try to do something better, in each project or stagnate, deteriorate, and fall into self-parody. The way to avoid that triple hazard is to keep your attachment to your past work a loose, unconfining one. Possessing confidence in the lessons you've learned, feel comfortable storing them in the background rather than constantly referring to them. What you're more interested in is the lessons of the future.

It's commonly said that writers learn to recognize and express their true feelings. That's so; and I'd go beyond that to add that it isn't just your own feelings you encounter and express, nor is it only the true feelings, nor is it just feelings in the narrow sense of the word, nor is it just what belongs to individuals. It's other people's feelings, and it's all their feelings whether deep or shallow, authentic or put-on; it's their cognitions, their views of the world, their assumptions, their beliefs, their conceptions and misconceptions; it's their culture, their time and place, as well as their personalities.

Let's say you're writing a story about a woman's relationship with her sister. You might start out remembering your own relationship with your sister; you might review the whole course of the relationship from early childhood to the present, even though the story will take place entirely in the present. The first morning of your work on the story, you sit back, recalling and jotting down incidents that well up spontaneously from the past. Maybe you call your sister on the phone, confirming your memories, eliciting ones you might have forgotten, refreshing your sense of who your sister is and how you interact. The feelings are strong and various and conflicting. You love your sister; you feel free with her; but you're competitive with her, and the freedom is in part a freedom to be mean. You wish you saw her more often but you're glad she lives far away. You love her children but you desperately want your children to do better than hers, and you feel a guilty little pleasure when hers get into trouble. You've done unselfish things for your sister and, at other times, have taken advantage of her. You share secrets with each other and keep secrets from each other; you agree in your opinions about your parents, except for the points on which each of you feels the other is being unfair. You think you know better than your sister, but she thinks she knows better than you, and each of you patiently endures the misguided advice the other gives. You dream of a perfect life in which you settle next-door to your sister—but you can't imagine how she can tolerate her lifestyle, and whenever you meet for the holidays you have an argument.

What are your feelings? How could you possibly label them? Which feelings are the "true" ones?

What writing teaches you is that all the feelings are true. It's inadequate to summarize them or to draw lessons from them; it's a distortion to rank them in order of authenticity. The only true way to know your feelings is to experience them in their fullness, in their contradictions. Being a writer gives you a way of doing that. You build a model made of words, and if it works, it doesn't simplify or codify or schematize your feelings, it adds to them.

If the process stopped there, it would be therapy—but the writing process is much more. To prepare to write your story, you study other sister pairs as well. You observe your friends' relationships with their sisters; you might interview them on the subject or at least raise the subject in a seemingly casual conversation. You read stories other writers have written about sisters, both to avoid duplicating their work and to absorb what can be generalized from it. You might read memoirs or psychology books that discuss sisterhood and anthropology or history books about sisterhood in other times and places. You might think about how being a sister, and having a sister, is both similar to and different from being, and having, a brother, cousin, friend, enemy, father, mother, lover. Through this, you develop a vision of the subject that is not limited to your personal feelings but can enrich your personal feelings.

You are not just getting material for a story, you are learning about the world. As a writer, you have the perfect excuse to learn anything and everything you ever want to—it's all research. If you want to learn about crime and justice, you don't have to become a criminal—you can write a crime novel. As preparation, you'll read lots of crime novels, read nonfiction about crime and justice, probably talk to cops or convicts or crime reporters or criminal lawyers, perhaps get a job teaching creative writing in a prison or doing paralegal work. The writer is a universal expert.

Whatever your subject, and whatever you learn about it through a combination of research and experience and imagination, you will probably be writing about its problems. Fiction is about human beings' mistakes and how they try to overcome them. Ideally, the writer—and the reader—can learn the overcoming without actually making the mistakes. Fiction can be a moral laboratory, a way of testing out the wrong ways to live and thus finding the right way.

WHY WRITERS FEEL GOOD

We read about characters who suffer, and it makes us happy. There is danger in this and also opportunity. The danger is voyeurism, sadism, getting pleasure from the pain of others; this leads to brutalization and can cheapen one's life and shorten one's lifespan. The danger is real when fiction tries to ignore the subjective fact of suffering, as in so many shallow works of violent entertainment. The opportunity is real when the fiction explores suffering honestly, when the person undergoing the suffering, the person inflicting it, and the person witnessing it are presented as human beings who are affected by the experience, not as pop-up targets at a shooting gallery or as superheroes who can get away with anything. The opportunity is greatest when the violence is recognizable as part of real human life, not wish-fulfillment: when the reader feels, "I have, or could have, suffered this" rather than "I wish I could bust up a barroom like that." It gives us the opportunity to transcend lies: the lie of simplistic right and wrong, the lie of blame and innocence, the lie of perfection, the lie of happy-ever-after and Mr. or Ms. Right, the lie of invulnerability and helplessness, the lie of us and them.

More than most people, the writer has the chance to become a fulfilled human being. Few writers have achieved it, but there are enough examples so that the rest of us can believe in the goal: Tolstoy, Chekhov, Colette, Stein, Gaskell, George Eliot, Byron, Keats, Whitman, Chaucer, Milton, Dante, Goethe, Schiller, Yeats, Lawrence, Woolf, Nin, Orwell, Stevenson, Thomas Mann, and, perhaps, if we knew enough about him, Shakespeare. None of these people were flawless, and too many died prematurely; Woolf, for one, suffered from a fatal mental illness (which probably could have been controlled with medication today). But they knew how they wanted to live, and they insisted on living that way—and it was a constructive way, increasing the intellectual and spiritual freedom of those around them. They knew what limitations were but, rather than surrendering, worked at the borders of those limitations to push them back. They were emotionally complex and vital, philosophically inquis-itive, daring in their work and honest in their lives.

It is not true that a writer must choose between perfection of the life and of the work. The man who said so, Yeats, had a life most people would trade theirs for (and he was probably better off for not marrying Maud Gonne). The way to become a better writer is to become a wiser human being.

What about the saying, "You have to suffer to sing the blues?" It's true that you have to know what suffering is in order to write about it—but all people know what suffering is. Writers don't require a special dose of suffering: the average human amount will do. Anyone who has lived through a childhood and adolescence and has struggled to become an adult has seen enough to write about. Add to that the occasional health problem or economic problem, and you've got a surplus. Besides, becoming a writer is hard enough in itself so that no writer needs to go in quest of extra strife.

What a writer does need, more than the average person, is awareness of suffering. Many Americans are deep in denial, spending untold life-energy convincing themselves that they feel good, that they're okay and we're okay, that there's no problem. This kind of thinking is necessary at times in order to keep going and not despair; as a philosophy of life, however, it's incompatible with writing. "Keep smiling!" will make you an insurance broker, not a writer. Writers must be aware of the ugliness in themselves, in others, and in society, and they must be fearless, even *comfortable,* about uncovering it. That's the only way to turn it into beauty. It's the writer's way of learning to feel good.

A great acting teacher used to tell his or her students (I forget which teacher it was!): "When there's a fire in a house, most people run out of the house as fast as they can, but there are some people whose job it is to run toward the flames, and they're called firefighters. When there's a fire in the human heart, most people try to run from it, but there are some people whose job it is to run toward the flames—and they're called artists."

That's why many writers have not lived up to the ideal: they've gotten burned. It's hard to keep your ideals when you know so many bad things. The best way to attain a balance is to believe in art.

Many writers have led unhappy lives, but, as a good meliorist, I believe they didn't have to—or wouldn't have to today. A large part of their suffering has been imposed from outside, by societies and families that denigrated their work. We like to think that our society is evolving past that. Even it if isn't, there are probably so many aspiring writers nowadays that they form a supportive subculture.

Writers have also suffered when they imagined they had to live what they wrote about instead of transcending it. (Readers have suffered for a similar reason, when they've identified with alienated characters such as Dostoyevsky's underground man or Meursault in Camus' *The Stranger*.) Accepting the false choice between perfection of the art and of the life, many have bargained away their happiness and found too late that it didn't make their art any better.

Writers have also suffered when they mistook the false rewards of fame for the real rewards of art.

Writers have also suffered because most of us, to begin with, are called to our vocation as compensation for some feeling of inadequacy or inhibition or misplacedness. We want to bellow our feelings freely, to hook up with those around us, to be recognized and admired, but the only medium in which we feel safe doing so is the silent written word. We're afraid we're not like other people (usually we're more like them than we want to admit). We feel we're in the wrong century or the wrong body or the wrong culture. These feelings can be useful, especially for the young writer. They can be the fuel that allows us to take off. What many of us don't realize is that they can be jettisoned like the first stage of a rocket, so that the next stage can propel us farther. To become a writer is to find your place; after you've done so, why keep telling yourself you can't?

Writers have also suffered because they became their own personae, putting on a rigid, false self, because they thought they needed armor or wanted to appear literary or glamorous or hip. It's fun to put on new selves, and part of the fun of being a writer is that we, second only to actors, can put them on more frequently than anyone. Believing that one *is* one's persona, or must live up to it, is a terrible trap, though.

The pressure to be hip has been a particular danger for American writers since World War II. I should say the pressure to be cool. By *cool* I mean "trendy and fun"; by *hip* I mean "engaged in a private search for values in opposition to the values of mass culture." Since 1966 or thereabouts, there has been some new form of coolness approximately every three months, with two-hundred-and-fifty million people simultaneously jumping on and off the bus at once. Hipness, in this same era, has become quaint—I mean, what kind of fool would want to engage in a private search for values that two-hundred-and-fifty million people didn't know about? Punk, grunge, college rock, white rap, cyberpunk, and poststructuralist criticism are all fun, but the energy that drives them is the energy of careerism. Compare this to Anaïs Nin, who kept a diary for decades and wasn't sure she ever wanted to publish it.

In a nation desperately trying to appear cool, the most desperate are the people who sell us athletic shoes, soft drinks, and telephone service plans. Bringing up the rear are the writers and publishers—a place writers and publishers should never be. Trapped in a time lag between inspiration and publication, beset by doubts about their medium, their frantic method of getting attention has been to depict to excess the toxic byproducts of cool: drug-taking and violence. The coolest-looking writers of today fully share the values of mainstream society; they are the antithesis of hip. In its most debased form, we find this in the work of certain "postmodern" (a marketing label rather than a substantive term) novelists who invent ever-more baroque forms of decadence but are themselves the pure products of academia, and whose idea of literary experimentation is to insert rhapsodic fantasies about how many copies they hope to sell. In contrast, the appearance in the early 1990s of rock bands who actively discourage publicity has been a hopeful sign. You'll only hear about them to the extent they compromise their values.

If every writer who aspired to coolness in the past thirty years had instead aspired to wisdom, we would have a stronger literature and possibly even a better world.

People will always do what's easier, of course.

Who gets to pursue the hard ideal? Who ought to be allowed to try to become a writer, to open the interface between individual and culture, to reshape the forces that shape us?

Anyone who dares.

There is no adequate definition of the qualifications for being a writer, and if there ever were one, it would be disproved by the next writer who came along. Art, literature, is that which evades definitions and categories and analyses—that which is *other*.

There are thousands of people nowadays who make their livings analyzing communications. They take a text, let's say *To the Lighthouse* by Virginia Woolf, and invariably find their own ideas in it. They subject it to feminist analysis, Freudian analysis, Marxist analysis, post-Marxist analysis, genre analysis, formal analysis, historical analysis, and who knows what else. Suppose that all the things they find there are really there. (I actually believe that this might be the case.) Nevertheless, there's one thing they haven't found, and it's the most important thing. What they haven't found is what makes *To the Lighthouse* art. They might as well have analyzed the London *Times* classified ads that Virginia Woolf perused at breakfast; they would have discovered as much (or more) evidence for feminist, Freudian, Marxist, post-Marxist, genre, formal, historical, and who known what else theories. What makes *To the Lighthouse* a work of art is what makes it different from, more beautiful than, the classified ads; and about this, the analysts haven't a clue. To the extent that they attempt an answer, they usually act as if the value of a work like *To the Lighthouse* lies in inspiring us to believe their theories; they reduce art to propaganda or to a kind of illustrated literary criticism.

What makes *To the Lighthouse* art is that Virginia Woolf was aware of *the other thing,* the thing that eludes analysis, and was capable of finding it in herself. Perhaps she had some of that capacity at birth; certainly it was strengthened by her upbringing and her deliberate efforts. There is no specifying the attributes that a writer needs at birth. I suspect that intelligence is the only universal requirement, but there are various kinds of intelligence, and different writers have surely possessed them to different degrees. Some have had extraordinary verbal talent, others only average. My hunch is that many writers have succeeded through a cross-fertilization of talents, the spatially or musically intelligent writer able to construct intricate plots, the physically or visually intelligent writer able to describe convincing scenes, the logically inquisitive writer skillful at mysteries, the intuitively intelligent writer leaning toward nature descriptions and fantasy. (This is meant to be a riff on possibilities and by no means a strict typology.) Writers have brought their educations, their special training and their temperaments to their fiction. There are fiction writers who seem like historians or essayists or poets or mystics or psychologists or anthropologists in disguise. Fiction is an all-encompassing form and not only is there no one kind of person qualified to participate, but the appearance of new and unexpected kinds of participants will enrich it.

So there's no point in asking, "Am I talented enough?" You can save yourself that grief. I don't think the question is answerable. Even if theoretically answerable, it wouldn't be answerable in practice until the end of a career anyway—not at the beginning. I do believe that something called "talent" exists, but I know that it's neither necessary nor sufficient for becoming a fiction writer. It helps, but coasting on it will hurt you and working on other strengths will help you. Nor does it show up at the same time in everyone's life or at all times in one individual's life. If I had judged by my own, and others', perception of my talent, I would have stopped when I was sixteen.

Writing ability is to a large extent created by the writer himself or herself and discernible only after the fact. It's created by self-programming. We all receive some programming before birth and during our childhoods, but after that we have the opportunity to rewrite many of our programs. That's the most important writing a writer does: the inner writing that makes the writing on paper possible. Every human being has different childhood programming, even identical twins. (I know more than one pair of identical twins where one twin is a writer and the other isn't.) Therefore, every aspiring writer needs to institute a different self-programming. There is no formula, but there are broad guidelines and observations that have been useful over time for a number of people: a fuzzy metaprogram. That is what this book consists of.

A writer is someone for whom living and writing are the same thing. Therefore, a writer is someone who is always learning to live.

Do It

1. Imagine you are on your deathbed. (Your age is up to you.) You look back over your life, remembering the things you've done and wondering about the things you never did. What did you accomplish? What are you proud of? What do you regret? What do you wish you'd done? Write it down. Keep it in case you find yourself in that situation someday—or in case you want to use the information before you get there.

2. Stare at yourself in the mirror for five minutes, looking right into your own eyes without fidgeting, laughing, making faces, fixing your hair, or otherwise disturbing the moment. Ask yourself the four questions: Who am I? Why am I here? Where do I come from? Where am I going? Let your thoughts arise as they will. Many people try to avoid looking at themselves. Others look at themselves constantly in a superficial way, anxious about trivial surface blemishes. It is rare to look at oneself steadily, calmly, acceptingly, as an observer. Done repeatedly, this exercise can be a meditation. It's a narcissistic kind of meditation, which might make it perfect for writers.

3. Imagine that you write a work of fiction that makes you rich and famous at an early stage of your career. How would you live after that, and what kinds of things would you write? Imagine that you write a work of fiction that fails to make you rich and famous at an early stage. How would you live after that, and what kinds of things would you write? At every point in your career, it is not a bad idea to ask yourself what you'd do if your current project ended up otherwise than expected. Should you keep on course,

doing the same kind of thing, or turn to something different? The correct answer differs for everyone.

4. Suppose you have set yourself the task of writing a book on a subject of importance to you. It might be about writing, or family life, or romance, or war, or commerce, or history, or medicine—it might be about anything human beings do. The only requirement is that you put everything you know about the subject into the book. You may devote anywhere from six months to your entire life to this task. How will you go about it? What do you know already that you can use as a starting point? What sorts of things must you learn in the future before you can accomplish the task? At what point do you think you could begin putting words on paper? At what point do you think you could tell people about your project or show it to them? What is your present vision of what the finished book might look like? In what ways do you think your vision of the book might change as you go about creating it? How do you think working on this project will make you feel while you are in the midst of it? After you're finished? What will be your criteria for success? Think about these questions as you go ahead and do it.

Writer's Bookshelf

Literary biographies, memoirs, autobiographies, letters, and diaries are a lifelong source of role models for writers. Some, such as the following, are works of literature in themselves.

The Journals of James Boswell, 1762–1795 (edited and introduced by John Wain, 1991).

Read it and wish you were in the eighteenth century! Has anyone ever been as complicated, as self-contradictory, as uninhibitedly self-revealing as Boswell, or written as likably about it? This selection skims the surface of the thirteen-volume edition, of which the most well-known volume is the first: Boswell's London Journal, 1762–63 *(edited by Frederick A. Pottle, 1950).* Boswell's The Life of Samuel Johnson *(1791), a three-volume study of the charismatic talker and stylist whom Boswell followed like a puppy dog, is generally considered the greatest biography in English.*

Henry James: A Life by Leon Edel (1985)

is a one-volume abridgement and enhancement of Edel's great five-volume biography of The Master.

The Life of Charlotte Brontë by Elizabeth Gaskell (1857).

The author of Wives and Daughters *on the life of her friend, the author of* Jane Eyre; *a landmark in the art of biography.*

The Diary of Anaïs Nin (6 vols., 1966–80)

may be Nin's most considerable achievement, though her fiction is evocative and poetic. Heavily edited from her original drafts (which contained some unsavory, later-published revelations), it's notable for lucid descriptions, astute psychological insights, and portraits of Nin's writer friends, especially Henry Miller.

Tolstoy by Henri Troyat (translated by Nancy Amphoux, 1967)

is a page-turningly readable study of a great novelist whose life resembled a great novel. Troyat has also written biographies of Pushkin, Dostoyevsky, Chekhov, Gogol, and Turgenev: a major service for lovers of the nineteenth-century Russian giants.

The Diaries of Virginia Woolf (1977–85)

run to five volumes and contain the most well-written gossip ever about some of the most interesting people ever. A further volume, A Passionate Apprentice: The Early Journals: 1897–1909 *is of special interest to young writers. Woolf's widower, novelist Leonard Woolf, issued a selection of the entries that dealt with writing, under the title* A Writer's Diary *(1954). Also recommended:* Congenial Spirits: The Selected Letters of Virginia Woolf *(edited by Joanne Trautman Banks, 1989), an abridgement of the six-volume complete letters.*

Index